The MIRACLE MORNING

for TRANSFORMING YOUR RELATIONSHIP

*How to Create an Unshakable LOVE
and Unleashed PASSION that
Lasts a Lifetime!*

Hal Elrod • Paul & Stacey Martino

With Honorée Corder

THE MIRACLE MORNING FOR TRANSFORMING YOUR RELATIONSHIP

Hal Elrod, Paul & Stacey Martino
with Honorée Corder

Interior Design: Christina Culbertson, 3CsBooks.com

ISBN-13: 978-1942589143

DEDICATION

HAL

I dedicate this book to my wife, Ursula, to our children, Sophie and Halsten, and to my co-authors, Stacey and Paul.

To Ursula, you have added more value to my life than any other person on earth. You are everything I've always dreamed of in a wife, and so much more that I never even imagined, but would never want to live without. Thank you for your unconditional love, your unending loyalty, and your friendship. Thank you for believing in me when I didn't believe in myself.

To Sophie and Halsten, you constantly inspire me to strive to become the best version of myself, and know that I love both of you more than anything in this world! May this book one day help you to create an unshakable love and unleashed passion that lasts a lifetime. (But not until you're much older, of course!)

To Stacey and Paul, your ability and commitment to helping individuals and couples to transform their relationships is inspiring! Your work has already been the catalyst for thousands of couples, to transform their relationship, and I'm so grateful that we could bring your knowledge and wisdom to millions of Miracle Morning Community members around the world!

STACEY

This book is dedicated to our students, our team, our kids, and my amazing husband Paul.

To all our students, your dedication to throw your whole self into your dream of living your life by design lights a fire w ithin me to serve you at 1000 percent! You inspire me, you make me laugh, you move me, and I just love you all. God bless you.

To our team, holy crap on a cracker, you are the best freaking team on the planet! Nothing in this book would be here without you. Your dedication to serve every family that comes to us is overwhelming. You step forward with your whole heart and your unique brilliance and you make everything better. Amy, Carmie, Jennifer, Jade, Theresa, and Carol … there is no book without you. I love you darlings! I thank God for bringing us together in service to all.

Gracie and Jake, we love you endlessly. Everything Daddy and I do, we do for you two. Jake, every day you teach me what love is. No one loves like you, Jake Martino. You embody unconditional love. You are a friend to all and the most generous giver that I have ever known. Gracie, you are MAGICAL. Your brilliance, fierceness, humor, and unique abilities amaze me. The way your mind works stops me in my tracks. You are like a rainbow unicorn. There's nothing else like you. Every day, you both inspire me and Daddy to be better versions of ourselves for you. Thank you for choosing us. We love you more than words. God bless you and keep you.

Paul, there are no words invented yet in our language to describe how much I love you and what you mean to me. You are my air. Everything in my world begins and ends with you. I am the woman I am today because you allow me to be exactly that. I admire your strength, fearlessness, integrity, brilliance, selflessness, passion, intensity, and insanely hysterical sense of humor! Thank you, God, for creating Paul Martino just for me. Every day I strive to be the woman who deserves such a blessing.

PAUL

This book is dedicated to my incredibly beautiful, brilliant, and awe-inspiring wife, Stacey, who created a path where none existed before. In addition, this book is dedicated to our two young children, Jake and Grace, our inspiring students, our team, and our many, many mentors.

To all our students, you consistently remind me of just how powerful, admirable, and magnificent humans can be! I love you for your bravery, commitment, and compassion even during the times where the path ahead wasn't always so clear, among so many other things.

To our team, we would be nowhere without you, including nowhere on this book! Thank you for your passion to help us get out there in a bigger way and for all you do to help our students. Clearly, God/ the Universe has put you with us because you each bring the perfect mindset and talents needed in order for us to do what we do! Amy, Carol, Theresa, Jade, Carmie, and Jennifer—we love you all for not only who you are and your many gifts, but also for your passion to shine the light forward!

Jake and Grace, not a single day goes by where I am not totally and humbly grateful to God for blessing us with you both as our children. I will always love you more than words can explain! You already have superpowers at your young ages. Jake, my handsome young boy, your capacity for giving love is endless. Every day you remind me of how powerful love can be. I'm so proud of you and your loving heart! You are a love superhero. Grace, my beautiful little girl, you are sugar, spice, and everything nice ... mixed in with some seriously bold and fierce energy! You are Wonder Woman in an eight-year-old wrapper. You are both a force for good in changing this world and I'm so grateful to be blessed to be your father, who eternally loves you.

Stacey, I love you from every molecule in my body. Not a single day goes by where I am not totally and humbly grateful to God for you! My entire world begins and ends with you. I wouldn't be a fraction of the person I am today if it wasn't for you inspiring me to be a better man every single day. Words cannot express how much I love you. I am beyond grateful to be so blessed to have you as my wife and mother to our children. Your divine gifts and passion to change the world for the better are nothing less than awe-inspiring!

CONTENTS

SECTION I: THE MIRACLE MORNING + LIFE S.A.V.E.R.S.

   Leveraging the most powerful force in relationships, one person is always shifting the relationship! Empower yourself to use that force to single-handedly transform your relationship ... all your relationships!

   The case for mornings and why they are critically important to a relationship's success (and what happens when you don't take advantage of them).

   Even if you've never been a morning person, here's the most effective way to overcome the challenges of waking up early, beat the snooze button, and maximize your mornings.

   Harness the life-changing power of the most effective, proven personal development practices known to man, which are guaranteed to save you from missing out on the levels of success (in every area of your life) that you truly want and deserve.

SECTION II: TRANSFORMING YOUR RELATIONSHIP

   Until you shift your perspective, nothing can change for you. In this chapter, Stacey will open your eyes to the real dynamics of love and passion. You will understand men and women in a way that you never have before. This shift in your perspective is the opening that will allow you to use the tools and strategies to come.

A SPECIAL INVITATION FROM HAL

Readers and practitioners of *The Miracle Morning* have come together to co-create an extraordinary online and offline community, made up of over 200,000 like-minded individuals from around the world, who wake up each day *with purpose* and dedicate time to fulfilling the unlimited potential that is within all of us while helping others to do the same.

As the author of *The Miracle Morning*, I felt that I had a responsibility to establish an online community where readers could come together to connect, get encouragement, share best practices, support one another, discuss the book, post videos, find accountability partners, and even swap smoothie recipes and exercise routines.

I honestly had no idea that the Miracle Morning Community would become one of the most positive, engaged, and supportive online communities in the world, but it has. I'm constantly astounded by the caliber and character of our membership, which presently includes people from over 70 countries and is growing daily.

Just go to **MyTMMCommunity.com** and request to join the Miracle Morning Community on Facebook. You'll immediately be able to connect with 80,000+ people who are already practicing the Miracle Morning. While you'll find many who are just beginning their Miracle Morning journey, you'll discover even more who have been at it for years and who will happily share advice and guidance to accelerate your success.

I'll be checking in regularly and helping to moderate the community, so I look forward to seeing you there! If you'd like to reach out to me personally on social media, follow **@HalEl-rod** on Twitter, @Hal_Elrod on Instagram, and on Facebook at **Facebook.com/YoPalHal**. I look forward to connecting with you, soon!

With Love & Gratitude,

- Hal

A SPECIAL INVITATION FROM STACEY AND PAUL

We are the founders of Relationship Development®, which is a segment of the personal development space focused on your relationships. Our proven process, including our strategic tools and strategies, work in real life for real families. Everything we teach is designed to empower you to create the transformation you want in your relationship without needing your partner to participate in the process with you.

Countless people around the world today are implementing the Relationship Development tools and strategies we teach. They believe in creating an unshakable love and unleashed passion. They want to be a role model to their children! They believe in living life by design and not living in a life by default.

And they have gathered with us in the most amazing community of like-minded, dedicated, positive, fun, and extraordinary individuals! Our Relationship Development Community is designed to give you support, encouragement, insights, compassion, accountability, and love. It is a safe, judgment-free zone where real people come to be who they are and do the work to create the relationship transformation that they desire. In our community, you will find inspiration, dedication, fun, and enlightenment that will uplift you each day.

Our Relationship Development team facilitates this group to ensure that it serves all who are a part of it. While Stacey and the team facilitate, it is the members of this amazing group that truly co-create this precious and unique community of men and women.

We invite you to join the Relationship Development Community. This is the secret advantage to big results! Surround yourself with like-minded people that are happily on this journey with you.

Just go to MyRelationshipDevelopmentCommunity.com and request to join the Relationship Development Community on Facebook. You will immediately be able to connect with people who are already doing this work.

If you would like to reach out to me and Paul personally, please email us at Support@RelationshipDevelopment.org and find me on Facebook at Facebook.com/StaceyMartinoLPC. Let's connect soon!

Sending love,

Stacey and Paul

A NOTE FROM HAL

Welcome to *The Miracle Morning for Tranforming Your Relationship.* I think it's safe for us to say that there is at least one thing we have in common (probably a lot more than just *one*, but at least one that we know for sure): *We want to improve our lives and ourselves.* This is not to suggest that there is anything necessarily "wrong" with us, or our lives, but as human beings we were born with the innate desire and drive to continuously grow and improve. I believe it's within all of us. Yet most of us wake up each day and life pretty much stays the same.

Whatever your life is like right now—whether you are currently experiencing extraordinary levels of success, enduring the most challenging time of your life, or somewhere in between—I can say with absolute certainty that the Miracle Morning is the most practical, results-oriented, and effective method I have ever encountered for improving *every* area of your life and doing so faster than you may believe is possible.

For achievers and top performers, the Miracle Morning can be an absolute game-changer, allowing you to attain that elusive *next level* and take your personal and professional success far beyond what you've achieved up to this point. While this can include increasing your income or growing your business, sales, and revenue, it's often more about discovering new ways to experience deeper levels of fulfillment and success in aspects of your life that you may have neglected. This can mean making significant improvements in your *health, happiness, relationships, finances, spirituality,* or any other areas that are at the top of your list.

For those who are in the midst of adversity and enduring times of struggle—be it mental, emotional, physical, financial, relational, or other—the Miracle Morning has proven time and time again to be the one thing that can empower anyone to overcome seemingly insurmountable challenges, make major breakthroughs, and turn their circumstances around, often in a short period of time.

Whether you want to make significant improvements in just a few key areas, or you are ready for a major overhaul that will radically transform your entire life—so that your current circumstances will soon become a memory of what was—you've picked up the right book. You are about to begin a miraculous journey using a simple, step-by-step process that is guaranteed to transform any area of your life ... all before 8:00 a.m.

I know, I know—these are some big promises to make. But the Miracle Morning is already generating measurable results for hundreds of thousands of people around the world, and it can absolutely be the one thing that takes you to where you want to be. My co-authors and I have done everything in our power to ensure that this book will be a truly life-changing investment of your time, energy, and attention. Thank you for allowing us to be a part of your life. Our miraculous journey together is about to begin.

A NOTE FROM STACEY

"I challenge you to make your life a MASTERPIECE, I challenge you to join the ranks of those people who live what they teach, who walk their talk."

—TONY ROBBINS, Best-selling
author and entrepreneur

Paul and I believe that everyone deserves to have an unshakable love and unleashed passion!

An unshakable love is one where you have rock-solid alignment with your partner, where nothing and nobody can come between you. You are each other's partners first and above all else. You receive and give unconditional support and are each other's greatest champions. It's you and your partner, indivisible, facing the world as a team!

An unleashed passion is one where you walk through your day charged up by desire, craving your partner. Your relationship is filled with playfulness, flirting, and romance. You have insane levels of sex, especially for how busy you are. Your ravishing and unleashed sex life satisfies a hunger so deep within you, you didn't know it was there. The deep satisfaction energy from this kind of sex lasts for days, shifting you into a better version of yourself. Unleashing your passion is about so much more than sex!

The great news is that everyone can have an unshakable love and unleashed passion! It's not just for some people! It's for all people. It's not that some people have it and others don't. The truth is that a magnificent relationship is *created*, not found! And while it's work to create it, it's totally worth it! Love is the purpose of life.

Nothing is more important than love. No matter what we tell ourselves, at the end of the day, love is what we are here for.

Right now, the state of your relationship impacts how you show up in every area of your life. Your work, parenting, finances, health, fitness, confidence, happiness, spirituality, and even your self-worth! Living in unshakable love and unleashed passion every day allows you to be your best and most authentic self!

And no matter how much personal development work and growth you do, if you haven't created an unshakable love and unleashed passion, you are simply not living your best and most authentic life ... *yet!*

The quality of your life is in direct proportion to the quality of your relationships. And your love relationship is the kingpin that impacts you more than any other.

You must learn to create outstanding relationships if you want to live your best life. You deserve it. Your partner deserves it, and your kids deserve it too!

Stacey & Paul's Mission

At RelationshipDevelopment®, our mission is to provide a *relationship education* and ultimately a *relationship transformation* for everyone on this planet who wants it.

We believe that everyone deserves a relationship education; a basic education of the differences between the masculine and the feminine, the dynamics of long-term committed love relationships, and the principles of how to create an unshakable love and unleashed passion that can last a lifetime.

Your relationship transformation happens when you implement this Relationship Education to shift the action you take in your day-to-day moments to get the results you want.

We love and adore the people we are blessed to serve, including *you*! And … . we also have a slightly hidden agenda. We have a mission to serve your *kids*!

We want them to grow up in a home where Mom and Dad have an unshakable love and unleashed passion, so that they will grow up knowing exactly how to create their own (and they won't need us when they are 40).

Then, we would truly be leaving this planet better than we found it—for them!

Who Is This For?

Our society has perpetuated the myth of the "fairy tale" romance. We grow up believing this myth, expecting that when we fall in love, we should just "have this fairy tale." Then real life starts. Much to our surprise, a committed relationship is really hard. At some point, most of us end up just trying to survive in our committed relationship and can't conceive of what it would feel like to thrive. The relationship gets hard. And we don't know what to do to turn things around.

This situation leaves good people stuck in a dilemma. Do we settle for how things are when we want so much more for our relationship, or do we put our family through the pain of separation over this?

It doesn't have to be that way.

What Paul and I offer you in this book is a third option. *Stay* and *transform* your relationship! We can show you how. It's not a million things; it's eight simple steps. Your partner doesn't need to do this with you. You can get the results you want without their participation in the process (your partner does *not* have to read this book). These tools work no matter where you are on the relationship continuum.

If your marriage is in a tough place right now, and this book is your last-ditch effort, you are in the right place. I'll be very direct with you, not every marriage is meant to last. However, every relationship can be rescued, whether or not you stay married to your spouse. If you have kids, you must rescue that relationship. You will be co-parenting with that partner for the rest of your life until you die. And your kids deserve to have peaceful and happy co-parents. In the chapters ahead, we will give you the tools and strategies you need to improve your relationship, stop the fighting, and create the alignment you need and deserve. Once the relationship is healed, you will have a much clearer understanding if you are with the partner you are aligned with long-term or not.

If you have a loving or caring relationship, you are good friends with your partner, and you parent well together, but the passion and excitement has fizzled or disappeared completely, you are in the right place. This is an epidemic right now. There's a very good reason why relationships everywhere are fizzling and most folks are not having in-credible sex anymore (more on that later). In the chapters that follow, my husband Paul and I will teach you what you need to implement to turn that passion back on! Here's the truth: you can have sex that is hotter, more satisfying, and takes you to levels of ecstasy that you didn't know were possible for humans to reach … and you can have that even after being together 20 years like us!

If you are a parent who is getting separated or divorced and realize that things with your ex are getting worse as you try to co-parent, you are in the right place. I know you are committed to giving your kids a harmonious family. And I'm a huge advocate for you. In the chapters that follow, we will empower you with specific tools and strategies you can begin using with your co-parent and partner to heal the relationship and create a peaceful and happy co-parenting experience for you, your co-parent-partner, and your children! What could be more important than your harmonious family? And while you are transforming your relationship with your co-parent, you will be learning the tools and strategies you need to attract and create the forever love that *is* aligned for you. The only thing better than two loving parents is four.

If you are a growth-oriented single person who wants an unshakable love and unleashed passion, you are in the right place. You must get crystal clear on what exactly is the right relationship for you so you can learn to trust yourself to pick the partner who is best aligned with you. You will need tools and strategies to create a magnificent relationship, and it would be nice to learn them before you meet that person. I can't tell you how many people have told me, "When I get into a relationship, Stacey, I'm going to do your program!" It's roughly the same number of people who have called or emailed me saying "Help! I didn't expect to meet someone, and now I fear I'm screwing this up already!"

In the chapters ahead, you will gain tremendous relief flowing from clarity on the dynamics of your past relationships, get crystal clear on what is right for you, and be empowered with the tools to attract, pick, and create the unshakable love and unleashed passion you deserve!

And if you have an extraordinary love and fantastic passion with your partner and want to take it to the next level? Well, buckle up, buttercup, because you didn't know it could be like this! Take every juicy bit of content in the pages of this book and implement it in your marriage, then watch as your levels of love escalate beyond your wildest vision. Revel in the delight as your ecstasy surpasses the most insane levels you've ever experienced in all your days! Everything you have always wanted and didn't know you could have is waiting for you.

It takes ONE partner to transform a relationship, *any* relationship! I'll explain this concept to you and show you how it works in chapter 1.

At this point, we have been blessed to serve thousands upon thousands of individuals from all around the world. We offer proven tools and strategies that work in real life for real families.

We work with people in every kind of relationship situation you could image, and some you will never imagine. There's nothing that can't be handled. The more common challenges people come to us with include the following:

- How to recover after an affair or get over infidelity
- A lack of time because of work, kids, or other commitments
- Partners who haven't had sex in many years or decades
- Fighting over money, financial stress on the marriage, partners facing bankruptcy
- Work challenges including massive working hour demands
- Family-of-origin drama stressing your relationship
- Long distance relationships or spouses who travel for work
- Sexual abuse (in the past or childhood)
- Kids with special needs making it difficult to get the time or space for the marriage
- Addictions causing havoc (substances or sex addiction)
- Dishonesty or transgressions that need to be healed
- And the most common challenge of all ... we are busy and overwhelmed parents who work a ton and have a lot of crap going on and no one ever taught us how to have a magnificent love affair in real life today.

Paul and I are real people. We did not start out as relationship experts. Far from it!

Our Story

Sixteen years ago, Paul came home one night to tell me that he was leaving. He said our relationship was over, and he was walking out the door.

I was not surprised that Paul was leaving. After all, our relationship was total crap, and my nickname back then was the Ice Princess. I was *shocked* at my reaction.

I became hysterical and broke down crying.

I had not cried in about 10 years before that moment, so it was unnerving for me. I once heard someone say that some people break down, and others break *open*. Well, that must be what happened to me, because through the intensity of my pain and despair, I felt a surge of love for Paul that I had never felt before.

In that moment, I had an awakening. I realized two life-changing truths at once. First, all this time I was living behind big walls I had created to protect myself, and none of it worked because I was brokenhearted over a man I didn't even know I was in love with until that moment. Clearly, thinking I could protect myself from pain was a lie I was telling myself. Second, the surge of love that I felt for Paul was unexplainable using the words that we currently have in our language. It was transcendent. It was as if nothing else in the world mattered except Paul. Before that moment, I had heard musicians sing about love in that way, but always dismissed their words as just "art" and not possible in real life. In one moment, I discovered that, in fact, it was possible to feel *love* like this for another human, and I feel this way for Paul.

I suddenly felt a new fear, the fear of missing the chance to experience this love again because of the mistakes I had made on the way to this moment. When I finally looked up at Paul, I quickly noticed that he wasn't having the same spiritual awakening I was having. He looked more shocked that things had gone so horribly wrong when he was trying to just end things and walk out.

Unequipped with any relationship skills, I did the only thing I could think to do in that moment. I begged Paul for a second chance. I told him what he said about me and our relationship was true. I told him I didn't know if I could turn it around, but I was committed to figuring out if it was possible. I begged him for one more chance.

Thank God, Paul decided to give me another chance that night.

Being a big personal development person, I dove into everything I could get my hands on to learn about men, women, relationships, and intimacy. I was shocked to find out how much of the "crap" in our relationship was actually caused by my own lack of understanding and appreciation for how the masculine is wired, how different Paul is from me. I also discovered that all my protecting and refusal to rely on anyone other than myself was actually blocking me from the relationship I wanted most with my man.

I transformed myself. I figured out ways to interact with Paul that honored his core wiring and brought out the best in him and in me. I shifted how I was showing up. It was a massive struggle, but I started melting my "ice" and opening to my feminine.

Don't get me wrong, I was doing a lot of trial-and-error, testing things out, including some things that I read in popular books and tried that caused so much damage we almost lost our relationship all over again.

Eventually, our relationship transformed.

The amazing thing was, *back then*, Paul wasn't reading the books, attending the events, or doing any of the programs I was doing to learn and shift. And yet, he was transforming too. I noticed him shifting in response to how I was now showing up.

Noticing so much change in me and our relationship, about a year later, Paul asked what I was reading and what he could learn because he was inspired by my change. He told me that, just through my shift, he already felt like a better man and wanted to do more for us.

From there, we dove in together. We invested nearly two decades and hundreds of thousands of dollars studying with the best of the best, transforming ourselves, and creating the unshakable love and unleashed passion we are blessed to have today.

Along our journey, we felt the calling to help others who were suffering the way we once had by sharing what worked for us. Eventually, it snowballed into the work we are blessed to do today.

What We Do Today

If, after reading this book, you want to take a deeper dive and do the work in your life, we invite you to join us for one of our online programs or live events. We provide step-by-step expert guidance, support, accountability, and community for our students who are all happily on this relationship development journey with you! If you want to explore our online programs or live events, please visit RelationshipDevelopment.org and click on "Programs" or "Events."

This book is an outstanding first step in your relationship education, but it doesn't stop there if you want lasting relationship transformation. You can't learn your way to a better relationship; you must implement this in your life to create the shift. It doesn't need to be hard, and you don't have to do it alone. We are here to help!

The Real Deal

When our students first come to us, we give them the same warning I'm about to give you. We teach adult content and use adult language. This language is never used to offend you. We have nothing but love for you.

We use direct and raw language as a strategic intervention tool to help you get the breakthrough you want. You can't get a breakthrough and be buttoned up at the same time. Cursing or real language is one of the strategic ways we keep reminding your nervous system to stay *real* and not button up. This methodology goes all the way back to techniques used by some of the greatest psychotherapists and NLP practitioners.

Whether that's a fit for your style or not, don't let our language or anything else about us get in your way of getting what you need.

As our students will tell you, Paul and I are the real deal. We don't walk our talk, we are *talking our walk*. We lived it first, and now we feel compelled to teach it. Our tools and strategies work, in real life, for real families.

If you apply what we teach you in the chapters ahead, you will experience a transformation in your relationships (all your relationships).

We will deliver on these promises.

Your unshakable love and unleashed passion is here for the taking. You deserve it.

Why The Miracle Morning

Once on QVC, Tony Robbins asked me what, after nearly two decades in personal development and transforming my life in every way possible, was the single greatest tool in my tool belt.

My answer ... my Daily Morning Ritual.

Every day, for too many years to count, I have done a daily morning ritual! Gratitude, visualization, affirmations, personal development, and writing!

As I told Tony, I don't have any days that aren't worth designing before I begin!

I've known Hal for about a decade now since our mutual friend Jon Vroman of the Front Row Foundation introduced us. I vividly remember getting a call from Jon one day when he told me that his buddy Hal was testing out a new morning ritual he had figured out. He asked me if I wanted to learn it and start using it. Of course I said yes!

I remember feverishly writing down each step of the early version of the Miracle Morning in a spiral notebook. Hal's process took everything I was doing to another level, while putting the process into a repeatable, digestible, and actionable format to create consistency in my development.

I was in, and so the Miracle Morning became part of my life. Never in a million years would I have guessed that one day I would be sitting here in the same office writing this book. Holy crap on a cracker ... life is awesome, isn't it?

I ask all my students to make the Miracle Morning part of their daily habit. Why? Because it works! I'm living proof!

A NOTE FROM PAUL

"When I let go of what I am, I become what I might be."
—LAO TZU

S tacey and I know that everyone can have an unshakable love and unleashed passion in their committed relationship. How do we know that? Because today we find ourselves on an unplanned mission to help people to transform their relationships, just as we have. We didn't simply transform our relationship; we also identified *exactly what it took* to transform our relationship. We didn't just happen to find "the right one," as we were brought up to believe would be the case: we created this. And you can too!

As we grew, we started noticing the same dysfunctional dynamics that we used to have in our relationship in so many other people's relationships around us. What happens when you know something that could not only make someone's life dramatically better, save marriages, and keep parents and their kids sleeping in the same homes, but also change the world by creating a new generation of happy marriages and passionate relationship role models for their children and more? You feel compelled to share what you have learned!

As I often say, if I see someone reading a newspaper while walking down the street, and there is an open man-hole cover directly on the path in front of them, I'm going to run over to prevent that accident. I couldn't imagine not doing something to prevent it, and I certainly can't sit back and watch it happen.

In a similar way, Stacey and I never planned to turn what we now do into business or our life's mission. Rather, just as we wouldn't let someone fall in a manhole, we could no longer sit back quietly, knowing what we know, without getting our message out to everyone who is willing to listen. Too many families we knew were suffering, our kids were friends with other kids whose parents were going through divorces, … and we knew that we could have done something to prevent it if only we had been able to share all that we know.

One day, while dropping our son off at preschool, I ran into another preschool parent who told me she was getting a divorce from her husband. I decided enough is enough! That was the day we began to create the formal teaching structure so that we could grow our reach and serve as many people as possible who wanted to transform their relationships. Stacey and I are thrilled that we have now reached you.

The most profound changes that impact our destiny happen in small moments. The decision to read this book to the end and apply what you learn will forever empower you with new awareness, skills, and habits to start transforming your love relationship and all relationships around you. Consequently, when you do, it will forever change your destiny for the better. The moment I fell in love with Stacey, my destiny changed. The night Stacey and I had our hanging-by-a-thread moment, not only did our destiny change, but so did the world.

You cannot unknow something once you become aware of it. When you know better, you do better. When you do better, you change your life for the better. When you change your life for the better, you positively change the world around you for the better. This world needs you now, all of you, and your happiness. Throughout this book, Stacey, Hal, and I are going to share some of the best secrets to our own happiness to contribute to yours.

My love for Stacey and our children is the fuel that drives me to serve you, to contribute to this book, to co-create our online programs, and to co-host our events. Stacey's commitment and passion to teaching everyone the skills and knowledge that she had to put together alone and without support over years of evolution and through massive investments has inspired me to the same dedication.

In hindsight, it's clear to me that the Universe or God (whatever that is for you) wanted Stacey and me to get this message out together. Initially, I was inspired to join Stacey in my own development in this area by the changes she started making in our relationship all by herself. My own path to development was not exactly the same as Stacey's, primarily because I am a man and I am obviously a different person.

As a masculine man, I know that other men typically do not see relationships the same way women do. Our needs as men are very different than those of women. Sadly, relationship work used to be perceived by men as a female topic and not relevant to them. Men, I can tell you that if you want to feel even more of a man, more of a hero, fired-up and capable, you need to know this.

As men, we hate not knowing how to fix our problems, right?

So why have men stayed away from learning the secrets to rocking their women's world through their thriving relationship? Primarily because of several false beliefs about this topic:

- **False Belief #1:** Relationship topics were perceived by us men to be something where we would have to spend time just talking about our feelings, which we don't want to do.

- **False Belief #2:** Participating in relationship work would feel feminine, which we don't want.

- **False Belief #3:** The process would be inherently man-bashing in nature or otherwise overly biased towards women.

- **False Belief #4:** Men would not be heard or otherwise would be minimized in the process.

- **False Belief #5:** We would have to change something fundamental about what makes us men to become better at this relationship stuff.

- **False Belief #6:** It seems like the process would simply suck (why would we do that?).

- **False Belief #7:** If I did some relationship work, I'd be the only guy.

- **False Belief #8:** We would not get anything useful or actionable out of it, which is all we really want.

While some so-called relationship experts may indeed create the kind of unproductive and unenlightened environment that men commonly dislike, I can assure you that Stacey and I do not. In fact, the Relationship Development work Stacey and I do is just the opposite! But don't take my word for it. Read this book to the end and draw your own conclusions.

We actually help you reconnect with your authentic masculinity to dramatically improve your relationship. We empower you with strategic and immediately actionable tools you can use to create a difference. Stacey will tell you how much she loves and celebrates the mature masculine (more on that later) and repeatedly states that she will not tolerate any man-bashing in her presence. Obviously, I'm in complete agreement with that.

This is no longer a topic only for women. Some of the most honorable, likable guys I've had the privilege to know are in our Relationship Development programs and events. These are great men that are doing this work to serve their women while simultaneously becoming better men.

Men and women have different needs, and we have different ways of speaking. What Stacey and I do together is teach in ways that honor men and women for who they are and allow them to get what they need in the way they need it.

This is not your grandmother's relationship development class, my friend! We know everyone will learn at a deeper level when the training is fun and immediately actionable—and we bring both. The other difference is that we are not a one-sided source; Stacey and I both contributed to all our training content as well as actively participate in teaching all of this together. We live this life together.

Throughout this book, you will read certain chapters or passages that are specifically written by me. It will say so on the page. Most of the time, Stacey is the voice behind the words you read. However, please know that Stacey and I wrote every page of this book together. My perspective, guidance, and words are reflected throughout to serve both men and women. We are a team.

As Stacey said, we talk our walk. Few people giving relationship advice, of any kind, have both the husband and the wife teaching what works together. Men, if you had any concerns about this being one-sided, or otherwise just half of the bigger picture needed, I can promise you that you have no need to fear learning or participating in what we are doing. Just the opposite—I challenge you as a brother not to let any false preconceptions about this topic get in your way of obtaining the knowledge you need to become the hero in your woman's world, to become a better father and a happier man, and to remove the unnecessary confusion that has most likely been clouding your ability to see and know what to do in your relationship.

For the magnificent women out there, I deeply love how you are wired and what makes you so different from us men. We so need *both* authentic energies, just as they are, to make this world a great place to live in. My contributions to our teaching will help you remove the unnecessary relationship confusion you may have about us men that most likely has been causing you a lot of frustration, hurt, and disagreements.

Nobody needs to change who they are in our process—that's not how we roll. We want you to become a better, more authentic version of yourself to create your unshakable love and unleashed passion. It is only through maintaining and supporting these different masculine and feminine energies that we can create the unshakable love and unleashed passion in your relationship!

Let's do this!

SECTION I:

THE MIRACLE MORNING
+
LIFE S.A.V.E.R.S.

— 1 —

IT ONLY TAKES ONE

BY STACEY MARTINO

"Magnificent love affairs are not found, they are created! So stop searching and start building! It is so worth it!"
—STACEY MARTINO

"We waste time looking for the perfect lover instead of creating the perfect love."
—TOM ROBBINS, Novelist

The question I've been asked to answer countless times by countless interviewers is one that may have arisen in your mind as you read our introductions.

*What do you mean it only takes **one** partner to transform a relationship, Stacey? That flies in the face of everything we've ever been taught, like it takes two to tango.*

Yes, it truly takes only *one* partner to transform a relationship!

What's more, you do *not* need your partner to do the work with you or you to get the results you want. This is great news for you because, in my experience, two people in the same relationship rarely want to do the work to transform their relationship at the same time. Here are two common reasons why:

1. One partner is unsatisfied with how things are, but the other partner thinks everything is fine.

2. Or, they both acknowledge that things aren't working so well, and one partner wants to do something about it, but the other partner wants no part in any of that.

This leaves good people feeling stuck in a dilemma. Do they settle for how things are, or put their relationship and family through the pain of separation?

Both of those choices suck, so many good people are left feeling stuck.

Our Relationship Development work provides a third option: *stay and transform!*

You don't need your partner to do this with you. In fact, in a moment I'm going to show you why couples work is actually counter-productive to the goal you want.

With our tools and strategies, you will be empowered to create the change you want to see in your relationship. It doesn't matter whether your partner wants to do this with you or not. You can create the positive shift you want in your relationship on your own. Even better, you can begin transforming things immediately because you don't have to wait for your partner to get on board with this.

It does *not* take two to tango!

One partner is always shifting the relationship. You're aware of this fact already, and when I explain the following scenario, you'll see the truth of it.

Have you ever had an experience like this?

You're going through the day, and you are in the zone! Everything is flowing and you are crushing it. Then you encounter your partner, and the minute you see them, they start complaining because they are in a crappy mood.

Question: What happens to your peak state when they do? It drops to the floor, right?

Why? Nothing changed in your world; why did your state tank?

Answer: They triggered you, and now you are in the toilet with them.

Next thing you know, you are saying something like, "I was rocking my day. Why do you have to be so negative?"

That usually triggers them to react with something like, "You don't understand what it's like. You have no idea what real problems feel like!"

You then retort, "Why do you always have to do this?"

Do you see what happened there?

Nothing changed in your world. Your partner just triggered you. Now you are going back and forth, and it's become about the two of you! It didn't start out that way, but do you see how quickly that spiraled into being personal?

It's critical that you understand this: Nothing actually changed for you, but they triggered you, and the relationship shifted *instantly*.

One partner is always shifting the relationship through triggers!

You already know this in your core. I can prove it. Ready? (This is going to be fun.)

Have you ever had the experience of listening to your partner, and while they were talking, you had a thought or a feeling about it, but you didn't bother telling your partner because in your head you heard, *Well, I already know how that would go. Forget it!*

Yes? Well guess what, cupcake, if you've been together for any length of time, they already knew what you were going to say next.

They also knew how they'd respond to what you were going to say, and even how you'd respond in return to *that*!

Round and round it goes because of triggers.

Triggers are one of the most powerful forces in human relationship today. Whether positive or negative, people and circumstances trigger us to feel a certain way.

Consider each statement below and fully associate with it for a moment; feel it as if you are in the moment. In ordinary life, what feeling would it trigger for you?

> Your kid comes home and says, "A boy in my class hit me today and called me a stupid head."
>
> Your partner says, "I love you so much. Every day I'm overwhelmed with gratitude that I get to spend my days next to the person I feel is the greatest person ever put on this earth. Thank you for loving me."
>
> Your friend says, "You lied to me. I can't believe you would do that!"
>
> Your boss says, "You broke the record for top performer! Everyone is blown away by your outstanding results."
>
> Your child says, "I don't feel good, Mommy/Daddy. Please help me," as they cry and throw up.

Each statement triggers a different emotion. That's how *one* person can trigger you and shift your state instantly. It happens all day, every day, and most of us are unaware it's happening.

Triggers are one of the most powerful forces in human relationship. As a result, in our Relationship Development work, we teach you how to leverage the power of triggers to bring out the *best* in your partner, instead of the worst.

By getting a relationship education you will understand how to stop doing what is triggering them negatively and what you can start doing to trigger them into being their best and most authentic self for you. When you do this, you will create the love and passion you desire.

The relationship education contained in this book is designed to help you do two things:

1. *Understand* exactly what you're doing that triggers the results you don't want from your partner.

2. *Empower* you with the real-life tools and strategies to trigger results you do want from your partner.

NOTE: While we often focus on your committed love relationship, the principle of triggers applies to every human relationship. Some of what we teach you will apply only to your love partner (like creating passion). But other things will affect every relationship in your world (like understanding the differences between masculine and feminine).

This is outstanding news! You can create the change you want to experience in your relationship. You don't need your partner to participate in the process. In fact, it's counterproductive to ask your partner to do this work with you. Why? Consider the following scenario.

> You're not satisfied with some aspect of your relationship, so you find something you hope will make things better, such as couples therapy.
>
> You tell your partner, "We need this. I want to go, and I need you to come with me."
>
> They don't respond favorably, and you take that as confirmation that things aren't going great, so it adds to your stress about the relationship.
>
> What just happened? There's an invisible dynamic at play, and it's best revealed through a different scenario, involving a friend instead of your partner.
>
> Your best friend calls you and says, "Hey, there's a 'Be Better Looking' event going on next month! I'm going,

and I really think you should go. We both need this. I'm going. Come with me!"

What is the first thought that comes up for you when your "friend" says you both need it?

It's probably something like, *WTF? Are you saying that I'm not good looking enough and that I need that? Screw you!*

Or it's something like, *OMG! (crying) I knew you thought I wasn't good looking enough! All this time! I knew it! I'm UGLY! You just proved it!*

Here's the thing, when you ask someone to participate in something that will *improve* things, by definition, you're implying that things are *not good enough*. Even worse, most humans will further interpret that to mean that *they* are not good enough!

In other words, you're triggering *defensiveness* or *unworthiness*, depending on the other person's level of self-confidence.

If they agree to go, it feels like an admission that they are not good enough. (They don't realize that consciously, but that is what you are triggering.)

That's why asking your partner to do this work with you is often counterproductive to the outcome you deeply want to experience: positive change.

Instead, focus on Relationship Development, which is personal development, for your relationships. We've designed this work to help you cultivate your best and most authentic self, empowered with the relationship tools and strategies to bring out the best in others. Do this for *yourself!*

You can shift any relationship in your life by shifting how you show up. We can show you how.

The Power Is Yours

Magnificent relationships are created, not found. So stop searching and waiting and start building. It's so worth it!

People don't simply find an unshakable love and unleashed passion, while others pick the wrong person. It doesn't work that way. You don't stumble upon this kind of relationship, you create it.

As you will see in the chapters of this book, every choice you make, every reaction or response, is either building up or breaking down your relationship. Moment by moment, all through your day, everything you do and say is having an impact.

Some of your reactions and responses are building up your relationship with your partner, and other actions are tearing it down. Up until now, this dynamic has been invisible to you.

Even with the best intentions, good people are unknowingly doing things that negatively impact their relationships all day long.

It's not your fault. No one gave you a relationship education. No one even mentioned the words relationship and education together. Until now.

By the time you are done with this book, you will know, for sure, that magnificent relationships are in fact created and not found. What you do with that is up to you.

Considering the following two truths:

1. Magnificent relationships are created, not found.

2. It only takes *one* partner to transform a relationship.

That being the case, the question is not, "*Can* you do this?" It's, "*Will* you do this?"

What's your answer? If you are a *giant* "yes" right now, *rock on!* You've got this, and we've got you.

If you feel resistance to saying yes, let me explain where that might be coming from and how you can move past it.

The number one objection people give for not wanting to say yes is, *"Why?"*

> "Why should I? My partner's the one who's screwed up."
>
> "Why can't my partner do something for a change? I do *all* the work for this relationship."
>
> "Why should I do this if my partner doesn't too? What's the point?"

If that's what you're wondering, then here are some great reasons why you should do the work to transform your relationship, no matter what your partner does or doesn't do.

- **This is *your* relationship**. You are in it every day. And it's impacting your happiness, well-being, confidence, and everything else in your life. You either have to live *in* it, or live *through* leaving it, so you might as well improve it.

- **Empower Yourself!** When you say, "I'm not going to do this unless my partner does it," you are handing your power over to someone else and rendering yourself powerless. What you are effectively doing is placing the fate of your relationship in their hands. Maybe they will do something about it, maybe they won't. Based on past performance, what do you think? Don't leave yourself at the whim of someone else; empower yourself to create the results you want.

- **Ditch Your False Belief**. Every day I see women and men who want to wait to start this work until their husband or wife wants to do it with them because they've assigned meaning to their partner's participation: *"If they really love me, they will ... "* They wait to see their partner take action so that they can prove that the partner really cares about the relationship. Wrong. That's a false belief. People often assign meaning to someone's action that isn't true. It's false. And it holds them back.

Perhaps one of those reasons resonated with you? If so, that's great, but that's not the primary reason you need to do the work!

Are you ready for the number one reason? Buckle up, buttercup, because we are going there …

The big *WHY* you should do the work: None of this work is for your partner. It's all for you!

It's true. This work is *not* for your partner. It's not even for your relationship. This is 100 percent *for you* because the challenges you're experiencing in your relationship are *not* only because of your partner. They're being triggered by you!

Even if you aren't currently in the forever love relationship that is aligned for you, you still do plenty to contribute to the state of the relationship you're in. You're not aware of what you're doing, so you think the other person is the problem.

Even worse, if you choose *not* to do the work, here's the kicker: You will take *you* (and all your triggers) with you to the next relationship. Then, about six months into it, *bam*, you'll realize you're dealing with the exact same crap and experiencing the *same* relationship you left before, just with a new face!

When that happens, you'll realize that your problem isn't only with your partner, it's with *all* women or *all* men!

At that point, you could decide that all women are crazy or all men are jerks, and there's no way to have a successful relationship. Unfortunately, that is a common misconception that is simply not true. A more empowered choice is to decide to learn about and master the differences between the masculine and feminine and create the relationships you really want.

To do this, you must shift your perspective so you see your partner and all of the stuff that's driving you crazy as the gifts that they truly are. You see, every *problem* that comes into your life is really an *opportunity* for your growth. My friend Jon Vroman calls them "challenge-tunities."

You are designed to want more from life. It's like Hal teaches us, "Don't settle for mediocrity when you want a Level 10 life."

You are wired for more. Everything on this planet is designed to grow and evolve.

If you want to grow and evolve, you must be willing to endure the *dis*comfort of leaving your current comfort zone in order to enter your next one.

Do you see that line between the two comfort zones? That's the *dis*comfort zone I'm referring to, where you leave your old comfort zone and grow into the version of you that can have all the things you want at your next level.

How do you go from your current level to the next level? You can't get there by staying the same. If you could reach the next level by being exactly who you are right now, you'd be there already.

The fact is things have to change in one of two ways to get where you want to go:

1. You willingly seek to learn and grow.

2. Learning opportunities (aka problems) find you and challenge you to grow. Every problem presents an opportunity to release the old and step into a new level. What you choose to do with that opportunity creates your destiny. Do you run away from problems, hoping they magically go away?

Or do you embrace the opportunity and break through the challenge?

Your love partner provides the greatest opportunity to grow into an even better version of yourself. Do they trigger you? Great, do the work and rewire that trigger.

My friend, I'm going to share a truth that will make your life a whole lot easier once you embrace it:

No one else was put here on this planet to please *you*.

Don't ask someone else to change to please you; it's not their job. Do the work for yourself.

Anytime you feel pain, it's merely the Universe telling you it's time to grow, and to do so, you need to do some work in the area that's the source of the pain.

Let's say your partner does something that triggers you and makes you feel bad. Up until now, you have wanted your partner to change so that they don't trigger you.

Let's step back for a minute. If that's what has to happen for you to be happy, can you imagine how many people in your life need to change so you don't get triggered anymore? Holy crap! There's your partner, the people at your work, your kids, your friends, your parents, your neighbors, your siblings, and even your pet!

Can you imagine the laundry list of things about your partner that they would need to change to make you blissfully happy, if that was the *way* to happy?

What are the chances they all will take *your* list of triggers and change everything about themselves so they don't trigger you? Ha! Not likely—I mean, are *you* going to change everything about yourself so that you never trigger them? That'd be ridiculous!

Keep in mind that every person has very different triggers, so you'd never be able to please everyone.

For the sake of illustration, let's pretend you live in a dream world where you could find people malleable enough to change everything on your trigger list. What if a trigger of yours changes, and something that never bothered you before starts to irritate the crap out of you? Are you going to distribute a new list to everyone and keep updating them on how they need to change to not trigger you?

Are you following me here?

By now it should be obvious that the person who triggers you isn't the problem, Lovie. The *trigger* itself is the problem, and it's not serving you—it's holding you back. So why are you trying to protect the trigger by asking people to stop bumping into it? Let's just pull it out! By taking action using the Relationship Development work that we will walk you through on these pages, you can do exactly that—pull out those triggers!

The relationship education contained in the chapters that follow will help you get back to your best and most authentic self while empowering you with the tools and strategies needed to bring out the best in others, too.

You can have it all! But we can't do it for you; you must do the work!

If you are willing to do the work, say, "*Yes!*"

Let's do this!

What's a great way to start? By doing this work during your Miracle Morning!

For two decades, I have practiced a daily morning ritual. I believe that every day is worth living by design, so during my Miracle Morning I design my day. It puts me in the best possible state to create the day I envision. That's why I was so excited when Hal asked us to partner with him in writing *The Miracle Morning to Transform Your Relationship*! I had already been recommending that my students do the Miracle Morning.

There are so many benefits to doing the Miracle Morning practice every day, and we will cover more of them in the chapters ahead. One of those benefits is starting each day by giving to *yourself* so you are ready to give to *others* the rest of your day. This is the ultimate way to put the oxygen mask on yourself first.

So often, our days run away from us (and with us). When you do the Miracle Morning at the beginning of each day, it will have lasting effects to help you master your state throughout the day.

Friend, this is a game changer, and I'm thrilled about the new possibilities that will unfold for your life and relationships!

While I've been doing a daily morning ritual for a long time and I am a self-proclaimed TMM'er (as we call ourselves), there's no one better to teach you about the Miracle Morning than my good friend and Miracle Morning creator, Hal Elrod.

In the next three chapters, Hal will teach you how to use the Miracle Morning to transform your life, and throughout these pages, I will also contribute with respect to how this will transform your relationships.

{Optional} Do the Work-Book (Available at DotheWorkBook.com): In your companion *Do the Work-Book*, please complete the section that goes with each chapter. This will allow you to take strategic action and integrate the content deeper!

Real Life Relationship Case Study

CATHERINE

Before

When I started Stacey and Paul's program, it was only a month or two after I was diagnosed with breast cancer. I was a cranky bitch, taking all of my frustration out on my husband and daughter. I knew that my relationship was swirling down the toilet and that it was my fault. Each night, my husband was working on the computer, while I was left wondering why he wasn't hanging out with me. Well, I sure wasn't filling his cup, was I? What an eye-opener that was!

For years, I bought into all those MYTHS—it takes two, it has to be 50-50, and, the most embarrassing of all, "I have to be just like Stacey and Paul to have an unshakable love and unleashed passion." It was all CRAP! It only takes ONE; I can be my quiet, authentic self and still have a wonderful relationship! I'm living proof of that!

Doing the Work

I started implementing Stacey and Paul's strategies right away. There are so many stories I could tell, but let me just talk about the shift in committing to be 100 percent ALL IN. Oh my God it was so flipping HARD. If Stacey says she was a "gold medal holder in score keeping," then I was definitely standing next to her on the podium holding the silver medal. I worked this program, fell flat on my face, then picked myself up and tried again.

I remember one night, my husband was out in the driveway getting the snow blower ready, even though it was 10 p.m. and he was exhausted. I didn't ask. I didn't nag. He just did it. (That never would have happened before I started this program.)

I was in the house folding laundry and I went upstairs to find a sink full of dishes. The OLD me would have gone to bed and left the dishes for HIM to do in the morning because, after all, it was HIS job. The NEW (still exhausted) me stepped up to the sink, singing a happy tune, in deepest gratitude to be able to GIVE this GIFT to my husband entirely freely—no strings attached—100 percent ALL IN! My husband was SO grateful!

After

Today, my husband and I have the most amazing marriage! We build bricks (Brick Conversations), we have date nights, we ask for what we want directly, and we honor one another. The man who never brought me flowers has not only brought me three bouquets in the last two months, but he told me that he plans to keep that vase filled! HEAVEN!

I am over-the-moon grateful to you, Stacey! Your process has changed our lives completely! Our household is more harmonious, we put each other first, our daughter is a thousand times happier, and all this while I was going through chemo and now about to start radiation. Really? Cancer would put ANY relationship to the test! I am mind-blown! Thank you a million times! Love you so much! MWAH!

Keys to Her Success

- **No excuses:** Catherine had just been diagnosed with breast cancer when she came to work with us. She could have easily said that she didn't have time or that she had to focus on SURVIVING instead of doing this work. She didn't use any excuses.

- **Wake up**: Catherine received the wake-up call from her illness. She chose to create a magnificent life with the time she had! She started transforming and taking massive action! She got big results!

- **Personal responsibility**: One of the things I admire the
  most about Catherine is her dedication to taking personal
  responsibility for everything in her world today! Every time
  she "fell on her face" she picked herself back up and asked
  herself, "What can I do to shift this?" If that's not *heroic*, I
  don't know what is!

Paul and I are thrilled to report that after a full year, Catherine
has triumphed! Today, she is cancer-free and her marriage and family have never been stronger!

— 2 —

WHY MORNINGS MATTER
(MORE THAN YOU THINK)

BY HAL ELROD

"'Life's too short' is repeated often enough to be a cliché, but this time it's true. You don't have enough time to be both unhappy and mediocre. It's not just pointless, it's painful."

—SETH GODIN,
New York Times best-selling author

"You've got to get up every morning with determination if you're going to go to bed with satisfaction."

—GEORGE LORIMER,
American journalist and author

How you start each morning forms your mindset and the context for the rest of your day. Start every day with a purposeful, disciplined, growth-infused, and goal-oriented morning, and you're virtually guaranteed to crush your day.

As Stacey says, "This is a key element to living a life by design instead of ending up in a life by default. There is no day given to you that is not worth designing!"

Do you start your day feeling overwhelmed? I'd be willing to bet that most people (in or out of relationships) do. Their day starts when their alarm goes off, the kids wake them up, or when they absolutely *have* to get up.

What if you could have the hour of peace and quiet you've been dreaming about? That clean, uncluttered mental space where you could regain your sense of elegance and dignity, where you're in total control and can proceed in an orderly, self-nurturing fashion? But you know you can't—or maybe you can, but not today. Maybe when you're independently wealthy or the kids have all grown up. Just not now.

It's no wonder most people start their days with procrastination, letting their life or even their job set the agenda, and sending a message to their subconscious minds that says they don't have enough energy or even the will to get out of bed. They think today will be another free-for-all where their personal goals go out the window in the usual scramble to meet the needs of others.

Add to this the fact that most people believe they aren't early risers, and the pattern of procrastination shows up early in life and lingers.

But what if you could change it?

What if, when the alarm clock starts beeping in the morning, you could consider it to be life's first gift? It's the gift of time that you can dedicate to becoming the person you need to be to achieve all your goals and dreams—for yourself and your relationship—while the rest of the world is still asleep.

You might be thinking, *All of this sounds great, Hal. But. I. Am. Not. A. Morning. Person.*

I understand. I really do! You're not saying anything I haven't told myself a thousand times before. And believe me, I tried—and failed— many times to take control of my mornings. But that was before I discovered the Miracle Morning.

Stay with me here. In addition to wanting to have a better relationship, I bet you also want to stop struggling and worrying about having more month than money, quit missing your goals, and release the intense and not-so-great emotions that go along with those challenges. These things get in the way of being an effective partner because they affect your self-esteem and prevent you from feeling good about yourself and your life.

I'm a firm believer in the advice given at the start of every airplane flight: Put your oxygen mask on first, and then help your child. You won't be able to help anyone if you pass out due to lack of oxygen.

Many people don't see this simple truth. They think success means putting your own needs last, and they have so much to do that they never get to those needs. Over time, they end up exhausted, depressed, resentful, and overwhelmed.

Sound familiar?

Then know this:

Mornings are the key to it all.

More important than even the *time* you start your day is the *mindset* with which you start your day.

Regardless of where you are in your relationship, learning to practice your Miracle Morning before anything else is important to make sure you get *your time*, uninterrupted. The good news is … it's worth it, and it's far more fun and rewarding than you might expect.

But, before I get into exactly *how* you can master your mornings, let Stacey and me make the case for *why*. Because, believe me, once you've uncovered the profound truth about mornings, you'll never want to miss one again.

WHY MORNINGS MATTER SO MUCH
By Stacey Martino

The more you explore the power of early rising and morning rituals, the more proof mounts that the early bird gets *a lot* more than the worm. Here are just a few of the key advantages you're about to experience for yourself:

You'll take advantage of the "break in momentum."

Metaphysics teaches us that sleep breaks the momentum you built up the day before. When you rise first thing in the morning, there is *no* momentum yet, and you have the greatest opportunity to set your new intention and bring it into your day. Sometimes it can feel like your relationship never changes, that yesterday rolls into today. There's an *opening* to change this, and it happens for you every morning with the break in momentum. Learning to maximize this opportunity each day is one of the keys to success in every area of your life and certainly in your relationships. Using the moments first thing in the morning to design your day gives you a massive advantage in creating positive change.

You'll increase your ability to be compassionate and patient.

Remember, you are constantly shifting your relationship through triggers. You are triggering your partner, and your partner is triggering you. As you learn new tools and strategies in this book, your capacity to remain compassionate and patient will help you tremendously in reducing old triggers. You will be more resourceful in the moment and increase your ability to positively shift your relationship.

You'll be more proactive and productive.

Oftentimes people think life is too busy to get in their Relationship Development learning time. While we teach strategies like listening to audios while you are driving, grocery shopping, or on the go, you also need *focus* time. The best time for that is before your day begins. Tony Robbins teaches us the difference between *must* and *should*. When you make your Relationship Development time a *must*, you will do the work and delight in the results. If you don't, then as Tony charmingly tells us, "You are shoulding all over yourself."

You'll have more energy.

People often tell me that they don't have *time* to get up an hour earlier than they normally do. This is a false belief and factually untrue. If anything levels the playing field among humans, it's time. You, me, Hal, Oprah, we all have the same 24 hours in each day. No more, no less. It's not that you don't have time, it's that you don't want to forgo something else to prioritize the time. And that *thing* in your mind is typically sleep. What you are really saying is that you don't have the *energy* to get up an hour earlier.

I hear you. There have been nights when I worked until 1:00 a.m., and Gracie, our daughter, woke me at 2:30 and 4:30. Then my alarm went off at 6:00 to start my day. Trust me. I hear you.

The truth is, if my alarm were going off at 6:00 a.m. because I was getting on the plane to go to Saint Lucia for our Breakthrough in Paradise™ event for the week, I would burst out of bed and happily grab my bags to head out the door!

It's amazing how much energy we have when we *love* what we are getting up for. When your nervous system experiences the *benefits* of your Miracle Morning and realizes that the practice actually makes every day better for you, you won't have any challenge getting up and getting going.

My Miracle Morning time does more for me than an hour of sleep does.

You'll have more to give to your relationship.

If two people come to relationship to *take*, then what's left? Nothing! A relationship is not somewhere you go to *take*, it's somewhere you go to *give*. Perhaps you find yourself in a place right now where you feel like you have given and given, and you are depleted, wondering when it's going to be your turn to receive. Don't worry, in the coming chapters of this book, I will show you how much of your giving is falling flat with your partner and how to tweak what you give so that it lands and you see results.

In the meantime, understand that you can't give from an empty tank. If you feel resistant to giving, coming from compassion, and doing the work during the day, you are not going experience the change that you desire. Transforming your relationship takes work. I'll give you shortcuts and proven methods, but you still must be the one to take action.

I've found that my clients who get the best outcome with this work are the ones who set up their day for success by giving to themselves *first* so their tank is full to start their day. The Miracle Morning is your tool for that. Give yourself an hour, fifteen minutes, or even just six minutes to fill yourself up, and you will create so much more progress in transforming your relationship that day.

You'll get better results from releasing your expectations before your day begins.

It's human nature to begin to expect a certain event after it has happened a few times. Right? We get stuck in our patterns, and we expect others to respond the way they always have. If this dynamic continues without positive change, it takes your relationship down. In the chapters ahead, I will teach you to shift *your* part, by helping you show up differently.

However, to get great results, you must also start shifting your expectation of how your partner will react or respond. You may not even realize it, but chances are that you often expect the negative response from your partner. If you expect the worst, you will surely find it. When you take time each morning to visualize a positive outcome, you start to break your neuro programming of negative expectation and replace it with possibility and eventually positive expectation. This creates greater progress in transforming your relationship.

As Hal says, "The evidence is in, and the experts have had their say. *Mornings contain the secret to an extraordinarily successful life.*" *Now let's hear more of his thinking on why this is.*

MORNINGS? REALLY?
By Hal Elrod

I admit it. To go from *I'm not a morning person* to *I really want to become a morning person* to *I'm up early every morning, and it feels amazing!* is a process. But after some trial and error, you will discover how to outfox, preempt, and foil your inner late sleeper so you can make early rising a habit. Okay, sounds great in theory, but you might be shaking your head and telling yourself, *There's no way. I'm already cramming 27 hours of stuff into 24 hours. How on earth could I get up an hour earlier than I already do?*

Let me ask you, *How can you not?*

The key thing to understand is that the Miracle Morning isn't about denying yourself another hour of sleep so you can have an even longer, harder day. It's not even about waking up earlier. It's about waking up *better*.

Thousands of people around the planet are already living their own Miracle Mornings. Many of them were night owls, but they're making it work. In fact, they're *thriving*. And it's not because they simply added an hour to their day. It's because they added the *right* hour. And so can you.

Still skeptical? Then let me tell you this: *The hardest part about getting up an hour earlier is the first five minutes.* That's the crucial time when, tucked into your warm bed, you make the decision to start your day or hit the snooze button *just one more time*. It's the moment of truth, and the decision you make right then will change your day, your success, and your life.

And that's why the first five minutes is the starting point for *The Miracle Morning for Transforming Your Relationship*. It's time for you to win every morning! When we win our mornings, we win the day.

In the next two chapters, I'll make waking up early easier and more exciting than it's ever been in your life (even if you've *never* considered yourself to be a morning person) and show you how to maximize those newfound morning minutes with the Life S.A.V.E.R.S.—six of the most powerful and proven personal development practices in existence.

In chapter 4, Stacey will give you a powerful perspective shift, after which you will never be able to see men, women, and relationships the same way again.

In chapter 5, Stacey will walk you through the proven methodology that she and Paul created to empower you to forgive *anything* that is keeping you held back. *Yes, anything.*

Then, in chapters 6 and 7, Stacey and Paul will give you tools and strategies to begin using today in order to create the shift you want in your relationship.

In chapter 8, Stacey gives us the Roadmap to Mastery that she and Paul created to empower you to get *lasting change* from all your personal development work. And the *next step solutions* to give you the most powerful results.

And finally, there's a bonus chapter from Stacey and Paul that I think you are really going to love!

We have a lot of ground to cover in this book, so let's jump right in.

— 3 —

IT ONLY TAKES FIVE MINUTES TO BECOME A MORNING PERSON

BY HAL ELROD

If you really think about it, hitting the snooze button in the morning doesn't even make sense. It's like saying, "I hate getting up in the morning, so I do it over, and over, and over again."

—DEMETRI MARTIN, Comedian

Have you ever considered that how we start our day could be the single most important factor in determining how we live our lives? When we wake up with excitement and create a purposeful, powerful, productive morning, we set ourselves up to win the day.

Yet most people start their day with resistance and procrastination, hitting the snooze button and waiting until the last possible moment to pry themselves out from beneath their cozy covers. While it may not be obvious, this seemingly innocent act may be sending a detrimental message to their subconscious minds, programming their psyches with the unconscious belief that they don't have the self-discipline to get out of bed in the morning, let alone do what's necessary to achieve everything else they want for their lives.

Could it be that how we wake up in the morning affects who we're becoming and thus changes every area of our lives?

When the alarm clock starts beeping in the morning, consider that as life's first *gift*, *challenge*, and *opportunity* to us—all three at the same time—each day. It's the gift of another day, the challenge of making the disciplined decision to get out of bed, and the opportunity to invest time in our personal development so each of us can become the person we need to be to create the life we truly want. And we get to do all of this while the rest of the world continues to sleep.

The good news is that it is possible to love waking up—and do it easily each day—even if you've *never* been a morning person.

I know you might not believe it. Right now, you think, *That might be true for early birds, but trust me, I've tried. I'm just not a morning person.*

But it is true. I know because I've been there. I used to sleep until the last possible moment, when I absolutely had to wake up. And even then, it took me a while to get out of bed. I was a "snooze-aholic" as I now call them. I dreaded mornings. I hated waking up.

And now I love it.

How did I do it? When people ask me how I transformed myself into a morning person—and transformed my life in the process—I tell them I did it in five simple steps, one at a time. I know it may seem downright impossible. But take it from a former snooze-aholic: you can do this. And you can do it the same way I did.

That's the critical message about waking up—it's possible to change. Morning people aren't born—they're self-made. You can do it, and it doesn't require the willpower of an Olympic marathoner. I contend that when early rising becomes not only something you do, but *who you are,* you will truly love mornings. Waking up will become for you like it is for me—effortless.

Not convinced? Suspend your disbelief a moment and let me introduce you to the five-step process that changed my life. Five simple, snooze-proof keys that made waking up in the morning—even early in the morning—easier than ever before. Without this strategy, I would still be sleeping (or snoozing) through the alarm(s) each morning. Worse, I would still be clinging to the limiting belief that I am not a morning person.

And I would have missed a whole world of opportunity.

The Challenge with Waking Up

Waking up earlier is a bit like running: You think you're not a runner—maybe you even *hate* running—until you lace up a pair of running shoes and reluctantly head out the front door at a pace that suggests you might be about to go for a run. With a commitment to overcome your seemingly insurmountable disdain for running, you put one foot in front of the other. Do this for a few weeks, and one day it hits you: *I've become a runner.*

Similarly, if you've resisted waking up in the morning and chosen to hit the *procrastination* button—I mean *snooze* button, then of course you're not *yet* a morning person. But follow the simple steps-by-step process that you're about to discover, and you'll wake up in a few weeks (maybe even a few days), and it will hit you: *OMG, I can't believe it ... I've become a morning person!*

The possibilities feel amazing right now, and you might be feeling motivated, excited, optimistic. But what happens tomorrow morning when that alarm goes off? How motivated will you be when you're yanked out of a deep sleep by a screaming clock?

We all know where motivation will be right then. It will be flushed down the toilet and have been replaced by rationalization. And rationalization is a crafty master—in seconds, we can convince ourselves that we need just a few extra minutes … and the next thing we know, we're scrambling around the house late for work, late for life. Again.

It's a tricky problem. Just when we need our motivation the most—those first few moments of the day—is precisely when we seem to have the least of it.

The solution is to boost that morning motivation and mount a surprise attack on rationalization. That's what the five steps that follow do for you. Each step in the process is designed to increase what I call your Wake Up Motivation Level (WUML).

First thing in the morning, you might have a low WUML, meaning you want nothing more than to go back to sleep when your alarm goes off. That's normal. But by using this simple five-step process (which takes about five minutes), you can generate a high WUML that makes you ready to jump up and embrace the day.

The Five-Step, Snooze-Proof Wake-Up Strategy

Minute One: Set Your Intentions Before Bed

The first key to waking up is to understand this: *Your first thought in the morning is usually the same as your last thought before you went to sleep.* I bet, for example, that you've had nights where you could hardly fall asleep because you were so excited about waking up the next morning. Whether it was when you were a kid on Christmas morning or the day you were leaving for a big vacation, as soon as the alarm sounded, you opened your eyes ready to jump out of bed. Why? It's because the last thought you had about the coming morning—before you fell asleep—was positive.

On the other hand, if your last thought before bed is, *Oh gosh, I can't believe I have to get up in six hours—I'm going to be exhausted in the morning,* then your first thought when the alarm clock goes off is likely to be something like, *Oh gosh, it's already been six hours? Nooo … I just want to keep sleeping!* Consider that it is a self-fulfilling prophecy and that you create your own reality.

The first step is to consciously decide—every night, before bed—to actively and mindfully create a positive expectation for the next morning. Visualize it and affirm it to yourself.

For help on this and to get the precise words to say before bed to create your powerful morning intentions, download "The Miracle Morning Bedtime Affirmations" free at **TMMBook.com**.

Minute Two: Move Your Alarm Clock Across the Room

If you haven't already, be sure to move your alarm clock as far away from your bed as possible. This will make it so you have to actually get out of bed and engage your body in movement to turn off the alarm. Motion creates energy, and getting out of bed and walking across the room naturally helps you to wake up.

Most people keep their alarm clock next to their bed. Think about it: if you keep your alarm clock within reach, then you're still in a partial sleep state after the alarm goes off, and your WUML is at its lowest point, which makes it much more difficult to summon the discipline to get out of bed. In fact, you may turn off the alarm without even realizing it! On more than a few occasions, we've all convinced ourselves that our alarm clock was merely part of the dream we were having. (You're not alone in that one, trust me.)

By forcing yourself to get out of bed to turn off the alarm, you are setting yourself up for early rising success by instantly increasing your WUML.

In that moment, however, on a scale of one to ten, your WUML may still be hovering around five, and you'll likely be feeling more sleepy than not, so the temptation to turn around and crawl back into bed will still be present. To raise that WUML just a little further, try . . .

Minute Three: Brush Your Teeth

As soon as you've gotten out of bed and turned off your alarm clock, go directly to the bathroom sink to brush your teeth. I know what you may be thinking. *Really? You're telling me that I need to brush my teeth?* Yes. The point is that you're doing mindless activities for the first few minutes and giving your body time to wake up.

After turning off your alarm, go directly to the bathroom sink to brush your teeth and splash some warm (or cold) water on your face. This simple activity will allow for the passing of more time to increase your WUML even further.

Now that your mouth is minty fresh, it's time to …

Minute Four: Drink a Full Glass of Water

It's crucial that you hydrate yourself first thing every morning. After six to eight hours without water, you'll be mildly dehydrated, which causes fatigue. Often when people feel tired—at any time of day—what they really need is more water, not more sleep.

Start by getting a glass or bottle of water (or you can do what I do, and fill it up the night before so it's ready for you in the morning) and drinking it as fast as is comfortable for you. The objective is to replace the water you were deprived of during the hours you slept. (And hey, the side benefits of morning hydration include better, younger-looking skin and maintaining a healthy weight. Not bad for a few ounces of water!)

That glass of water should raise your WUML another notch, which will get you to …

Minute Five: Get Dressed in Your Workout Clothes (or Jump in the Shower)

The fifth step has two options. *Option one* is to get dressed in your exercise clothing so you're ready to leave your bedroom and immediately engage in your Miracle Morning. You can lay out your clothes before you go to bed or sleep in your workout clothes. (Yes, really.) And for some people, the prep you do the night before is especially important to help you go straight into your practice. You can make this part of your bedtime ritual.

Option two is to jump in the shower, which is a great way to take your WUML to the point where staying awake is much easier.

However, I usually opt to change into exercise clothes, since I'll need a shower after working out, and I believe there is something to be said for *earning* your morning shower! But a lot of people prefer their shower first because it helps them wake up and gives them a fresh start to the day. The choice is completely yours.

Regardless of which option you choose, by the time you've executed these five simple steps, your WUML should be high enough that it requires very little discipline to stay awake for your Miracle Morning.

If you were to try to make that commitment the moment your alarm first went off—while you were at a WUML of nearly zero—it would be a much more difficult decision to make. The five steps let you build momentum so that, within just a few minutes, you're ready to go instead of feeling groggy.

I have never made it through the first five minutes and decided to go back to bed. Once I am up and moving with intention through the morning, I can more easily continue being purposeful throughout the day.

Miracle Morning Bonus Wake-Up Tips

Although this strategy has worked for thousands of people, these five steps are not the only way to make waking up easier. Here are a few others I've heard from fellow Miracle Morning practitioners:

- **Bedtime Affirmations:** Available at TMMbook.com, you can download these re-energizing, intention-setting bedtime affirmations to help you program your subconscious mind, before bed, and ensure that you will wake up focused and ready to maximize your day.

- **Set a timer for your bedroom lights:** One member of the Miracle Morning Community shared that he sets his bedroom lights on a timer (you can buy an appliance timer online or at your local hardware store). As his alarm goes off, the lights come on in the room. What a great idea! It's a lot easier to fall back to sleep when it's dark—having the light on tells your mind and body that it's time to wake up.

Regardless of whether you use a timer, be sure to turn your light on first thing when your alarm goes off.

- **Set a timer for your bedroom heater:** Another member of the Miracle Morning Community says that, in the winter, she keeps a bedroom heater on an appliance timer set to go off fifteen minutes before she wakes up. She keeps it cold at night, but warm for waking up so she won't be tempted to crawl back under her covers.

Feel free to add to or customize the five-minute, snooze-proof wake-up strategy, and if you have any questions you'd like to ask more experienced Miracle Morning practitioners, please don't hesitate to post them in *The Miracle Morning Community* at **MyTMMCommunity.com**.

Waking up consistently and easily is all about having an effective, predetermined, step-by-step strategy to increase your WUML in the morning. Don't wait to try this! Start tonight by reading "The Miracle Morning Bedtime Affirmations" to set a powerful intention for waking up tomorrow morning, move your alarm clock across the room, set a glass of water on your nightstand, and commit to the other two steps for the morning.

Taking Immediate Action

There's no need to wait to get started implementing the power of early rising. As Tony Robbins has said, "When would NOW be a good time for you to do that?" Now, indeed, would be perfect! In fact, the sooner you start, the sooner you'll begin to see results, including increased energy, a better attitude, and, of course, a happier home life.

Step One:

Set your alarm for 30–60 minutes earlier than you usually wake up for the next 30 days. That's it, just 30–60 minutes for 30 days, starting now. And be sure to write into your schedule time to do your first Miracle Morning … *tomorrow morning*. That's right, don't use *waiting until you finish the book* as an excuse to procrastinate on getting started!

If you're feeling resistant at all, because maybe you've tried to make changes in the past but haven't followed through, here's a suggestion: turn now to chapter 10, The Miracle Morning 30-Day Transformation Challenge, and read ahead. This will give you the mindset and strategy to not only overcome any resistance you may have to getting started, but also the most effective process for implementing a new habit, and sticking with it. Think of it as beginning with the end in mind.

From this day forward, starting with the next 30 days, keep your alarm set for 30–60 minutes earlier than you typically wake up so you can start waking up when you *want* to, instead of when you *have* to. It's time to start launching each day with a Miracle Morning and becoming the person you need to be to take yourself and your relationship to extraordinary levels.

What will you do with that hour? You're going to find out in the next chapter, but for now, simply continue reading this book during your Miracle Morning until you learn the whole routine.

Step Two:

Check out *The Miracle Morning Community* at **MyTMMCommunity.com** to connect with and get support from more than 80,000 like-minded early risers, many of whom have been generating extraordinary results with the Miracle Morning for years.

Many new readers of The Miracle Morning head to the online Community to find an accountability partner. —someone who will to join you on this new adventure so you can encourage, support, and hold each other accountable to follow through until your Miracle Morning has become part of who you are.

Okay, now let's get into the six most powerful, proven, personal development practices known to man (or woman) … the Life S.A.V.E.R.S.

— 4 —
THE LIFE S.A.V.E.R.S.
FOR YOUR RELATIONSHIP

BY HAL ELROD

What Hal has done with his acronym S.A.V.E.R.S. is take the best practices—developed over centuries of human consciousness development—and condensed the "best of the best" into a daily morning ritual. A ritual that is now part of my day.

*Many people do one of the S.A.V.E.R.S. daily. For example, many people do the **E**, they exercise every morning. Others do **S** for silence or meditation, or **S** for scribing or journaling. But until Hal packaged S.A.V.E.R.S., no one was doing all six ancient "best practices" every morning. The Miracle Morning is perfect for very busy, successful people. Going through S.A.V.E.R.S. every morning is like pumping rocket fuel into my body, mind, and spirit ... before I start my day, every day.*

—ROBERT KIYOSAKI, Best-Selling author of *Rich Dad Poor Dad*

Most people live their lives on the wrong side of a significant gap that separates *who we are* from *who we can become*, which holds us back from creating the life we truly want. Often we become frustrated with ourselves and our lack of consistent motivation, effort, and results in one or more areas of life. We spend too much time *thinking* about the actions we should take to create the results we want, but then we don't take those actions. More often than not, we know what we need to do ... we just don't consistently do what we know.

Do you ever feel like that? Like the life and relationship that you want, and the person you know you need to be to create both, are just beyond your grasp? When you see other people who are excelling in an area, or playing at a level that you're not, does it ever seem like they've got it all figured out? Like they must know something you don't because if you knew it then you'd be excelling too?

When I experienced the second of my two rock bottoms (the first was when I died for six minutes in a car crash, and the second was when my business failed due to the financial collapse of 2008), I felt lost and depressed. I tried to apply what I already knew wasn't working. Nothing I tried improved my situation. So, I began my quest for the fastest, most effective strategy to take my success to the next level. I went in search of the best personal development practices used by the world's most successful people.

After discovering and assembling a list of six of the most timeless, effective, and proven personal development practices, I first attempted to determine which one or two would accelerate my success the fastest. However, my breakthrough occurred when I asked, *what would happen if I did ALL of these?*

So, I did. Within just two months of implementing all six practices, nearly every single day, I experienced what you might call miraculous results. I more than doubled my income and went from someone who had never run more than a mile to training to run a 52-mile ultramarathon—because I *wasn't* a runner and actually despised running. I thought, *What better way to take my physical, mental, emotional, and spiritual capacities to another level?*

So, whether you're already very successful, like multimillionaire entrepreneur Robert Kiyosaki (who practices the Miracle Morning and the Life S.A.V.E.R.S. almost every day), or if you've ever felt like the life you want to live and the person you know you can be are just beyond your grasp, the Life S.A.V.E.R.S. are virtually guaranteed to save you from missing out on the extraordinary life you truly want.

Why the Life S.A.V.E.R.S. Work

The Life S.A.V.E.R.S. are simple but profoundly effective daily morning practices that will enable you to become more so that you can fulfill your potential. They also give you space to gain heightened levels of clarity to plan and live life on your terms. They're designed to start your day by putting you in a peak physical, mental, emotional, and spiritual state so you continually improve and will feel great and *always* perform at your best.

I know, I know. You don't have time. Before starting the Miracle Morning, I would wake up to pure chaos with barely enough time to get dressed and out the door to work. You probably think you can hardly squeeze in what you have to do already, never mind what you want to do. But I didn't have time before the Miracle Morning either. And yet, here I am with more time, more prosperity, and a more peaceful life than I've ever had.

What you need to realize right now is that your Miracle Morning will create time for you. The Life S.A.V.E.R.S. are the vehicle to help you reconnect with your true essence and wake up with purpose instead of obligation. The practices help you build energy, see priorities more clearly, and find the most productive flow in your life.

In other words, the Life S.A.V.E.R.S. don't take time from your day, but ultimately add more to it.

Each letter in Life S.A.V.E.R.S. represents one of the best practices of the most successful people on the planet.

That's what makes the Miracle Morning so effective: you're harnessing the game-changing benefits of not just one, but all six of *the best practices, developed over centuries of human consciousness development*, and combining them into a concise, fully customizable morning ritual.

The Life S.A.V.E.R.S. are:

Silence

Affirmations

Visualization

Exercise

Reading

Scribing

Leveraging these six practices is how you will accelerate your Relationship Development during your newfound Miracle Morning ritual. They're customizable to fit you, your lifestyle, and your specific goals. And you can start implementing them first thing tomorrow morning.

Let's go through each of the Life S.A.V.E.R.S. in detail.

S is for Silence

Silence, the first practice of the Life S.A.V.E.R.S., is a key habit for happy relationships. If you've been guilty of starting your day by immediately grabbing your phone or computer and diving into email, phone calls, social media, or text messages, then this is your opportunity to learn the power of beginning each day with peaceful, purposeful *silence.*

Like I did before the Miracle Morning, most people start the day when they absolutely have to, as opposed to choosing when to wake up. And most people run from morning to night, struggling to regain control for the rest of the day. It's not a coincidence. Starting each day with a period of silence instead will immediately reduce your stress levels and help you begin the day with the kind of calm and clarity that you need to focus on what's most important.

Remember, many of the world's most successful people are daily practitioners of silence. That shows you how important it is. It's not surprising that Oprah practices stillness—or that she does nearly all the other Life S.A.V.E.R.S., too. Musician Katy Perry practices transcendental meditation, as do Sheryl Crow and Sir Paul McCartney. Film and television stars Jennifer Aniston, Ellen DeGeneres, Jerry Seinfeld, Howard Stern, Cameron Diaz, Clint Eastwood, and Hugh Jackman have all spoken of their daily meditation practices. Hip-hop mogul Russell Simmons meditates with his two daughters every morning for 20 minutes. Even famous billionaires Ray Dalio and Rupert Murdoch have attributed their financial success to the daily practice of stillness. You'll be in good (and quiet) company by doing the same.

If it seems like I'm asking you to do nothing, let me clarify: you have a number of choices for your practice of silence. In no particular order, here are a few to get you started:

- Meditation
- Prayer
- Reflection
- Deep breathing
- Gratitude

Whichever you choose, be sure you don't stay in bed for your period of silence, and better still, get out of your bedroom altogether.

———

Here is Stacey's practice in her own words:

For the last two decades, I have started my daily morning ritual with a practice called the Gratitude Flood. For about three minutes, I flood myself with declarations of gratitude. Starting with myself, all the things I'm grateful for about who I get to be today, the life I get to lead, my incredible optimal health and wellness, etc. Then I go into gratitude for Paul, and how grateful I am for who he is as a man. Then I flood myself with gratitude for Jake and for Grace. Each time, I focus on specific things about them that I'm truly grateful for. And I keep going from there. Sometimes it ends up lasting 15 minutes! By the time I'm done, my vibration is so high I feel as if I'm levitating off the pavement as I walk or run through the neighborhood! People probably think "There's that crazy girl who smiles while she runs."

———

The Benefits of Silence

How many times do we find ourselves in stressful situations? How many times do we deal with urgent needs that take us away from our vision or plan? Stress is one of the most common side effects of a rocky relationship. We face the ever-present distractions of a dissatisfying relationship, combined with other people encroaching on our schedule and the inevitable fires we must extinguish. Lots of people have the uncanny ability to push our stress buttons.

Excessive stress is terrible for your health. It triggers your fight-or-flight response, which releases a cascade of toxic hormones that can stay in your body for days. That's fine ... *if* you experience that type of stress only occasionally.

According to Christopher Bergland, a world-record holding triathlete, coach, and author, "The stress hormone, cortisol, is public health enemy number one. Scientists have known for years that elevated cortisol levels: interfere with learning and memory, lower immune function and bone density, increase weight gain, blood pressure, cholesterol, heart disease ... The list goes on and on. Chronic stress and elevated cortisol levels also increase risk for depression, mental illness, and lower life expectancy."

Silence in the form of meditation reduces stress and, as a result, improves your health. A major study run by several groups, including the National Institutes of Health, the American Medical Association, the Mayo Clinic, and scientists from both Harvard and Stanford, revealed that meditation reduces stress and high blood pressure. A recent study by Dr. Norman Rosenthal, a world-renowned psychiatrist who works with the David Lynch Foundation, even found that people who practice meditation are 30 percent less likely to die from heart disease.

Another study from Harvard found that just eight weeks of meditation could lead to "increased gray-matter density in the hippocampus, known to be important for learning and memory, and in structures associated with self-awareness, compassion, and introspection."

Meditation helps you to slow down and focus on you, even if it's for only a short time. Start your meditation practice and say goodbye to feeling scattered and wandering aimlessly without intention and purpose through your day.

"I started meditating because I felt like I needed to stop my life from running me," singer Sheryl Crow has said. "So meditation for me helped slow my day down." She continues to devote 20 minutes in the morning and 20 minutes at night to meditation.

When you are silent in the morning, it opens a space for you before you encounter anyone else. The benefits are extraordinary and can bring you much-needed clarity and peace of mind so you bring your best self to any interaction. Practicing silence, in other words, can help you reduce your stress, improve cognitive performance, and become confident at the same time.

Guided Meditations and Meditation Apps

Meditation is like anything else. If you've never done it before, it can be difficult or feel awkward at first. If you are a first-time meditator, I recommend starting with a guided meditation.

Here are a few of my favorite meditation apps that are available for both iPhone/iPad and Android devices:

- Headspace
- Calm
- Omvana
- Simply Being
- Insight Timer

There are subtle and significant differences among these meditation apps, one of which is the voice of the person speaking. Experiment and choose what works best for you.

If you don't have a device that allows you to download apps, simply go to YouTube or Google and search for the keywords "guided meditation." You can also search by duration (e.g., "five-minute guided meditation") or topic (e.g., "guided meditation for increased confidence").

Miracle Morning (Individual) Meditation

When you're ready to try meditating on your own, here is a simple, step-by-step meditation you can use during your Miracle Morning, even if you've never done this before.

- Before beginning, it's important to prepare yourself and set expectations. This is a time for you to quiet your mind and let go of the compulsive need to be thinking about something—reliving the past or worrying about the future, but never living fully in the present. This is the time to let go of your stresses, take a break from worrying about your problems, and be here in this moment. It is a time to access the essence of who you truly are, to go deeper than what you have, what you do, or the labels you've accepted as who you are. If this sounds foreign to you, or too "new agey," that's okay. I've felt the same way. It's probably because you've never tried it before. But thankfully you're about to.

- Find a quiet, comfortable place to sit on the couch, a chair, the floor, or a pillow for added comfort.

- Sit upright, cross-legged. You can close your eyes, or you can look down at a point on the ground about two feet in front of you.

- Begin by focusing on your breath, taking slow, deep breaths. Breathe in through the nose and out through the mouth. The most effective breathing causes your belly to expand and not your chest.

- Now start pacing your breath. Breathe in slowly for a count of three seconds (one one thousand, two one thousand, three one thousand), hold it in for another three counts, and then breathe out slowly for a final count of three. Notice your thoughts and emotions settling down as you focus on your breath. Be aware that, as you attempt to quiet your mind, thoughts will still come in to pay a visit. Simply acknowledge them and let them go, always returning your focus to the breath.

- Allow yourself to be fully present in this moment. Some people refer to this state as *being*. Not thinking, not doing, just *being*. Continue to follow your breath and imagine inhaling positive, loving, and peaceful energy and exhaling all your worries and stress. Enjoy the quiet. Enjoy the moment. Just breathe … Just be.

- If you find that you have a constant influx of thoughts, it may be helpful for you to focus on a single word, phrase, or mantra to repeat to yourself as you inhale and exhale. For example, you might try something like this: "I inhale confidence …" (on the inhale) "I exhale fear …" (as you exhale). You can swap the word confidence for whatever you feel you need to bring more of into your life (love, faith, energy, strength, etc.), and swap the word fear with whatever you feel you need to let go of (stress, worry, resentment, etc.).

Meditation is a gift you can give yourself every day. My time spent meditating has become one of my favorite parts of the Miracle Morning routine. It's a time to be at peace and to experience gratitude and freedom from my day-to-day stressors and worries.

Think of daily meditation as a temporary vacation from the challenges of life. Although your problems will still be there when you finish each day, you'll find that you're more centered and better equipped to solve them.

A is for Affirmations

Have you ever wondered how some people seem to be good at *everything* they do and consistently achieve at a level so high, you can hardly comprehend how you're ever going to join them? Or why others seem to drop every ball? Time and time again, it is a person's *mindset* that has proven to be the driving factor in their results.

Mindset is the accumulation of beliefs, attitude, and emotional intelligence. In her bestselling book, *Mindset: The New Psychology of Success*, Carol Dweck, Ph.D., explains it this way: "For twenty years, my research has shown that the view you adopt of yourself profoundly affects the way you lead your life."

Others can easily sense your mindset. It shows up undeniably in your language, your confidence, and your demeanor. Your mindset affects everything! Show me someone with a successful mindset, and I'll show you someone who has a better chance of having a successful relationship.

I know firsthand, though, how difficult it can be to maintain the right mindset—the confidence and enthusiasm, not to mention motivation—during the roller coaster ride that comes with being in a committed relationship. Mindset is largely something we adopt without conscious thought. At a subconscious level, we have been programmed to think, believe, act, and talk to ourselves a certain way.

Our programming comes from many influences, including what others have told us, what we repeat to ourselves, and all of our good and bad life experiences. That programming expresses itself in every area of our lives, including the way we show up in our relationships, and that means that, if we want to be better at how we relate, we need to upgrade our mental programming.

Affirmations are a tool for doing just that. They enable you to become more intentional about your goals while also providing the encouragement and positive mindset necessary to achieve them.

Science has proven that affirmations—when done correctly—are one of the most effective tools for quickly becoming the person you need to be to achieve everything you want in your life—for yourself, your partner, and your relationships. And yet affirmations also get a bad rap. Many people have tried them only to be disappointed with little or no results. You can, however, leverage affirmations in a way that will absolutely produce results for you. I'll show you how.

By repeatedly articulating and reinforcing to yourself *what* result you want to accomplish, *why* accomplishing it is important to you, *which* specific actions are required to produce that result, and, most importantly, precisely *when* you commit to taking those actions, your subconscious mind will shift your beliefs and behavior. You'll begin to automatically believe and act in new ways, and eventually manifest your affirmations into your reality. But first …

Why The Old Way Of Doing Affirmations Doesn't Work

For decades, countless so-called experts and gurus have taught affirmations in ways that have proven to be ineffective and set people up for failure. Here are two of the most common problems with affirmations.

Problem #1: Lying to Yourself Doesn't Work

I am a millionaire. Really?

I have 7 percent body fat. Do you?

I have achieved all of my goals this year. Have you?

Creating affirmations as if you've already become or achieved something may be the single biggest cause of affirmations not being effective for most people.

With this technique, every time you recite the affirmation that isn't rooted in truth, your subconscious resists it. As an intelligent human being who isn't delusional, lying to yourself repeatedly will never be the optimum strategy. *The truth will always prevail.*

Problem #2: Passive Language Doesn't Produce Results

Many affirmations are designed to make you feel good by creating an empty promise of something you desire. For example, here is a popular money affirmation that's been perpetuated by many:

I am a money magnet. Money flows to me effortlessly and in abundance.

This type of affirmation might make you feel good in the moment by giving you a false sense of relief from your financial worries, but it won't generate any income. People who sit back and wait for money to show up magically are cash-poor.

To generate the kind of abundance you want (or any result you desire, for that matter), you've got to actually do something. Your actions must be in alignment with your desired results, and your affirmations must articulate and affirm both.

Four Steps to Create Miracle Morning Affirmations (That Produce Results)

Here are four simple steps to create and implement results-oriented Miracle Morning affirmations that will program your subconscious mind, while directing your conscious mind to upgrade your behavior, so that you begin to produce results and take your levels of personal and professional success beyond what you've ever experienced before.

Step One: The Ideal Result You Are Committed to and Why

Notice I'm not starting with what you *want*. Everyone wants things, but we don't get what we want: we get what we're committed to. You want an unshakable love? Who doesn't? Join that nonexclusive club. Oh wait, you're 100 percent committed to transforming yourself to be your best and most authentic self, empowered with the tools and strategies that really work to bring out the best in your partner and transform your relationship into an unshakable love? Okay, now we're talking.

Action:

Start by writing down a specific, extraordinary result or outcome—one that challenges you, would significantly improve your life, and one that you are ready to commit to creating—even if you're not yet sure how you will do it. Then reinforce your commitment by including your *why*, the compelling reason you're willing to stay committed.

Examples:

- *I take 100 percent personal responsibility to transform my relationship. I choose to empower myself to become the hero of my family, and I no longer blame my partner!*

- *I am dedicated to and grateful for <u>living</u> the Relationship Development tools and strategies. Every day that I progress in implementing what I have learned, I become an even better, happier, and more authentic version of myself.*

- *I am 100 percent committed to learning to understand and appreciate the differences between my partner and me so that I can elevate our relationship.*

Step Two: The Necessary Actions You Are Committed to Taking and When

Writing an affirmation that merely affirms what you *want* without affirming what you are committed to *doing* is one step above pointless and can actually be counterproductive by tricking your subconscious mind into thinking that the result will happen automatically and without effort.

Action:

Clarify the (specific) action, activity, or habit that is required for you to achieve your ideal outcome and clearly state when and how often you will execute the necessary action.

Examples:

- *To ensure that I don't fall into blame with my partner, in moments when I find myself frustrated or unhappy I will ask myself "What's my role in this? How can I shift this?"*

- *To ensure that I implement and* live *these tools instead of just learning them, I will get an accountability buddy within three days and check in with them regularly to celebrate my progress and stay accountable!*

- *To ensure that I stay committed to learning the differences, I will make time in my schedule to dedicate X hours per week to my Relationship Development learning! If I need to put a pause on things like TV, extra social time, or other nonessential activities for a while, I will absolutely do so!* (Write your schedule in your journal and schedule it in your calendar NOW.)

The more specific your actions are, the clearer your programming will be so that you consistently take those actions required to move you closer to your goals. Be sure to include *frequency* (how often), *quantity* (how many), and *precise time frames* (when you will begin and end your activities).

Step Three: Recite Your Affirmations Every Morning with Emotion

Remember, your Miracle Morning affirmations aren't designed only to make you *feel good*. These written statements are strategically engineered to program your subconscious mind with the beliefs and mindset you need to achieve your desired outcomes while directing your conscious mind to keep you focused on your highest priorities and taking the actions that will get you there.

For your affirmations to be effective, however, it is important that you tap into your emotions while reciting them. Mindlessly repeating an affirmation without intentionally feeling its truth will have minimal impact for you. You must take responsibility for generating

authentic emotions such as excitement and determination, and powerfully infuse those emotions in every affirmation you recite.

You must affirm who you need to be to do the things you need to
do so that you can have the results that you want. I'll say this again: it
isn't magic. This strategy works when you connect with *the person you
need to become* on the way to achieving your goals. It's who you are
that attracts your results more than anything else.

Action:

Schedule time each day to read your affirmations during your
Miracle Morning to program your subconscious and focus your
conscious mind on what's most important to you and what you are
committed to doing to make it your reality. That's right, you must
read them daily. Reading your affirmation occasionally is as effective
as an occasional workout. You'll start seeing results only when you've
made them a part of your daily routine.

A great place to read affirmations is in the shower. If you laminate
them and leave them there, then they will be in front of you every day.
Put them anywhere you can to remind you: an index card under your
car's sun visor, a sticky note on your bathroom mirror—you can even
write them directly on a mirror with dry erase markers. The more you
encounter them, the more the subconscious mind can connect with
them to change your thinking and your actions.

———

Here is Stacey's practice in her own words:

*Over the last four years I have catapulted the effectiveness of my
affirmation process by using note cards. When I find an opportunity to
crush a belief system that is not serving me or find a new goal or intention that I want to solidify in my life, I write an affirmation card about
it. I keep my cards in a stack on my nightstand. I have one for every key
area of my life. I typically have between 6 and 9 cards in my stack at
any given time. Every night before bed, I put myself into a passionate*

and intentional state, and I read every card as the very last thing I do before I close my eyes. Then I release and allow my other-than-conscious mind to keep doing the work for me while I sleep. When I wake up in the morning, the first thing I do is pop out of bed and intensely incant my affirmation cards to start my day!

Every time I manifest the affirmation on one of my cards, I put a big check mark across the card with a thick marker and put it in a pile of done cards in my nightstand drawer. I love how ginormous that stack of done cards is today!

Ninja Secret: *Whenever I write a new affirmation card that feels like a stretch compared to my current human reality, I go back and read all my done cards. At one time, each of those felt like a big stretch too, and now I've blown by them as my new normal! It helps me strengthen my faith.*

———

Step Four: Constantly Update and Evolve Your Affirmations

As you continue to grow, improve, and evolve, so should your affirmations. When you come up with a new goal, dream, or extraordinary result you want to create for your life, add it to your affirmations.

Like Stacey, I have affirmations for every single significant area of my life (finances, health, happiness, relationships, parenting, etc.), and I continually update them as I learn more. And I am always on the lookout for quotes, strategies, and philosophies that I can add to improve my mindset. Anytime you come across an empowering quote or philosophy and think, *Wow, that is an area where I could make a huge improvement,* add it to your affirmations.

Remember, your affirmations should be tailored to you and what you are *personally* committed to. They must be specific to work on your subconscious.

Your programming can change and improve at any time, starting right now. You can reprogram any perceived limitations with new beliefs and create new behaviors so you can become as successful as you want to be in any area of life you choose.

In summary, your new affirmations articulate the extraordinary results you are committed to creating, why they are critically import- ant to you, and, most importantly, which necessary actions you are committed to taking and when to ensure that you attain and sustain the extraordinary levels of success you truly want (and deserve) for your life.

Affirmations to Create a Level 10 Relationship

In addition to the formula to create your own affirmations, Stacey has provided this list of sample affirmations, which may help spark your creativity. Feel free to include any of these that resonate with you.

- I am just as worthy, deserving, and capable of achieving an unshakable love and unleashed passion as any other person on earth, and I will prove that today with my actions.

- Magnificent relationships are *created*, not found. It's a *skill*, and it can be learned! Many other people have learned how to do this, and I can too!

- The relationship I have today is a result of the decisions and actions I took in the past. I did the best that I could with what I knew then. Now I know better, and I can do better. I am proving that with every shift I make in my day-to-day life!

- As I do this work, I am becoming a better and more authen- tic version of myself every day. This work is a gift that I give myself.

- Only good can come from healing my relationship. I have faith that all the positivity I pour into this relationship will be the best thing for me, my partner, and our children.

- Every moment of the day, the Universe is giving me more opportunities to practice my new skills and tools. I am grateful for these learning opportunities, and I see them as *gifts* for my growth!

These are just a few examples of affirmations. You can use any that resonate with you, but do create your own using the four-step formula described in the previous pages. Anything you repeat to yourself over and over again with emotion will be programmed in your subconscious mind, help you form new beliefs, and manifest through your actions.

V is for Visualization

Visualization has long been a well-known practice of world-class athletes who use it to optimize their performance. Olympic athletes and top performers in many sports incorporate visualization as a critical part of their daily training. What is less well known is that other top achievers use it just as frequently.

Visualization is a technique by which you use your imagination to create a compelling picture of your future, providing you with heightened clarity and producing the motivation that will assist you in making your vision a reality.

To understand *why* visualization works, it helps to look at mirror neurons. A neuron is a cell that connects the brain and other parts of the body, and a mirror neuron is one that fires or sends an impulse when we take an action *or* observe someone else taking action. This is a relatively new area of study in neurology, but these cells seem to allow us to improve our abilities by watching other people perform them *or* by visualizing ourselves performing them. Some studies indicate, for example, that experienced weight lifters can increase muscle mass through vivid visualization sessions, and mirror neurons get the credit for making this possible. In many ways, the brain can't tell the difference between a vivid visualization and an actual experience.

I was always a little skeptical about the value of visualization because it sounded a little too *new agey*. Once I read about mirror neurons, my whole attitude changed!

What Do You Visualize?

Most people are limited by visions of their past results. They replay previous failures and heartbreaks. Creative visualization, however, enables you to *design* the vision that will occupy your mind, ensuring that the greatest pull on you is your future—a compelling, exciting, and limitless future.

Many people don't feel comfortable visualizing success and are scared to succeed. They may experience resistance to this practice. Some may even feel guilty that they will leave colleagues, friends, and family members behind when they become successful.

This famous quote from Marianne Williamson is a great reminder for anyone who feels mental or emotional obstacles when attempting to visualize:

Our deepest fear is not that we are inadequate. Our deepest fear is that we are powerful beyond measure. It is our light, not our darkness, that most frightens us. We ask ourselves, "Who am I to be brilliant, gorgeous, talented, fabulous?" Actually, who are you not to be? You are a child of God. Your playing small does not serve the world. There is nothing enlightened about shrinking so that other people won't feel insecure around you. We are all meant to shine, as children do. We were born to make manifest the glory of God that is within us. It's not just in some of us; it's in everyone. And as we let our own light shine, we unconsciously give other people permission to do the same. As we are liberated from our own fear, our presence automatically liberates others.

Consider that the greatest gift you can give to those you love is to live to your full potential. What does that look like for you?

After I've read my affirmations during my Miracle Morning practice, I sit upright, close my eyes, and take a few slow, deep breaths. For the next five to ten minutes, I simply visualize the *specific actions* that are necessary for my long- and short-term goals to become a reality.

Notice that I do *not* visualize the results. Many people will disagree on this, but scientific evidence shows that merely visualizing the result you want (e.g., the new car, the dream house, crossing the finish line, standing on stage, etc.) can actually diminish your drive because your brain has already experienced the reward on some level. Instead, I highly recommend focusing your visualization on the necessary actions. Visualize yourself performing these actions—especially those that you habitually resist and procrastinate on—in a way that creates a compelling mental and emotional experience of the action. For example, I despised running, but I'd made a commitment to myself (and publicly) to run a 52-mile ultramarathon. Throughout my five months of training, I used Miracle Morning Visualization to see me lacing up my running shoes and hitting the pavement—*with a smile on my face and pep in my step*—so that when it was time to train, I had already programmed the experience to be positive and enjoyable.

You might picture yourself feeling fully supported by your partner. Spend time imagining how proud you feel as the one who is creating this improvement in your relationship. What does it look like? How does it feel as you see yourself coming from compassion and appreciation, where you used to get frustrated? Picture yourself responding to triggers and issues with ease.

If experiencing a transformation in your relationship feels like an impossibility for you, imagine what it will feel like to give yourself the relationship education that no one ever gave you before. Imagine the role model you are being for your children. Feel the freedom of being your best and most authentic self and being at peace with the state of your relationship.

You can pick anything that is a critical action step or skill that you may not be performing at your best yet. Envisioning success and what it takes to get there will prepare you for, and almost ensure, a successful day.

Three Simple Steps For Miracle Morning Visualization

The perfect time to visualize yourself living in alignment with your affirmations is right after you read them.

Step One: Get Ready

Some people like to play instrumental music in the background during their visualization, such as classical or baroque (check out anything from the composer J. S. Bach). If you'd like to experiment with music, put it on with the volume relatively low. Personally, I find anything with words to be distracting.

Stacey, on the other hand, has shared that she blasts her favorite music over and over again when she visualizes. The words don't distract her at all; she's conditioned herself to thrive with it. Perhaps that's her feminine wiring (more on that in later chapters).

Now, sit up tall in a comfortable position. This can be on a chair, the couch, or the floor with a cushion. Breathe deeply. Close your eyes, clear your mind, and let go of any self-imposed limitations as you prepare yourself for the benefits of visualization.

Step Two: Visualize What You Really Want

What do you really want? Forget about logic, limits, and being practical. If you could reach any heights, personally and professionally, what would that look like? See, feel, hear, touch, taste, and smell every detail of your vision. Involve all your senses to maximize effectiveness. The more vivid you make your vision, the more compelled you'll be to take the necessary actions to make it a reality.

Step Three: Visualize Yourself Taking And Enjoying The Necessary Actions

Once you've created a clear mental picture of what you want, begin to see yourself doing precisely what you need to do to achieve your vision, doing it with supreme confidence, and enjoying every step of the process. See yourself engaged in the actions you'll need to take (dropping your expectations, putting your partner first, coming from heartfelt understanding, loving without measuring, etc.). Imagine the look and *feeling* of supreme confidence as you experience the results of the positive shifts you are creating in your relationship. See and *feel* yourself smiling as you navigate the moments of your day with more ease and happiness, filled with a sense of pride for your self-discipline to follow through on your commitment. In other words, visualize yourself doing what you must do, and thoroughly enjoying the process, especially if it's a process you don't naturally enjoy. Imagine what it would look and feel like if you did enjoy it.

Visualize the joy and happiness you feel as each day gets better and better. Visualize your family, friends, and spouse responding to your positive demeanor and optimistic outlook.

Seeing yourself as the person who has it all together is the first step in actually getting it all together. Imagine yourself creating the rock-solid relationship that you want to live in. See yourself laughing and enjoying playful moments once again.

Final Thoughts on Visualization

Visualization can be a powerful aid in overcoming self-limiting beliefs, as well as self-limiting habits like procrastination, and get you consistently performing the actions necessary to achieve extraordinary results in your relationship. When you combine reading your affirmations every morning with daily visualization, you will turbocharge the programming of your subconscious mind for success through peak performance. Your thoughts and feelings will align with your vision so that you can maintain the motivation you need to continue to take the necessary actions to transform your relationship.

E is for Exercise

Exercise should be a staple of your Miracle Morning. Even a few minutes of exercise each day significantly enhances your health, improves your self-confidence and emotional well-being, and enables you to think better and concentrate longer. You'll also notice how quickly your energy increases with daily exercise, and the people you spend the most time with will notice it, too.

Personal development experts and self-made multimillionaire entrepreneurs Eben Pagan and Tony Robbins (who is also a New York Times best-selling author) both agree that the number one key to success is to start every morning with a personal success ritual. Included in both of their success rituals is some type of morning exercise. Eben is adamant about the importance of *morning* exercise: "Every morning, you've got to get your heart rate up and get your blood flowing and fill your lungs with oxygen." He continued, "Don't just exercise at the end of the day, or at the middle of the day. And even if you do like to exercise at those times, always incorporate at least 10 to 20 minutes of jumping jacks, or some sort of aerobic exercise in the morning." Hey, if it works for Eben and Tony, it works for me!

Lest you think you have to engage in triathlon or marathon training, think again. Your morning exercise also doesn't need to replace an afternoon or evening regimen if you already have one in place. You can still hit the gym at the usual time. However, the benefits that flow from adding as little as five minutes of morning exercise are undeniable, including improved blood pressure and blood sugar levels and decreased risk of all kinds of scary things like heart disease, osteoporosis, cancer, and diabetes. Maybe most importantly, a little exercise in the morning will increase your energy levels for the rest of the day to help you keep up with the ups and downs of life.

You can go for a walk or run, follow along to a yoga video on YouTube, or find a Life S.A.V.E.R.S. buddy and play some early morning racquetball. There's also an excellent app called 7 Minute Workout that gives you a full body workout in—you guessed it—seven minutes. The choice is yours, but pick one activity and do it.

With as busy as our lives are today, to be successful, you need an endless reserve of energy to make the best of the challenges that come your way, and a daily morning exercise practice is going to provide it.

Exercise for Your Brain

Even if you don't care about your physical health, consider that exercise is simply going to make you smarter, and that can only help your problem-solving abilities. Dr. Steven Masley, a Florida physician and nutritionist with a health practice geared toward executives, explains how exercise creates a direct connection to your cognitive ability.

"If we're talking about brain performance, the best predictor of brain speed is aerobic capacity—how well you can run up a hill is very strongly correlated with brain speed and cognitive shifting ability," Masley said.

Masley has designed a corporate wellness program based on the work he's done with more than 1,000 patients. "The average person going into these programs will increase brain speed by 25–30 percent."

I chose yoga for my exercise activity and began practicing it shortly after I created the Miracle Morning. I've been doing it and loving it ever since.

———

Here's how Stacey's exercise routine differs.

For the last decade, I have been doing cardio outside in the morning before I start my day. Whether I can schedule an hour or just 20 minutes, one of the gifts I give myself is breathing that fresh morning air, outside in nature, as I move my body. Other than the writing, I do all my Miracle Morning Life S.A.V.E.RS. out on that street! I even listen to the portion of my audiobook that I have scheduled for that day as my reading. Then, before my shower, I take a few minutes to write in my phone journal or paper journal, and capture my "downloads" from the morning!

Find what resonates with you, and make it a part of your Miracle Morning.

———

Final Thoughts on Exercise

You know that if you want to maintain good health and increase your energy, you must exercise consistently. That's not news to anyone. But what also isn't news is how easy it is to make excuses. Two of the biggest are "I don't have time" and "I'm too tired." And those are just the first two on the list. There is no limit to the excuses you can think of. And the more creative you are, the more excuses you can find!

That's the beauty of incorporating exercise into your Miracle Morning—it happens before your day wears you out and before you've had hours to come up with new excuses. Because it comes first, the Miracle Morning is a surefire way to avoid those stumbling blocks and make exercise a daily habit.

Legal disclaimer: Hopefully this goes without saying, but you should consult your doctor or physician before beginning any exercise regimen, especially if you are experiencing any physical pain, discomfort, disabilities, etc. You may need to modify or even refrain from an exercise routine to meet your individual needs.

R is for Reading

One of the fastest ways to achieve everything you want is to find successful people to be your role models. For every goal you have, there's a good chance an expert has already achieved the same thing or something similar. As Tony Robbins says, "Success leaves clues."

Fortunately, some of the best of the best have shared their stories in writing. And that means all those success blueprints are just waiting for anyone willing to invest the time in reading. Books are a limitless supply of help and mentorship right at your fingertips.

Occasionally, I hear somebody say, "I'm just not a big reader." I get it. I never considered myself a big reader either. And think about this challenge—and solution—shared by Stacey:

After Jake was born, I used to refer to myself as having "reader's narcolepsy" because I couldn't stay awake for more than two sentences without nodding off. To my delight I have found that audiobooks are a fantastic solution for this. I listen while I'm exercising, out running errands, or even doing my makeup in the morning. By doing so, I'm able to consume a lot of books considering how full my days are. I always buy the physical book as well so I can highlight and make my notes after I listen to the book on audio.

Here are some of Stacey's favorite personal development books to support you in your relationship development journey.

- *The Go Giver: A Little Story About a Powerful Business Idea* by Bob Burg and John David Mann

- *Untethered Soul: The Journey Beyond Yourself* by Michael A. Singer

- *The Rhythm of Life* by Matthew Kelly

- *Inspiration for a Woman's Soul Series: Choosing Happiness, Cultivating Joy and Gratitude and Grace* by Linda Joy and co-authors (Stacey Martino, contributor)

- *Keys to the Kingdom* by Alison A. Armstrong

- *A Return to Love: Reflections on the Principles of A Course in Miracles* by Marianne Williamson

- *The War of Art: Break Through the Blocks and Win Your Inner Creative Battles* by Steven Pressfield

- *Start with Why: How Great Leaders Inspire Everyone to Take Action* by Simon Sinek

- *Ask and It Is Given* by Abraham and Esther Hicks

- *The Game of Life and How to Play It* by Florence Scovel Shinn

- *A Happy Pocket Full of Money* by David Cameron Gikandi

- *Money: Master the Game: 7 Simple Steps to Financial Freedom* by Tony Robbins

- *Profit First: A Simple System to Transform Any Business from a Cash-Eating Monster to a Money-Making Machine* by Mike Michalowicz

Hal's List:

- *The Art of Exceptional Living* by Jim Rohn
- *The One Thing: The Surprisingly Simple Truth Behind Extraordinary Results* by Gary Keller and Jay Papasan
- *The 7 Habits of Highly Effective People: Powerful Lessons in Personal Change* by Stephen R. Covey
- *Mastery* by Robert Greene
- *The 4 Hour Workweek: Escape 9-5, Live Anywhere, and Join the New Rich* by Tim Ferriss
- *The Compound Effect* by Darren Hardy
- *Taking Life Head On: How to Love the Life You Have While You Create the Life of Your Dreams* by Hal Elrod
- *Think and Grow Rich* by Napoleon Hill
- *Vision to Reality: How Short Term Massive Action Equals Long Term Maximum Results* by Honorée Corder
- *Finding Your Element: How to Discover Your Talents and Passions and Transform Your Life* by Sir Ken Robinson and Lou Aronica

In addition to finding confidence in yourself, you can transform your relationships, increase your self-esteem, improve your communication skills, learn how to become healthy, and improve any other area of your life you can think of. Head to your library or local bookstore—or do what I do and visit Amazon.com—and you'll find more books than you can possibly imagine on any area of your life you want to improve.

How Much Should You Read?

I recommend making a commitment to read a minimum of ten pages per day (although five is okay to start with if you read slowly or don't yet enjoy reading).

Ten pages may not seem like a lot, but let's do the math. Reading ten pages a day adds up to 3,650 pages per year, which stacks up to approximately eighteen 200-page books that will enable you to take yourself to the next level so you can take your relationship to the next level. All in just 10–15 minutes of daily reading, or 15–30 minutes if you read more slowly.

Let me ask you, if you read 18 personal and professional development books in the next twelve months, do you think you'll improve your mindset, gain more confidence, and learn proven strategies that will accelerate your success? Do you think you'll be a better, more capable version of who you are today? Do you think that will be reflected in your relationship? Absolutely! Reading ten pages per day is not going to break you, but it will absolutely make you.

Final Thoughts on Reading

- Begin with the end in mind by considering this question: What do you hope to gain from the book? Take a moment to do this now by asking yourself what you want to gain from reading this one.

- Books don't have to be read cover to cover, nor do they have to be finished. Remember that this is your reading time. Use the table of contents to make sure you read the parts you care about most, and don't hesitate to put it down and move to another book if you aren't enjoying it or gaining value from it. You have too many options for incredible information to spend time on the mediocre.

- Many Miracle Morning practitioners use their reading time to catch up on their religious texts, such as the Bible, Torah, Quran, and others.

- Unless you're borrowing a book from the library or a friend, feel free to underline, circle, highlight, dog-ear, and take notes in the margins of the book. The process of marking books as you read allows you to come back at any time and recapture the key lessons, ideas, and benefits without needing to read the book again. If you use a digital reader, such as a Kindle, Nook, or iBooks app, you can easily review your notes and highlighted passages each time you flip through the book, or go directly to a list.

- Summarize key ideas, insights, and memorable passages in a journal. You can build your own summary of your favorite books and revisit the key content anytime in just minutes.

- Rereading good personal development books is an underused yet very effective strategy. Rarely can you read a book once and internalize all its value. Achieving mastery in any area requires repetition. Why not try it out with this book? Commit to rereading *The Miracle Morning for Transforming Your Relationship* as soon as you're finished to deepen your learning and give yourself more time to master the practices.

- From Stacey: *Personally, there are some programs from Tony Robbins that I have consumed more than 25 times. "Repetition is the mother of skill," Tony tells us. And I will tell you that no one ever achieved mastery by hearing something once.*

- Audiobooks count as reading! You still get the information, and you can do it while exercising or during your commute. If you want to study a book carefully, listen to the audio while reading the text. As Stacey mentioned earlier, she regularly consumes her books on audio and simultaneously takes notes and highlights text in the physical book. Audiobooks are her primary strategy for repetitive consumption of books.

- Most importantly, make a plan to quickly implement what you've read. Schedule time for action steps based on advice you want to incorporate in your life while you're reading it. Keep your calendar next to you and schedule time blocks to put the content into action. Don't become a personal development junkie who reads a lot but does very little. I've met many people who take pride in the number of books they read, as if it's some badge of honor. I'd rather read and implement one good book than read 10 books and do nothing other than start reading the 11th book. While reading is a great way to gain knowledge, insights, and strategies, it is the application and practice of what you learn that will advance life and love. Stacey has said many times, "You can't learn your way to a better relationship." Are you committed to using what you're learning in this book by taking action and following through with the 30-Day Challenge at the end?

Glad to hear it. Let's get to the final *S* of the S.A.V.E.R.S.

S is for Scribing

Scribing is simply another word for writing. Let's keep it real—I needed an *S* for the end of S.A.V.E.R.S. because a *W* wouldn't fit anywhere. Thanks, thesaurus, I owe you one.

The scribing element of your Miracle Morning enables you to write down what you're grateful for, as well as document your insights, ideas, breakthroughs, realizations, successes, and lessons learned, including any areas of opportunity, personal growth, or improvement.

Most Miracle Morning practitioners scribe in a journal for five to ten minutes during their Miracle Morning. By getting your thoughts out of your head and putting them in writing, you'll immediately gain heightened awareness, clarity, and valuable insights that you'd otherwise forget or be oblivious to.

If you're like I used to be, you probably have at least a few half-used and barely touched journals and notebooks. It wasn't until I started my Miracle Morning practice that scribing quickly became one of my favorite daily habits.

Writing will give you the daily benefits of consciously directing your thoughts, but what's even more powerful are the insights you'll gain from reviewing your journals, from cover to cover, afterwards—especially at the end of the year. Tony Robbins reminds us that "A life worth living is a life worth recording."

It is hard to put into words how overwhelmingly constructive the experience of going back and reviewing your journals can be. Michael Maher, *The Miracle Morning for Real Estate Agents* co-author, is an avid practitioner of the Life S.A.V.E.R.S. Part of Michael's morning routine is to record his appreciations and affirmations in what he calls his Blessings Book. Michael says it best:

"What you appreciate … APPRECIATES. It is time to take our insatiable appetite for what we want and replace it with an insatiable appetite and gratitude for what we do have. Write your appreciations, be grateful and appreciative, and you will have more of those things you crave—better relationships, more material goods, more happiness."

There is strength in writing down what you appreciate, and reviewing this material can change your mindset on a challenging day. A great practice to add to your routine is to write what you appreciate about your relationship, your partner, and your life. When we slow down and notice the things we appreciate about our relationship, even (and particularly) when we feel less than wonderful about it, it's easier to focus on the positive aspects or qualities we might otherwise miss.

———

For more on this, let's hear from Stacey again:

Paul and I teach our students to look for the gift in the challenge so they can learn and progress. It can be tough to find the empowering meaning at times, but it's there.

For example, Tim is one of our clients who once came to me struggling because, after all the work he did in his marriage to his wife, Joanne, he was struck with the realization that he would actually be really hurt if he lost his marriage or Joanne—and he didn't like that feeling. After so many years of "I could take it or leave it" indifference to his wife, Tim was uncomfortable with the looming fear that, if his marriage to Joanne were to end or if something were to happen to her, he would be devastated.

As I often do with our students, instead of helping him to stop the uncomfortable feeling, I helped him to shift the meaning he was giving the situation to a more empowered meaning where he could find the gift.

With Tim it was simple, because the empowered meaning is "Congrat-ulations! You have created a relationship worth caring about!" That was a celebratory milestone in his relationship development journey. Going from "not giving a crap" to "I would be devastated if she wasn't my wife" is massive progress.

That was the gift. Appreciate your progress. That may sound simple to you as someone who is not feeling the pain of his situation. Tim was so focused on his newfound discomfort that finding something positive about it was simply not within his lens at the time.

What I did for Tim in our coaching call was to reflect back to him all his progress along the journey as a reminder that doing the work and going through the discomfort is "worth it" for him. You can do this same process for yourself through journaling.

I completely understand the feeling Tim had. I remember the day when that same feeling came over me about Paul for the first time. I know where I was standing in my house the moment I realized it. It had scared me so much that thoughts of ending my relationship with Paul had gone through my mind that day.

Actually, today I see that happen all the time. Often people reach out to me after they take damaging action from within a critical mo-ment like that. Where they get scared or hurt and from within that pain they react by doing or saying something that they can't "take back." It's a common pattern of reacting to pain.

I was grateful that Tim had me to call when it happened to him so I could congratulate him and break him out of his pattern …

With this empowered reframe, Tim was able to continue on his journey to create an unshakable love with Joanne, where nothing and no one could come between them! I know it was another milestone the day that he heard Joanne declare that he was the only thing that mat-tered in her world and told him they were unshakable! He might not have reached that milestone if he hadn't found the gift in his painful experience!

These moments will always come on your journey. When you get the positive meaning, write it down and capture it in a journal that is dedicated to progress and celebrations. On days when you are feeling unsure, frustrated, or dissatisfied with your progress (or lack thereof), go back and read your journal.

Sometimes we progress so much but stay focused on how far we have yet to go. If you don't capture the small but important grateful moments and the things in a regular day that "never used to happen for you before you started doing this work," you will forget them and, worse, forget the progress you have made. Make it part of your practice to write it down!

Recording your appreciations helps you focus on the positive, which will help you stay flexible and solution-focused even when circumstances are challenging.

———

While many worthwhile benefits flow from keeping a daily journal, including the ones Stacey just mentioned, here are a few of my favorites. With daily scribing, you'll:

- **Gain Clarity**—Journaling will give you more clarity and understanding of your past and current circumstances, help you work through present challenges you're facing, and allow you to brainstorm, prioritize, and plan your actions each day to optimize your future.

- **Capture Ideas**—You will be able to capture, organize, and expand on your ideas and avoid losing the important ones you are saving for an opportune moment in the future.

- **Review Lessons**—Journaling provides a place to record, reference, and review all of the lessons you're learning, both from your wins and any mistakes you make along the way.

- **Acknowledge Your Progress**—Rereading your journal entries from a year or even a week ago and observing how much progress you've made can be hugely beneficial. We often accomplish a task or goal and move on to the next without appreciating our efforts. Noticing how far you've come truly is one of the most enjoyable, eye-opening, and confidence-inspiring experiences, and it can't be duplicated any other way.

- **Improve Your Memory**—People assume they will remember ideas, actions they want to take, and questions they have, but if you've ever gone to the grocery store without a list, you know this is simply untrue. When we write something down, we are much more likely to remember it, and if we forget we can always go back and read it again.

Effective Journaling

Here are three simple steps to get started with journaling or improve your current journaling process:

1. **Choose a format: physical or digital.** You'll want to decide up front if you prefer a traditional, physical journal or a digital journal (on your computer or an app for your mobile device). If you aren't sure, experiment with both and see which feels best.

2. **Obtain the journal of your choice.** Almost anything can work, but when it comes to a physical journal there is something to be said for a durable one that you enjoy looking at—after all, ideally you're going to have it for the rest of your life. I like to buy high-quality leather journals with lines on the pages, but it's your journal, so choose what works best for you. Some people prefer journals without lines so they can draw or create mind maps. Others like to have a pre-dated book with a page for each day of the year to help them stay accountable.

Here are a few favorite physical journals from TMM Facebook Community:

- *The Miracle Morning Companion Planner* is your hands-on guide for building a happier and more fulfilling life and career. This 12-month, undated planner allows you to start at any time of the year! Incorporating and tracking the Life S.A.V.E.R.S. each day will help you to be more present and intentional in each moment, own every aspect of your day, and to get the most out of your life. Check out a free preview here: MiracleMorning.com/PlannerSample.

- *The Five Minute Journal* has become popular among top performers. It has a very specific format for each day with prompts, such as "I am grateful for …" and "What would make today great?" It takes five minutes or less and includes an evening option so you can review your day. (FiveMinuteJournal.com)

- *The Freedom Journal* gives you a structured daily process that is focused on helping you with a single objective: Accomplish Your #1 Goal in 100 Days. Beautifully designed by John Lee Dumas of the Entrepreneur On Fire podcast, it's designed specifically to help you set and accomplish one big goal at a time. (TheFreedomJournal.com)

- *The Plan: Your Legendary Life Planner* was designed by friends of ours, and it is a goal-setting and habit-tracking system and planner for people who are ready for life balance and are willing to be intentional about achieving Level 10 in all areas of life. (LegendaryLifePlan.com)

- *The Miracle Morning Journal* is designed specifically to enhance and support your Miracle Morning and to keep you organized and accountable while you track your S.A.V.E.R.S. each day. You can get a copy of *The Miracle Morning Journal* on Amazon or download a free sample at TMMbook.com to make sure it's right for you.

If you prefer to use a digital journal, many choices are available. Here are a few favorites:

- *Five Minute Journal* also offers an iPhone app, which follows the same format as the physical version, but allows you to upload photographs to your daily entries, and also sends you helpful reminders to input your entries each morning and evening. (FiveMinuteJournal.com)

- *Day One* is a popular journaling app, and it's perfect if you don't want structure or limits on how much you can write. Day One offers a blank page for each daily entry, so if you like to write lengthy journal entries, this may be the app for you. (DayOneApp.com)

- *Penzu* is a popular online journal that doesn't require an iPhone, iPad, or Android device. All you need is a computer. (Penzu.com)

  Again, it really comes down to your preference and the features you want. If none of these digital options resonate with you, type "online journal" into Google, or simply type "journal" into the app store for your device, and you'll get a variety of choices.

3. **Scribe daily.** You'll find endless things you can write about. Notes from the book you're reading, a list of things you're grateful for, and your top three to five priorities for the day are good items to start with. Write whatever makes you feel good and optimizes your day. Don't worry about grammar, spelling, or punctuation. Your journal is a place to let your imagination run wild; so keep a muzzle on your inner critic, and don't edit—just scribe!

Customizing Your S.A.V.E.R.S.

I know that you might have days when you can't do the Miracle Morning practice all at once. Feel free to split up the Life S.A.V.E.R.S. in any way that works for you, and include your kids in your practice as well. Here is an example. If your kids are old enough to meditate with you, invite them to join you. But if they're too young, it's probably best to practice silence by yourself.

I want to share a few ideas specifically geared toward customizing the Life S.A.V.E.R.S. based on your schedule and preferences. Your current morning routine might allow you to fit in only a 6-, 20-, or 30-minute Miracle Morning, or you might choose to do a longer version on the weekends.

Here is an example of a fairly common 60-minute Miracle Morning schedule using the Life S.A.V.E.R.S.

Silence: 10 minutes

Affirmations: 5 minutes

Visualization: 5 minutes

Exercise: 10 minutes

Reading: 20 minutes

Scribing: 10 minutes

You can customize the sequence, too. Some people prefer to do the reading and scribing first because it takes the most focus. Others prefer to do exercise first to get their blood pumping and wake themselves up. I prefer to start with a period of peaceful, purposeful Silence so that I can wake up slowly, clear my mind, and focus my energy and intentions. However, this is your Miracle Morning, not mine—feel free to experiment with different sequences to see which you like best.

Ego Depletion and Your Miracle Morning

Have you ever wondered why you can resist sugary snacks in the morning, but your resistance crumbles in the afternoon or evening? Why is it that sometimes willpower is strong and other times it deserts us? It turns out that willpower is like a muscle that grows tired from use, and at the end of the day it is harder to push ourselves to do activities that serve us and avoid those that don't.

The good news is that we know how this works and can set ourselves up for success with some advance planning. And the great news? The Miracle Morning is an integral part of your plan. To see how this works, we need to understand ego depletion.

Ego depletion is a term to describe "a person's diminished capacity to regulate their thoughts, feelings, and actions," according to Roy F. Baumeister and John Tierney, the authors of *Willpower: Rediscovering the Greatest Human Strength.* Ego depletion grows worse at the end of the day and when we are hungry, tired, or have had to exert our willpower too often or for long durations.

If you wait until the end of the day to do important things that give you energy and help you become the person and partner you want to be, you'll find that your excuses are more compelling and your motivation has gone missing. But, when you wake up and do your Miracle Morning first thing, you gain the increased energy and mindfulness that the Life S.A.V.E.R.S. provide and keep ego depletion from getting in your way.

When you perform the Life S.A.V.E.R.S. habit every day, you learn the mechanics of habit formation when your willpower is strongest, and you can use this knowledge and energy to adopt small and doable habits at other times of the day.

Final Thoughts on the Life S.A.V.E.R.S.

Everything is difficult before it's easy. Every new experience is uncomfortable before it's comfortable. The more you practice the Life S.A.V.E.R.S., the more natural and normal each of them will feel. My first time meditating was almost my last because my mind raced like a Ferrari, and my thoughts bounced around uncontrollably like the silver sphere in a pinball machine. Now I love meditation, and, while I'm still no master, I'm decent at it.

———

Consider this from Stacey:

When I first started doing Visualization practice, I would drift off into thoughts that questioned how can I do that? Fifteen minutes later, I would snap out of it and realize that I had taken myself on a journey listing all the reasons why I couldn't have what I had tried to visualize. It took practice, repetition, and dedication to get to the place with my visualization where I could see and feel things as I want them to be with zero attachment or speculation about how they would happen.

I invite you to begin practicing the Life S.A.V.E.R.S. now, so you can become familiar and comfortable with each of them and get a jump-start before you begin The Miracle Morning 30-Day Challenge in chapter 10.

The Six-Minute Miracle Morning

If you don't have ten minutes, you don't have a life.
—TONY ROBBINS,
speaking about a daily morning ritual

If your biggest concern is finding time, don't worry. I've got you covered. You can actually do the entire Miracle Morning—receiving the full benefits of all six Life S.A.V.E.R.S.—in only six minutes a day. While six minutes isn't the duration I'd recommend on a daily basis, for those days when you're pressed for time, simply do each of the Life S.A.V.E.R.S. for one minute each:

- **Minute One (S):** Close your eyes and enjoy a moment of peaceful, purposeful silence to clear your mind and get centered for your day.

- **Minute Two (A):** Read your most important affirmation to reinforce *what* result you want to accomplish, *why* it's important to you, *which* specific actions you must take, and, most importantly, precisely *when* you will commit to taking those actions.

- **Minute Three (V):** Visualize yourself flawlessly executing the single most important action that you want to mentally rehearse for the day.

- **Minute Four (E):** Stand up and engage in some high energy jumping jacks or drop and do push-ups and crunches to get your heart rate up and engage your body.

- **Minute Five (R):** Grab the book you're reading and read a page or paragraph.

- **Minute Six (S):** Grab your journal and jot down one thing that you're grateful for and the single most important result for you to accomplish that day.

I'm sure you can see how, even in six minutes, the Life S.A.V.E.R.S. will set you on the right path for the day—and you can always devote more time later when your schedule permits or the opportunity presents itself. Doing the six-minute practice is a way to start a mini-habit to build your confidence or a way to bookmark the habit on a tough morning. Another mini-habit you could do is to start with one of the Life S.A.V.E.R.S. and once you get used to waking up earlier, add more of them. Remember that the goal is to have some time to work on your personal goals and mindset, so if you are overwhelmed, it's not going to work for you.

Personally, my Miracle Morning has grown into a daily ritual of renewal and inspiration that I absolutely love!

In the coming chapters, Stacey will build on the benefits of the Life S.A.V.E.R.S. and cover loads of life-changing relationship education tools and strategies that have the potential to transform your love and life!

I have witnessed firsthand the incredible transformations that Paul and Stacey have empowered people to create in their marriages, their families, and their lives. Marriages that appeared too far gone to save brought back from the edge. Parents that lost the passion and started to slip rejuvenating to a rock-solid team with reignited passion. Couples going through separation that couldn't talk to each other civilly transforming into a harmonious co-parenting family for their kids. And singles who want an outstanding relationship gaining the clarity on the missing piece that allows them to attract and create their forever love relationship.

When it comes to relationships, Stacey and Paul are my go-to experts. They truly are changing the way relationship is done, and I'm thrilled to introduce you to them. I can't wait for you to take in all that they have to offer you in the chapters ahead.

Real Life Relationship Case Study

James & Alicia

James's Story

Before

When Alicia found you, our relationship was dead. We had been physically separated for six months (living in separate homes), but emotionally separated for over two years.

Our 25-year-long marriage was a shamble; we were both wrecked emotionally; our three kids and our families were all suffering. We were in a downward spiral that we didn't understand and couldn't arrest.

Doing the Work

I didn't know that Alicia had discovered the program and was doing some work on her own, but I could see some differences. I wasn't sure why they were happening … I was just glad!

Six months after beginning the work, Alicia invited me to one of the live events with Stacey and Paul. At that event, we had a breakthrough and decided to take a leap of faith and join the RelationshipU program.

After

One year later, our marriage is alive, passionate, hopeful, fun, messy, authentic, and in some ways better than it has ever been! We have our marriage back! And I moved back into our home! Our family is back together. Astonishing!

Talk about 'changing your story'; I'm so glad that we changed ours, from "25-year marriage that ended in a painful divorce" to "They fought through adversity, never gave up on each other, and made their relationship new and better."

That's the story I want our kids to tell about us. That's the example I want to be for them.

Second chances are a rare thing in life. Each morning when I wake up, I thank God that He's given me another chance to be the husband and the man that I want to be to serve the woman I love. And when I thank Him for that, I also thank Him for bringing Stacey and Paul into our lives and making all of this possible.

Thank you both so very much.

Their story has had an *amazing* turnaround! But what if Alicia hadn't been willing to be the one to start doing the work first? What if she'd felt it was hopeless and too far gone because James had already moved out?

Alicia's Story

Before

I knew I didn't want to get divorced, but I didn't see a way out. I didn't think that James would change. I was terrified, hurt, and resentful. I didn't know what I was going to do.

Had it not been for my friend Kelly sharing some of Stacey's videos with me, my marriage would be over by now. I thought Stacey had made those videos just for me! I sat in my chair with my hand over my mouth thinking, Holy shit …! *For the first time, someone was explaining WHY we were in this mess! It wasn't that I had turned into a terrible person or that I was being unreasonable in my discontent! But I also had as much responsibility as James did in getting to where we were in our relationship; something that my closed, "spouse-punishing" attitude hadn't considered before.*

I got an enormous amount of validation for my feelings ... I am not alone! Others are going through this! And most importantly, that day I felt a glimpse of HOPE for the first time in two and a half years. I needed to do this for me! I needed to stop waiting to see what James was going to do and take control of my destiny and happiness.

Doing the Work

I decided to do this work because I needed to heal. I didn't tell James anything about what I was doing because we really weren't talking at the time. I also didn't want to give him false hope because I wasn't even sure I wanted to save the marriage!

I remember the day that I walked into my first live event with Stacey and Paul. I was a mess. I was crying before I even opened my mouth, and Stacey just opened her arms and said, "We got you." From that moment on, I felt safe and like someone was going to help me along the way!

After

Committing to do the RelationshipU program with Stacey and Paul was a leap of faith, not knowing if it was going to work or not. After a year, I can tell you, it was the best thing we have ever done. We have our marriage back and my husband has moved back into our home, after one and a half years of living apart. I have learned that everything is possible! The minute that Stacey made me realize my responsibility, it was a game changer, because I went from being a victim to seeing that I had helped us get there. It's not that I had chosen the wrong person—we just didn't know how to navigate our way.

Today we are creating the marriage we want. We are doing it because it's a choice!

I can't believe how far we have come in a relatively short time. I am certain that we could have never gotten here without Stacey and Paul's commitment, hard work, and love. I love you both and I am forever grateful for your love and support.

Keys to Their Success

- **She did it herself:** Instead of looking at this as "couple's work," Alicia decided that this work was for her and began without including James. This empowered her to move forward.

- **Freedom:** Before beginning this work, Alicia was stuck. She came to me with a fear that doing the work somehow meant that she was saying that she wanted to stay in her marriage. When she began this work, the way things were, she did *not* want to commit to staying in her marriage; she had already begun the divorce process. I reassured her that this work was for *her* and for her to heal her *family* with James; whether or not their marriage survived this, their family needed this no matter what. She agreed with that and felt the *freedom* to start taking action without the commitment to stay in her marriage.

- **Don't give up:** There were many times on this journey when James and Alicia each had their stumbles, fears, and pains. They stayed plugged into the RelationshipU community, they came to Paul or me for guidance, and they harnessed their courage to move forward. I can think of several key moments when it could have easily fallen apart if one of them gave up and walked away. But they stayed with it, came to us for guidance, and broke through! Not for their marriage, but because they each needed this growth, or else they were destined to encounter the same pains in the next relationship.

- **Breaking her own ice:** Forgiving and forgetting was a challenge for Alicia, as it is for so many people who have been through so much. Through the decay of her marriage, she had surrounded herself with walls of protection and become an "Ice Princess" inside. Part of her healing was to be courageous to be vulnerable again. At one of our live meetings I remember Alicia saying that she made the decision to start "Breaking my own ice!" She had turned her fear and helplessness into courage and empowerment! We still say that phrase in our work! I invite *you* to start breaking *your* own ice!

SECTION II:

TRANSFORMING YOUR RELATIONSHIP

— 5 —
PERSPECTIVE:
SEE YOUR RELATIONSHIP WITH NEW EYES

BY STACEY MARTINO

*"If you change the way you look at things,
the things you look at change."*

—DR. WAYNE DYER, Best-selling author and speaker

*"It takes courage ... to endure the sharp pains of self-discovery rather
than choose to take the dull pain of unconsciousness
that would last the rest of our lives."*

—MARIANNE WILLIAMSON, Best-selling author
of *A Return to Love*

Sixteen years ago, all I wanted was to get out of the pain I was suffering in my love relationship. I wanted a rock-solid relationship with lots of passion and fire!

I wanted the dream.

A dream relationship where my man supported me one thousand percent! He would protect me, defend me, and stand up for me in the world.

His greatest joy would be to help me, support me, and clear a path for me to achieve my dreams.

I wanted him to cherish me, love me in spite of my flaws, and be my number one. (Of course, I would do all of these things for him, too.)

I wanted us to face the world together and triumph!

My man would be the person in the world I loved to be with most. We would go on adventures exploring the world together. We would delight in bringing fun, laughter, and excitement into each other's lives.

I dreamt of sizzling hot, unleashed passion with amazing sex that would take us to dizzying heights of ecstasy!

Sounds great, right? The only problem was, I didn't really know if any of that was possible because I had never seen anyone with a relationship like that in real life. Even if it *was* possible, I had no idea how to create it!

Perhaps you can relate? If so, you're not alone.

After interacting with thousands of people through this work, I know that most people want some version of the dream I had (*if* they're being honest with themselves).

While the specifics of their dream may sound different from mine, the bottom line is that they want it all—love, support, alignment, fun, playfulness, intimacy, and *amazing* sex!

Now, if they're *not* being honest with themselves, they will tell you flat out that they don't want that dream. But they're lying to themselves.

I know because I used to be one of those people. In my 20s, I told people I didn't believe in marriage or even in *love* itself.

I tried to convince myself I didn't need love and that my life was full without it, but the truth is, I was lying to myself.

Why do people lie to themselves about not wanting the dream?

- Some are bitter and jaded.
- Others are terrified and living in self-protection.
- Many are disconnected from desire and numbing out through distractions and addictions.

Love and passion have become associated with too much pain, so people distance themselves from their dream.

In fact, just admitting that they *have* that dream has become too painful, so they lie to themselves in one form or another and decide that they don't want it.

Sweetie, it's human nature to want love and passion! The research shows that it's wired into our DNA.

The fact is, love is a human *need*. If we don't have it, we start to wither and die, as evidenced by studies done on babies in orphanages. In institutions where only basic, physiological human needs were met without love, physical touch, and human connection, almost half of the babies died, despite the absence of a physical reason for death.

Love is the only transcendent emotion. It has a power that no other *feeling* has to take us to another place, another level. It creates *euphoria*.

Every human needs love, but what about passion?

Passion isn't optional either!

Passion is the life force of any love relationship. If the passion has fizzled or vanished, the relationship is dying.

Every day, I hear busy parents trying to tell themselves they can do without sex. Upon further questioning, I find that the sex and passion have fizzled in their marriage, and they have no idea how to get it back. The idea of living the rest of their lives without passion terrifies them, and so does the thought of ending their marriage.

They're stuck in the dilemma that they are too tired to have sex and too busy to put any time into it. They're absolutely exhausted and don't need *one more thing* to have to do.

So they decide that the honorable thing to do is to "grow up" and decide that sex isn't all that important. They throw themselves into their work, the kids, the house, and the abundance of "busyness" that is available to everyone.

Before they know it, months and years slip by, and they're rarely having sex anymore. When they do, it definitely isn't hot!

It breaks my heart to see well-meaning people erode perfectly good, loving relationships by doing this. They end up hanging by a thread, with no idea how it happened.

I teach a tool to help arrest this decline in its tracks: Salad or Garbage?

What does salad or garbage have to do with your relationship?

There's an old joke that goes, "What's the difference between salad and garbage?"

The punchline is "TIME! The difference between salad and garbage is time!" (Get it?)

It's the same with a caring or loving (yet passionless) relationship, and one that's hanging by a thread (where one or both partners consider leaving the relationship): Time.

Why?

When you stop experiencing passion and having sex with the only person that you're supposed to be able to have "the sex" with, pain eventually starts to build between you. You feel rejected and hurt, and in time that rejection turns into resentment. From there, the distance builds.

Eventually, you begin to live parallel lives, living under the same roof, raising kids together, going through the motions, and trying not to bump into each other. Each bump is a painful reminder of what you are no longer sharing together.

You continue in quiet desperation until the thing that was keeping you together disappears (often it's the day the kids move out), and you reflect on your relationship and ask yourself, "Can I really keep living like this for another 40 years?"

Then it hits you ... BOOM ... that over time your relationship has gone from salad to garbage! Now you're left wondering if you can stay in the relationship or whether this is even the right partner for you.

Unfortunately, salad to garbage is an organic progression. Without training and strategic action, this is how committed, long-term relationships naturally progress.

That's why Paul and I are *so* passionate about helping people to get the passion back into their relationship!

Listen, passion is not just about having *sex* for sex's sake. Sure, sex is awesome, and you will be a lot happier when you are having loads of great sex! But this is about so much more than sex. Sex is a symptom, not a cause.

We want to stop the epidemic of relationships that are decaying from salad to garbage due to the loss of the *life force* of passion!

If that's you, I want you to know you're not alone.

News flash! Even a quick Google search of the latest research reveals that busy parents are *not* having sex.

So if you are not having sex, or you are having very little sex (in your opinion), or if you are not having hot sex ... you are *not alone*.

And it's not your fault!

Why do committed, long-term love relationships organically lose their passion over time?

To explain this phenomena, I created a tool called the Love and Passion Seesaw.

Simply put, love and passion work like a seesaw—in an inverse relationship.

Sameness creates *love*, and *difference* creates *passion*.

In other words, having things in common creates friendship, and friendship is the foundation for your love relationship.

As a love relationship deepens, you start to accumulate more and more things in common: shared experiences as well as activities and people. Eventually, you start living together and raising children, and you share almost every aspect of your lives.

As what you have in common grows, you are going deeper and deeper into love, which is great! But do you know what this is not so great for? You guessed it, cupcake … *passion*!

Passion comes from differences!

When a relationship is new, there are lots of differences between partners. The things they say and do, the people they know, where they live, and the places they go are all different and new to one another. The newness and differences create lots of sparks and passion.

Over time, the newness fades and the differences disappear, causing a loss of passion in your relationship.

Your love gets stronger, yet your passion goes dim because of the Love and Passion Seesaw. When one goes up, the other goes down.

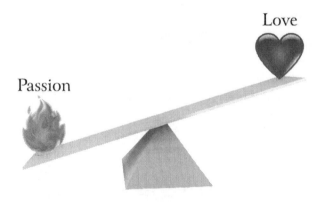

Please don't despair if that's happened to you. Although it's the natural progression of a committed relationship, you *can* turn it around!

You can create a *height* of passion that matches the *depth* of your love by *cultivating the differences*!

Bonus Download: To watch the "Salad vs. Garbage" training video and dive deeper into *Masculine and Feminine Energy*, visit RelationshipDevelopment.org/tmmonus..

We teach many tools and strategies to help students cultivate the differences and reignite the passion. However, *cultivating the difference between masculine and feminine energy is by far the most powerful* and will give you the biggest bang for your buck (pun intended)!

Everyone has both masculine and feminine energy inside. But most humans have one authentic core energy that is dominant—either masculine or feminine. (It doesn't matter what body you come in, it's about your dominant core authentic energy).

NOTE: At times, I will use the shortcut of referring to men for masculine energy and women for feminine energy. That is not always the case; gender does not always dictate your authentic core energy. Please don't let my vocabulary trip you up. Get what you need from this material. If you are a woman with a masculine core or a man with a feminine core please switch my vocabulary so that it serves you. All that matters for this content is your authentic core energy inside ... not your wrapper!

Masculine Energy and Feminine Energy are *wildly* different.

Are they equal? *Yes!*

Are they the same? Oh, *hell no!*

What is Masculine Energy?

Masculine energy is all about being rooted, unwavering, decisive, taking action, facing obstacles, and breaking through. What's more, mature masculine is wired to serve, protect, and provide, while being fueled and driven by integrity, honor, and freedom. Paul will go deeper into the differences between immature masculine and mature masculine in chapter 8.

What is Feminine Energy?

Feminine energy is all about being open, vulnerable, receptive, creative, helpful, collaborative, and communicative.

When you can cultivate the difference between masculine and feminine energy in your relationship, you can reignite the passion and bring the spark back!

In chapter 8, Paul and I will take you into a deeper dive into feminine and masculine energy and how to realign with yours. I can't stop you from skipping ahead to that point, as I know many people will do that anyway. But this book is designed the way it is for a reason. Your greatest opportunity for success in shifting your own energy is to *first understand and appreciate* the differences between you and your partner.

That lesson begins now.

KEY LESSONS ON THE DIFFERENCES BETWEEN MASCULINE AND FEMININE

Lesson #1: Men and Women are completely equal, yet totally different!

Our modern western culture has taught us to minimize or dismiss the differences—as if being different makes us inferior. But we are *not* the same, and trying to suppress our core energy and live inauthentically takes a toll—especially in our love relationship!

After working with thousands of people, I can attest that the root of a great deal of pain in relationships is a lack of understanding about the differences between the masculine and the feminine.

We expect our partners to think and behave like we do, so whenever they do, say, feel, or process something in a way that we would *not*, we judge them, make them wrong for it, and we feel angry, hurt, or frustrated.

We start having thoughts like:

"Why would you say that ..."

"It's so annoying when you ..."

"You never ..."

"Why can't you just ..."

Sound familiar?

That's *you* evaluating your partner based on your own blueprint instead of understanding and appreciating how they are wired.

Everyone has their own blueprint, which is comprised of mindset, rules, values, beliefs, patterns, triggers, meanings, and emotions. Think of it as the software that runs your show.

When your partner doesn't think, do, feel, or process the way you would, you react negatively because you're evaluating their behavior through the lens of *your* blueprint. They didn't do what you thought they should, so you interpret it to be bad behavior.

I'll give you an example of the principle using the differences between my two children because it's easier to understand than it would be if I used your partner and less likely to bring up resistance for you.

Our son Jake is a gentle, loving, sensitive, funny kid. He likes to read or play video games. A hug can pretty much fix anything. He's quick to give you a compliment, tell you how much he loves you, and be super considerate of your feelings. He is a loyal and trusted friend.

Our daughter Gracie is a firecracker. She is a force of nature to be reckoned with. She has an extraordinary level of protective instincts. She's bold, assertive, confident, and adventurous. She's wired for survival. She's strong, independent, and feisty.

It's my job to be the parent that my kid needs me to be. Jake and Grace are as different as night and day. Beyond their masculine and feminine energy, they are just completely different kids.

As a result, I can't use a one-size-fits-all approach.

When Jake is struggling, I offer him a hug and sit with him, snuggling and saying loving and positive things as he processes how he feels and moves through to a better state.

When Gracie is struggling, I give her more space and I sit quietly near her while she processes internally, on her own, until she gets into a better state.

I could insist on treating them the same way, but that would come from me being stubbornly attached to the way I want to be with them, expecting them to compromise their authenticity to accommodate the way I want to parent. That would lead to only frustration and misery for all of us. Furthermore, it would make me a very unenlightened, selfish, and unhappy parent.

By committing to learn about the differences between my kids and parenting them each accordingly, I can bring out the best in both, help them thrive as individuals, and enjoy parenting a hell of a lot more with *much* less struggle!

It's my choice, and this approach is more work for sure, but it leads to the kinds of results that are worth living for. After all, I didn't have kids to live selfishly and struggle every day as a parent as a result. I became a parent knowing it would be the hardest thing I would ever take on, and I committed to doing the best I possibly could … not for me, for *them*!

Well, it's the same in your love relationship. Your partner is completely different from you, just like children are all different from each other.

You can keep treating your partner as if they are just like you, making everything harder on yourself, struggling with your lack of results, and being miserable all of the time. Or you can commit to understanding the differences in your partner and shifting yourself so you bring out the best in them. This approach will give you outstanding results and create more joy in the experience of your relationship.

The choice is yours.

Lesson #2: Understanding the differences between the masculine and feminine happen on a spectrum.

You don't go from A to Z on these differences in a moment. It's a process, and just like all change, it happens on a spectrum.

SPECTRUM OF CHANGE

Step Zero: Unaware

You are unaware of the differences between the masculine and feminine and how to work with them. You are not really *on* the spectrum to mastery at this point, so it's step zero.

This is where the differences that your partner brings tend to drive you batshit crazy because they just don't make sense to you. You find yourself thinking, *Why the F would you do that?* That's the pain of being at Step Zero on the spectrum of change. The good news is, as you learn better, you can do better.

Step One: Awareness

You're on step one after reading this far. You are now aware that there are differences, but you aren't sure what they are, or how to use them. (Congratulations! You are on the spectrum, baby!)

Step Two: Understanding

This is where you understand the key differences between the masculine and feminine. It happens only after you receive a thorough relationship education.

This is what it looks like when you stop at understanding without progressing to acceptance of the differences:

> In this scenario, a husband and wife had gone to Home Depot together, and she commented to him about how much she *loves* hydrangea bushes, hoping he would take the hint and buy her one for Mother's Day. The husband heard only that his wife likes hydrangea bushes. Duly noted. He was reminded when they walked by the dryer vents that she needed a new one, and he's wired to serve her, so he picked one up. She was hurt that not only did he *fail* to get her what she wanted, but also that he gave her a thoughtless, boring gift. After all, it was something for the house, not her.
>
> So she said, "Oh, I get it. I understand that you don't pick up on implied communication, and you only understand direct communication. But I *told* you how much I love hydrangea bushes when we were walking through Home Depot yesterday! You can't even pick up a freaking hydrangea bush for me the next damn day for Mother's Day? Oh *no* … not you! You come home with a new dryer vent. A new freaking dryer vent! Seriously? I know, I know, you guys aren't even capable of picking up on something *blatantly* obvious. I get it."

Understanding without acceptance and appreciation won't get you a magnificent love affair. It will only *magnify* the problems as you begin to use your new tools and understanding as weapons against your partner.

Understanding is not enough, and unfortunately, that's where most relationship expertise, advice, and research stops.

Step Three: Acceptance

This is where you fully accept the differences in your partner. After getting a relationship education and understanding how you and your partner are wired differently, you release all judgments about masculine versus feminine. You fully accept that, although we're equal, we're different, and *it is supposed to be this way*. One is not better than the other. One is not wrong or right. This is acceptance without judgment.

This is how the example from above would play out differently between a husband and wife where the wife was at the level of Acceptance of the differences between the masculine and feminine.

> Again, they are walking through the Home Depot store, and she notices the hydrangea bushes and thinks to herself, *That would make a great gift for me for Mother's Day.* She squeezes her husband's hand (since he responds best to physical touch) and says "Babe, I really love hydrangea bushes. Would you please get one for me for either Mother's Day or another upcoming holiday? I would really enjoy that."
>
> "Absolutely! Consider it done." He tells her, as he pulls out his phone and enters a reminder for himself so he doesn't forget. He snaps a picture of the bush because he will never remember what it looked like, and he feels good about his ability to deliver on that gift at a Level 10!
>
> He was reminded when they walked by the dryer vents that she needed a new one, and he's wired to serve her, so he picked one up. As he puts it in the cart, she smiles a huge smile and squeezes his arm. She says, "Thank you so much for taking such good care of me, baby. I'm so grateful for you."
>
> "It's my pleasure and my job, baby!" he tells her.

Perhaps you are thinking that this scenario sounds too hard to believe? People don't actually talk like that to each other, right?

That scenario actually happened between me and Paul many years ago!

Paul did get me the hydrangea bush. I killed it (I can't keep a plant alive to save my life). Do you know what he bought me for Mother's Day this year? A *fake hydrangea bush.* I freaking love it! It's still looking gorgeous on my deck … through rain and snow. Ha! That man knows me so well.

Step Four: Appreciate

Once you see how the difference between you and your partner is really a gift, you experience a deep appreciation for them.

When you reach this level, your partner will feel it, and you begin to experience a much better quality of life, day to day.

To create an unshakable love and an unleashed passion, however, you can't stop there.

Miracle Morning Opportunity: During your Miracle Morning time, create affirmations that remind you of the things you appreciate about the differences your partner brings.

Step Five: CHERISH!

The ultimate goal is to become *so* grateful for everything that is different about your partner that you cherish the gifts they bring to your relationship and your life!

In this magical state, you'll find that you actually cherish the stuff that used to drive you batshit crazy!

Lesson #3: Three Key Differences Between the Masculine and the Feminine

In our programs and events, we teach our students dozens of key differences and the tools to navigate them.

For the sake of the limited time we have together, I'm going to teach you three that you can use right away so you can start experiencing the power you have to create positive change in your relationship.

While we will certainly focus on using these in your love relationship, the impact of mastering these tools extends way beyond. Understanding, accepting, appreciating, and cherishing these differences will dramatically improve how you relate to all of the people in your world.

DIFFERENCE #1: OUTCOME VS. JOURNEY

The masculine is outcome-focused.

They desire to find the solution, achieve the outcome, and get results. They want to achieve the goal, so they can get to the peace, calm, or "nothingness."

The feminine is experience-focused.

We are designed to enjoy the journey and experience it all. Sure, we like to get outcomes too, but not for the sake of getting to nothingness. When we achieve our goal, we get more "somethingness." (Yes, that's a word! My editor left it in, so it must be a word.)

There are moments on the journey that the feminine just wants to enjoy the experience—like when I just made that playful joke about my editor.

That comment didn't need to be in that paragraph. It didn't have a purpose, and it wasn't necessary. Paul would have edited it out. If he was looking at this manuscript purely from a masculine lens, he would have removed that superfluous sentence (see, I know some big-ass words) because it wasn't necessary to get to the outcome.

Since I'm a feminine energy girl, I like to play, have fun, and leave *more* words in so I can experience *more* on my journey of writing, and you can experience *more* on your journey of reading.

If you are masculine core, reading the past few paragraphs might have frustrated the heck out of you. You just wanted me to get to the freaking point!

If so, Paul has a great strategy you can use to learn how to *appreciate* the inefficient, feminine style of communication.

STRATEGIES FOR NAVIGATING OUTCOME VS. JOURNEY—FOR MEN

Strategy #1 from Paul: Appreciate Her Zest for Life

The feminine is designed to put some *color* in your otherwise black-and-white world. The first step to appreciating this aspect of the feminine is to learn how to see the world through her eyes and find enjoyment in seeing her so happy.

Miracle Morning Opportunity: Create an affirmation for your Miracle Morning to remind yourself of how much you appreciate her zest for life.

Tool: If you struggle with this concept, recognize the way you can appreciate how your kids enjoy all aspects of life and each new experience. Your kids don't need to be somewhere by a certain time or achieve any particular outcome. They can find fun for hours with simple things like a cardboard box, the spray from a lawn sprinkler, and some craft materials.

When you see them having the adventure and boldly defending their cardboard fort, do you tell them not to be so bold because it is just a cardboard box? I hope not … especially if you want them to grow up and *be* bold!

When they shriek and giggle uncontrollably at the feeling of the sprinkler streams hitting their little bodies, do you tell them it's just water, so they shouldn't find the physical feelings or experience fun because it is just water?

When they create something all by themselves with a hodgepodge of craft materials, and then proudly come running over to you to show you their cool creation, do you shake your head and point out how the corners are not symmetrical or that they should have used different materials to make it stronger and more durable? I freaking hope you don't! If you did, you would not only be showing up as a total ass in the face of that sensitive little child, but you would be equally missing out on the massive gift they are showing you. You would totally miss out on the opportunity to see the world through their eyes!

When you can sit back and clearly see the world through their eyes as they play, you have opened the gift that will transform even your own life experience. I'm solidly rooted in my mature masculine energy, and I can promise you that allowing myself to enjoy watching children play and laughing with their laughter, their excitement, their boldness, their creativity, and their pride all makes me a stronger and wiser man. At the same time, it makes me more whole in ways that reconnect me with opportunities to have fun again in my adult life and seriously fuel my sense of purpose in making their lives better.

You enjoy watching them, so enjoy watching her. She is not like us, and she is able to find the enjoyment in life that would have been lost on us otherwise ... until you start appreciating how she sees it.

Practical Tip: Sometimes taking a longer route when you drive is part of the goal. Stop by her favorite coffee place or take her past the farm stand so she can see the flowers and decorated pumpkins. This is a great way for you to serve her and win. Enjoy watching how happy you can make her!

Let's be honest, guys: if all we had on this planet were a bunch of guys, life would eventually become so dull, cold, and machinelike that we wouldn't want to live in it long-term. You do not want women to be like you.

Strategy #2 from Stacey: Make Her Journey Your Outcome

It will be much easier for you to appreciate her when you decide to make her *journey* your desired *outcome*.

How? Take shopping, for example.

A woman goes to the store to shop. Her goal is to take her time exploring and experiencing the joy of the journey.

Ladies go shopping. Guys don't go shopping. Guys pick up stuff.

A man goes to the store to get something specific. His goal is the outcome: finding exactly what he needs and getting it home in the most efficient way possible. He doesn't want to shop.

———

Paul Says: *Masculine men will not happily just go shopping. But a masculine man can gladly go shopping with you if he can find a purpose for himself in your shopping experience.*

Example: Paul will take me shopping and be happy doing so if he has decided that the way he can best serve me is to take me shopping.

He wants to escort me to the store, protect me while I'm there, make sure I get coffee or a snack if I need it, pay for everything I want, and take me home safely.

He takes pride in providing that service for me. I enjoy the journey, and he gets his outcome of making me happy. It's win-win.

Paul Says: *So, guys, if you decide to focus on your partner's journey of the shopping experience as an inefficient waste of time, you will suffer through each moment, add unnecessary distance between you and your woman, and ensure that everybody loses. If her satisfaction, protection, and comfort during the journey becomes your desired outcome, you can create a win-win experience for both of you. It's always a choice; when you decide to score a victory here and to add to her experience, you both win.*

STRATEGIES FOR WOMEN BY STACEY

Strategy #1: Appreciate How Efficient He Is

Men are wired to get stuff done! The truth is, we all have more stuff on our plates than we can ever accomplish. That being the case, enjoy how damn efficient he is at getting so much done.

Miracle Morning Opportunity: Another great affirmation for your Miracle Morning is "I am so grateful for the efficiency and productivity that my husband brings to my world."

Practical Tip: If you're tempted to feel slighted when your husband criticizes or performs the task differently than you would have when he strips it down to the bare minimum and removes the "fluff," stop and appreciate how much more efficient he is than you are. Be grateful for the results he gets by moving things through to the desired outcome quickly.

Strategy #2: Leverage His Skill Set to Help You with Your Huge List

Practical Tip: When you are overloaded, give him some of your to-do list and allow him to do what he does best: take stuff and get it done. Let's face it, there's too much crap on your to-do list. Hand it over to him and marvel at his effectiveness at getting stuff done.

Ninja Strategy: When he gets your crap done for you, shower him with appreciation! Don't simply shrug it off and definitely *do not* criticize the man for *how* he got it done! Just lavish him with your appreciation (and release your controlling grip a bit). It's for your own growth.

Strategy #3: Tell Him When You Want to Be Feminine and Enjoy the Journey

Practical Tip: When you are operating from your feminine and taking in the experience and he's getting frustrated, take a moment and help him. Tell him what you're doing so he knows what the outcome is. Don't expect him to enjoy the same things you do. Use direct communication to tell him how he can best serve you. (We will take a deep dive on when you operate from your feminine versus when you operate from your masculine in chapter 8.)

Sample Script:

> *Babe, I would really love to have 30 minutes to walk around and just explore the different kitchen gadgets in this store. That would make me so happy right now. I'm not looking for anything in particular, I just want to explore. Do we have time for me to do that right now? Would you please get me a coffee while I look around? Thank you, baby!*

DIFFERENCE #2: SINGLE FOCUS VS. DIFFUSED AWARENESS

The masculine has single-focused attention.

When they focus their attention on something, they go deep into that one thing, tuning out everything else around them.

Researcher Alison Armstrong once described this as a man descending "deep into a well" with his focus.

In order for him to focus on something else, he needs to come all the way up to the surface, get out of the well, shift his focus to something new, and then go deep into the well with the new focus.

The feminine has diffused awareness.

No matter what we're doing, we are aware of everything within a certain radius of ourselves, at all times.

Here's a peek inside my head at what diffused awareness looks like in a scenario when I'm walking through the house, getting ready to leave and run errands ...

I'm aware already that one kid doesn't have shoes on yet. I tell him to go find his shoes. I want to empower him, so I just say, "Go find your shoes, bud." Of course, I know they are under the table in the living room because he took them off there last night when he was doing his English homework. There's a mysterious red sock under that table too, and I'm sure it's still sitting there.

Anyway, I pack a bag, grabbing bags of cereal for snacks because it's going to be about two hours before we get back, and the little one didn't finish her waffle. To avoid a meltdown, I'll pack these goldfish too.

I notice that the painted rock is still sitting on the kitchen counter—I thought they were going to put that upstairs in the fish tank.

"Did you find your shoes, buddy? No? Try under the table in the living room, maybe? Okay, you found them. Awesome!"

I grab an extra charger from the kitchen counter because I want to be sure to charge his iPod before the ride home so he doesn't fight with his sister over what movie to watch.

"Get a long sleeve zip-up, sweetie. It's going to be cold by the time we leave!" I'm already handing her the one from yesterday that was hanging on the back of the door.

I notice the old winter coats by the door—I really should have packed them into the donation bin already. Those won't fit them by the time December gets here.

"Okay, guys, let's head out!"

Oops, those boxes should have gone into the recycling on Wednesday. Oh yeah, I wasn't here Wednesday night, that's why!

"Buddy, get the door for your sister, okay?"

I must call that tree guy this week! That stump is still here, and he never came back to pick it up.

What a beautiful day! Just look at that sky!

Men, you're probably exhausted just reading through that. I wish that was all that went on in a feminine zone of awareness in a three-minute time span, but if I attempted to include everything … even the ladies would go running screaming to another room!

Diffused awareness means that we can't tune everything else in the world out and focus on only one thing.

Sure, we can we focus, but it takes a lot of effort, and after a while, it depletes us. In fact, a woman who operates from her feminine will find it painful and exhausting to focus on only one thing for long periods of time.

Very often when I teach this in our programs and events, a woman will say, "But I totally can focus. I don't think this applies to me."

I know you *can* focus. You can pay attention to one thing and be diligent about that one thing. That's not what I'm talking about here.

The masculine has *single* focus. They focus on only one thing at a time.

Ladies, single focus means that you must block out any other thoughts that might drift in. You have no awareness of where your kids are, no random thoughts pop in. You are aware of nothing other than the *one* thing. How long do you think you can hold that kind of focus?

Example: Even while writing this book, I'm super focused in that I've made writing this book my only objective and put everything else aside for the morning. However, as I wrote this last passage, I heard someone walk up the stairs and wondered if it was Paul or my assistant. I also felt the cold air come in the window and wondered if I should close it or get fuzzy socks, and I remembered once again that my coffee cup is empty, even though I don't remember finishing it. I didn't stop writing, and it didn't interrupt myself. I'm just aware of all of it as I work.

I'm focused … in a feminine way.

That's not what the masculine does. The masculine goes deep into the well and maintains *single* focus.

Are you starting to gain an appreciation of this difference?

STRATEGIES FOR NAVIGATING SINGLE FOCUS VS. DIFFUSED AWARENESS

Strategy #1 from Paul: Men, stop asking her to focus so much.

She's not wired for it. Letting that aggravate you is setting yourself up for a lot of unnecessary frustration.

To help you understand this in reverse, think about what it is like to be a guy who is trying to focus on getting something done. In the process, your kids keep pulling at you for your attention, the phone calls keep coming in, and your wife needs your help in the kitchen to relocate some items from the high shelves. Most guys would find all these interruptions to their focused efforts as frustrating and exhausting, right? Women can operate comfortably with all of those distractions and be fully present for all of them because they operate with diffused awareness. When you ask her to unnaturally focus deeply on one thing, it is as difficult and frustrating for her to do that as it is for you to try and focus when so many distractions pull you away from your focus.

Strategy #2 from Paul: Men, observe her ability to be aware of everything that is going on around her and stand in awe of how much she takes in at once.

It's pretty impressive. A man might take in all that data, but he would delete it immediately as irrelevant and not necessary for the outcome at hand. Because that is how we operate, we tend to miss so much of the life experience going on around us. Guys, start appreciating the strength that your woman has to take that all in and hold onto it. She carries a lot.

Practical Tip: Replace your frustration with an appreciation of how she is wired. This will rewire your natural blueprint of judging her lack of focus.

Miracle Morning Opportunity: During your Visualization time, visualize yourself appreciating her diffused awareness.

Strategy #3 from Stacey: Ladies, stop interrupting him.

Develop your sensory acuity to pick up on when he's focused on something else and stop interrupting him.

Miracle Morning Opportunity: During your Visualization time, see yourself noticing his focus and cultivating your sensory acuity.

When he is thinking, speaking, or doing something, he is deep in his focus on *that* thing. Don't interrupt him by talking to him while he is focused on something else.

This is a skill set that may take you some time to cultivate. In the beginning, please accept the fact that you are going to continue to interrupt him all the time because you have no idea that certain behaviors are actually interruptions. Pay attention to his reaction to you and start building your sensory acuity.

Example: Many years ago, when I first started practicing this with Paul, we were standing in the kitchen, and I had just remembered that my car was due for inspection, but I didn't know where the registration form was.

I was about to blurt that out when I noticed Paul was looking something up on his phone. You can laugh if you want, but I remember my eyes getting big, as if I were having a moment of panic! I had something to say, but I knew I shouldn't interrupt him (sensory acuity), but I didn't know what to *do* with myself in the meantime. It felt like pressure was building up: *I have to say this, or I'm going to explode.*

It sounds silly, but for a woman there are twenty-five more thoughts behind this one, so stopping this one from flowing out is like plugging up a crack in a dam. Everything behind it feels as if it's backing up, and something is going to blow.

I was committed to figuring out how to implement this strategy. So, I wrote "Car inspection and form" on the notepad in the kitchen and felt a *huge* rush of relief come over me.

By the time I finished writing, he looked up and focused on me. It was like four freaking seconds, but it felt like a journey of a thousand miles for me.

I looked at my note and said, "My car is due for inspection, but I don't know where the registration form is, babe. Can you do this for me please?"

He said, "Absolutely!" and opened his phone to schedule it in for himself.

I wanted to tell him the thirty-minute story of what I had navigated in the last four seconds, but he was already focused on something else, a fact which I found both hysterically funny and ironic, so I laughed out loud.

He looked up from his phone to see what I was laughing at, and I realized, *Shit! I interrupted him after all.* And that made me laugh again. He laughed too, but he had no idea why.

I was on the spectrum with it.

Our students have a phrase they commonly use to describe when they are still learning a new strategy or tool and have not yet mastered it. Since there is a spectrum to every change, as we are developing and falling on our faces a bit, we use the phrase "I'm on the spectrum with it."

It's our way of being compassionate with ourselves and our partners as we work to make progress without perfection. Just do the best you can each time. You're "on the spectrum with it."

Strategy #4 from Stacey: Ladies, stop judging him for not having the capacity to take in multiple things at once.

It takes a lot of work and energy for your man to take in more than one thing at a time, just as it takes a lot of energy and work for you to focus only on one thing and block everything else in the world out (including your barrage of thoughts). You can do it, but it's not easy, and it's exhausting. It's the same for him to try to perceive a lot of things at once—he can't be in two wells at the same time.

Strategy #5: Teach Your Kids about Single Focus

It's important to help your kids learn that Daddy has single focus and Mommy has diffused awareness. This knowledge will particularly help your family at times when your man gets triggered by too many kids talking to him at once. Instead of getting frustrated that he is set off by the kids, take the opportunity to teach your kids about single focus.

Sample Script, said with a happy and non-judgmental tone:

> *Hey guys, Daddy has Single Focus, and he can't hear two voices at once. So pause … and speak one at a time. This way Daddy can hear* everything *you have to share.*

After a bunch of times of repeating that script, one day I overheard our daughter, Gracie (around age 4), say to our son, Jake, "Hey Jake, Daddy can't hear you at the same time, and I'm already talking, so please wait for his 'One Big Focus' to be your turn." Love it!

Gracie and Jake both learned at a young age that boys have single focus, girls have diffused awareness, and *both* are valuable and needed.

Strategy #6: Use these tools and strategies while interacting with other men and women in the workplace!

The masculine and feminine peeps in your world will really appreciate you for it (even if they don't know why).

Practical Tip: Ladies, stop interrupting the guys in your workplace and appreciate their ability to focus. This is a very valuable skill set, so leverage it.

Practical Tip: Men, stop asking ladies to focus in your workplace and start appreciating their ability to take in a lot of detail. This is a very valuable skill set; leverage it.

Leverage It: When it comes to leveraging these skill sets at work, understanding how your peers or team members are wired and allowing them to thrive by using their strengths is *key*.

For instance, when you have an assignment that requires taking in a lot of detail and being able to juggle many different things at once, that's an excellent place for the feminine to thrive. On the contrary, when you want a masculine man on your team to thrive, give him the space to focus without distraction.

DIFFERENCE #3: HELP!

The Masculine does *not* want help unless he asks for it.

The Feminine wants help all the F'ing time, even when she turns down an offer.

This is a *big* 'Kerfuffle'-causer in relationships!

Ladies, imagine that your sister is washing dishes at the sink and you say, "Can I help you dry?" If she says, "No, I got it, you sit and relax," what happens next?

You take a dishtowel out of the drawer, pick up a wet dish, and start drying, as you say, "So tell me, what's going on with you?" She smiles, feeling supported.

As a woman, if you took her at her word and actually sat down, grabbed another piece of pie and ate it while *watching* her wash and dry dishes ... you'd be perceived as a total bitch!

That's how the scene would play out between two women.

Now replace your sister with your man in that scenario. Oh boy! Can you say kerfuffle?

Dialogue between a man and woman:

> **You**: "Can I help you dry, sweetie?"
>
> **Him:** "No, I got this. You sit and relax."
>
> **You:** Go into the drawer, grab a towel, start drying and ask him, "So tell me, what's going on with you, sweetie?"
>
> **Him (brow furrowed, looking totally pissed):** "Fine! Then *you* do the dishes." And he walks away, leaving you wondering WTF just happened.

Let me explain.

You were being a "good girl" by offering help, and then stepping in to help, even when it was refused.

Your man, on the other hand, was trying to serve you by doing something for you. *He meant what he said!* (Read that one more time.)

His desire was to *watch* you enjoy him serving you. He wanted you to sit back, relax, and appreciate his stepping up to serve you. He wanted to be your hero!

By ignoring his request to serve you, he felt like you were stepping in to take over and emasculating him. Whether he took it to mean that you had no confidence in his ability to get the dishes done, or you merely ruined his experience of trying to serve by unwittingly cutting him off at the knees, it's ruined for him. He doesn't want to fight with you after that blatant act of emasculating behavior, so he throws his hands up and walks away.

You're baffled.

He's baffled.

Neither of you understand WTF just happened.

(It's a miracle men and women ever get together in the first place!)

But that's not the end of this kerfuffle!

Unfortunately for our species, women are raised from birth to offer help all the freaking time.

The paradox is that to be the "good girl," women have been trained *not* to ask for help unless it's a life-or-death situation.

She's supposed to demonstrate to everyone that she's got it all together. Everything is under control, and she shouldn't need to ask anyone for help.

The problem is that, underneath, she *does* want help with everything all the time. That fact is completely off the radar of most men. They have no idea that ladies want help because most women do such great job of demonstrating that they don't *need* any help.

That's where the trouble escalates between us. Ladies won't ask men for help. (They feel he should be able to see what she needs help with and *just do it!*)

Now, let's bring together a few facts ...

1. Women want help all the time, yet they give off the impression that they don't need help, and they won't ask for it.

2. Men don't want help *unless* they ask for it.

Can you see where I'm headed with this one?

Without a relationship education about the differences between masculine and feminine, most men will treat their women like she's another guy!

A man would *never* offer unsolicited help to another man unless he wanted to get hit. So, out of respect for his woman, he would *never* offer her unsolicited help because that would imply that she doesn't have her shit together. He would never disrespect her that way.

Combine these dynamics together and we have one giant mess!

Welcome to Kerfuffle-Town—population 8 billion!

Fortunately, we have strategies to successfully navigate the help dynamic.

Strategy for Women from Stacey

Do *not* **offer a man unsolicited help or, worse yet, help anyway after he's told you he doesn't want it.** It can be perceived by the man as emasculating, implying that you don't have confidence in his abilities to get this done on his own.

Practical Tip: When you see him doing something, fight the urge to offer help. This is harder to implement than it sounds. In the beginning, I would do all kinds of things to help train myself: bite my lips to keep myself from speaking, put a hand over my mouth, count to 100 and breathe deeply.

Ninja Strategy: Ladies, if you're tempted to offer help, say my proven ninja statement exactly like this: "Babe, I know if you need my help with that you will ask. Love you!"

Practical Tip: Keep on walking by him as you say the ninja statement and leave the room. Just keep on steppin'! That's a key piece of that strategy. *Why?* Because if you pause or linger, you will say something *after* that sentence, and then you will fall down the rabbit hole. Yes, you will, you know it. So keep on stepping, and as you walk by, use my ninja sentence.

Whatever you do, stop offering help when he hasn't asked for it. And please, for Pete's sake, stop taking over and helping when he didn't ask.

Strategy for Men from Paul

Help her! The good news is that she wants help all the freaking time, and you like serving her. So stop waiting for her to ask you and just serve her. It's pretty simple. You'll get used to it.

1. Offer her help all the time.
2. When she says no, start helping her anyway.
3. Repeat.

Practical Tip: Help her even when she says "no thanks." Develop your sensory acuity. When you offer help and she says no, pay attention to how she is feeling and stop listening to the words. She wants help, but she struggles with asking for it.

Miracle Morning Opportunity: Here's an Affirmation for your Miracle Morning "Today I seek out opportunities to provide unsolicited help to my wife. Through each opportunity, I know I will learn more about how I can best serve her, so I can never fail!"

BONUS TIP: Learn how to translate the implied communication from your woman! It's illogical for a man to hear someone say they don't want help and then to jump in and help them anyway. This is because *men talk to each other using direct communication.* We say what we mean, and we mean what we say. *Women communicate using implied communication.* Other women understand this implied communication clearly, whereas men will often miss the real meaning because they take the words at face value.

Example: Here's your feminine to masculine translator. We use the word Manslator, which came from a very funny video on YouTube with the same name. (Google it and enjoy!) Here is our custom example for you:

Man says: "Need help with that?"

Woman says: "No, I got it, thanks."

Manslator: Yes, I want help! I want help *all* the time, so why wouldn't I want help now. I did the nice thing and refused your help. Why aren't you helping me now, you big jerk?

Now, if you're anything like our students, at this point you're wondering, *OMG, Stacey do I have to think about what I'm going to say before I speak* every *time?*

The answer is yes, if you want to improve your relationships!

When you first begin doing this work, it requires a lot of effort! You need to put intention, time, and energy into creating this change.

Change happens on a spectrum, but luckily for you, life will offer you lots of opportunities to do the work. With practice, guidance, and repetition, you will progress from learning this material to living it. It will become second nature for you. Before you know it, what was once impossible will become easy!

But that's *only* if you choose to do the work and grow. The truth is, you live through those practice opportunities anyway. Most people call those opportunities problems. If you don't choose to grow, you will continue to see the same problems over and over in your life until you either give up or do the work!

Since you have to live through these opportunities anyway, why not *use them* as catalysts to create the change you want?

My hope is that you now have a greater understanding of masculine and feminine energy, and you realize that the problem is not just your wife, your husband, or your ex!

It's *not* a "you and your partner" problem. This is a masculine and feminine challenge.

You can either learn now how to master yourself and bring out the best in your current partner—through mastering tools that honor their masculine or feminine energy—or you can learn it with your next partner. Your choice!

There's no way around doing the work, and you won't escape unnecessary suffering in your love relationships until you master this. It's not about your partner. You don't just *find* the right one and it somehow magically works out or doesn't. That bullshit fairy-tale thinking that we've been handed has left a lot of pain and damage in its wake.

I'm here to take a stand and put an end to the unnecessary suffering in love relationships today. And I'm starting with you!

An unshakable love and unleashed passion is *created*, not found! The great news is that it's a *skill* that can be learned. It only takes one partner to create a transformation. And we can show you exactly how.

The question is: will you choose to be the one to create it?

When you decide to do the work, it can feel like a real struggle. It requires an incredible amount of intentional effort and can feel overwhelming at times. To help our students navigate this dynamic and stay the course, we teach a "Mega Strategy" to make the process much easier.

State Mastery

In order to get the greatest results from doing relationship transformation work, you need to understand that your *state* (emotional and energetic) impacts your ability to access the tools and strategies you learn from us. Therefore, a key tool that we teach our students is state mastery.

What do we mean by State Mastery?

Mastering your state means that you come from a high state the majority of the time, and few things can trigger you into a low state. What's more, during the times when you do get triggered, you have mastered the ability to get out of that low state in a matter of moments and *not* stay stuck there for prolonged periods of time.

If you want to have magnificent relationships, you *must* learn to master your state.

State mastery affects the quality of *all* the relationships in your life, and it massively impacts your experience of life itself. Every time you make progress on mastering your state, you simultaneously improve your ability to create an impact with all the other strategies.

To help you master your state, I'd like to share the State-O-Meter tool that I developed to help our students.

Think of your state as the thermometer in this image.

At the top of the thermometer is your high state. This is where you are when in the zone: you are rocking it, and everything is awesome!

At the bottom is your crap state. This is where everything sucks: you feel like a loser, and everything is going wrong!

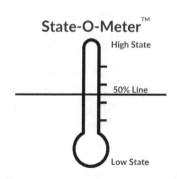

At the middle of the thermometer lies one of the most important invisible forces in your life: The 50 Percent Line™.

When your state drops below that line, you get emotionally hijacked. You're triggered into primal fight-or-flight reactions, and you're unable use any of the tools and strategies to grow. (Forget about putting your partner first, meeting their needs, and coming from heartfelt understanding. You have lost all capacity to do *any* of that!)

Key Strategy for State Mastery

When your state drops below the 50 Percent Line, you have only *one job:* get back above the 50 Percent Line!

That's it. That's *all* you need to do.

This is critical! Please listen up because this is a vitally important life skill.

When you've dropped below the 50 Percent Line in your state, stop "efforting" or pushing yourself to produce results and achieve your goals. When you take action from below the 50 Percent Line, your focus is in the *wrong* place, and your output is going to be crap. That's *not* the time to try to use your personal growth tools, and it's not the time to talk to your partner about your relationship.

Train yourself to *stop* whatever you're doing when you drop below the 50 Percent Line, and get back above it.

Once you're above 50 percent, take all the action you want: reach for your tools, have that difficult conversation, make those important calls, or deal with your kids.

Are you starting to feel how important it is to learn how to master your state?

If you're being honest, how much time is your state below the 50 Percent Line every day? I'm pretty confident that the state of your relationships today mirror that percentage, my friend.

The fact is, if you have wired yourself to be easily triggered below the 50 Percent Line, the results in your life and relationships will reflect that.

Please don't beat yourself up for it, though. First of all, that's counterproductive because it puts you further below the line. Second, it's not your fault. Most of us were taught when we were young (by well-meaning but misinformed adults) to wire ourselves in a way that makes it easy to feel bad (below 50 percent) and difficult to feel good (above 50 percent).

Rewiring yourself to feel good and stay above the 50 Percent Line so that you can use new tools and strategies to create the life and relationships that you want is a crucial part of doing the work, my friend!

We call State Mastery a "Mega Strategy" for your life, because your level of state mastery impacts your success, or failure, in every area of your life.

You must cultivate your ability to master your state, in any situation, regardless of the environment. It's absolutely possible, because it's a skill set, and it can be learned!

In the coming chapters, we will take a deeper dive into "Doing the Work" of creating an unshakable love and unleashed passion, but before we do that, I need to offer you a powerful shift into freedom.

In my experience, the number one resistance that keeps people held back from doing the work is the inability to forgive themselves or others for what has happened in the past.

If you can't release the past, set yourself free, and wipe the slate clean, you will stay stuck where you are.

You can only create this unshakable love and unleashed passion from a clean slate, but clean slates *don't just happen* to you. No one is going to show up on your doorstep and wipe your slate clean for you. You have to create a clean slate intentionally—just like you do with a magnificent relationship.

In the next chapter I will show you exactly how to create a clean slate by walking you through our unique and proven **Five-Step Forgiveness Process.**

Let's create that clean slate together!

Real Life Relationship Case Study

LEA

Before

After about a decade of issues and challenges, my husband and I had a huge rupture in our relationship and we both slammed our hand on the exit button! In a moment of feeling really hopeless, somehow I got an email from someone named Stacey Martino and the subject line was, "How do you know when it's time to walk away?"

*I was expecting more of the same stuff I had been bombarded with ... articles about how you **have to** work things out" or you **have to** walk away" ... but this was very different!*

Stacey had written a letter from the heart all about how, if you have children, you will be co-parenting with this person until the day you die, so you better heal what's between you, no matter what decision you are going to make about your marriage. And that really hit home for me.

Doing the Work

I started the program and realized that I had made every mistake in the book. While I didn't know if this was going to save my marriage, I realized that I still had work to do.

All I knew was that I didn't want to draw a line down my life and down my son's face—which is what you see when people divorce.

After

While it may not sound like a celebration to you, today, one year later, I am celebrating that my husband and I consciously decided to end our marriage BUT stay a family. It's so beautiful, because this time last year, we could have walked away a mess, fighting and spiteful.

Today, we both agree that we are fully committed to co-parenting our son harmoniously and that his parents will always be best friends. Our relationship is actually the most loving and supportive it has EVER been. We have awakened to the fact that we are not aligned with each other long-term as lovers, but we are so grateful to be parents together to our son!

Even though I have been the only one doing this program, my relationship has transformed. We have open, honest, and real conversations now, using the tools that I learned from Stacey and Paul. It's productive, it's beautiful, and it's friendly. I have learned how to come from my feminine and bring out his masculine to support me. We are in a better place now then we were even in the beginning of our relationship. And we have that for LIFE now and I'm forever grateful!

Through doing the work with Stacey and Paul, I realized that the purpose of this program was not to "fix us" so we could limp along forever, it was for us to heal so we could come to this place, so we could now move on and expand our family in a loving way, which I feel is beautiful. And the skills that I got from doing this work, I get to keep them forever!

Keys to Her Success

- **Rescued the relationship, even though the marriage was not aligned to last:** What I want you to get from Lea's story is that every relationship can be rescued. Not every marriage was meant to be your forever love. But if you have children together, that relationship is until you die. And you *owe* it to your children to give them harmonious peaceful co-parents who can be in the same room and enjoy each other while they move on, ready and healed and whole, to attract their forever love and bring more beautiful love and parents into the family. And that is the heroic journey that Lea has been on.

- **Did the work to transform herself:** Lea did the work. Instead of spending tens of thousands of dollars on divorce lawyers and battles, Lea and her ex-husband have been able to peacefully work with a mediator (for just a few thousand dollars) and preserve their family's financial stability.

We deeply honor the work that Lea has done to rescue her relationship with her ex-husband so she can harmoniously co-parent with him.

If you do the work, you *will* rescue your relationship. You may not rescue the marriage, but you will rescue the relationship. Either way, you will be at peace with your decision when you get there.

I share this story with you today, because this is what divorce *can* look like! You can release your unaligned marriage, while healing yourself and keeping your *family* together!

Real Life Relationship Case Study

JENNIFER & TOM

Jennifer's Story

Before

Before working with Stacey, my husband and I were in a very dark place. We were strangers to each other. We were in the same house out of necessity, but sleeping in separate bedrooms (living on different floors).

I wasn't sure if I was even in love with my husband anymore, even though I deeply cared about him. I was terrified that I had destroyed my marriage and wasn't sure if anything could be done.

When I went to Stacey and Paul's live event, it was my last-ditch effort. It was going to be either "give this a try" or go see the attorneys.

Doing the Work

Through the work I have done in this program, I have learned how to recover from past hurts, effectively communicate with my husband, and create a rock-solid foundation!

We've rescued our marriage, and in many ways our relationship now is better than when we were dating!

We also now enjoy a VERY passion-filled relationship. I love feeling crazy about my husband! We have so much fun with each other now. We have dates, and hand holding, and cuddling, and laughter, and flirting, and just a deep soul-satisfying happiness with each other.

After

Knowing that my husband is first in my life, and that I am first in his, makes it very easy to see what's important, what's less important, and what's not important at all. I feel unstoppable in my life because of my relationship today. This helps me—especially in my business. I used to try and be a people pleaser all the time, but now I have clearer priorities and am a much more effective leader with my employees. This allows me to spend more time doing what I love, while getting the support I need, and far less time managing.

The greatest result I am enjoying from being a student in RelationshipU is a level of intimate connection with my husband that I never dreamed was possible. The intimacy and passion that I now experience in my relationship is what puts a sparkle in my eye, a smile on my face, and a spring in my step—even when my husband isn't next to me. This feeling fuels me all day, every day, and provides me with an inner peace; I go through my day feeling much more relaxed and content.

I tell people, "Whatever you THINK is possible for your relationship … it's SO much more! You just can't even imagine WHAT is possible for you, from living in an unshakable love and an unleashed passion!"

Tom's Story

Before

Before working with Stacey and Paul, my marriage just existed. It was slowly withering, so slowly that I hardly noticed. Nothing was obviously bad or wrong, but nothing was really happening either. I could have just as easily walked away.

After

Doing this work has gotten me to a place where I can see how this process happened and how to change it. It's not always easy to change my ways, but it is always worthwhile.

The biggest change that has occurred for me is that I feel responsible for my marriage. Rather than taking it for granted or trying to ignore or shift blame for anything that might have gone wrong, I now feel responsible for what has happened before and what is happening now. This is empowering; it's a simple distinction but it changes everything!

I feel very fortunate to have made this change and to recognize how amazing and important my wife is. She always was and I just couldn't see it.

Keys to Their Success

- **Doing the work individually:** Jennifer had started doing the work about 6 months before she invited Tom to start one of our programs. Once they were both enrolled in the program, they continued to do the work *individually*, which was a *key* to their success!

- **Never miss a call (or event):** Jennifer and Tom never miss a live coaching call or event! They keep themselves immersed each week, getting the mentorship, answers, and support that they need to learn how to navigate their moments differently, and get the results that they want!

- **Start anew:** Paul and I suggested something to Jen & Tom that we invite you to consider on your Relationship Development journey, if it serves you.

  Sometimes we realize that our marriage is not the right marriage for us, and we don't want to stay in that marriage. But we love our spouse and we have hope. Jen & Tom didn't want to stay in their marriage under the conditions they started with, but both had hope and were committed to doing the work. They transformed their relationship and their marriage was healing.

  In order to help them get unstuck from the past, Paul and I suggested that they consider starting a second marriage—only with the same person! It would allow both of them to say, "We don't want to bring our old marriage into today, we want to start fresh—as the people we are today!" It was magnificent and inspirational when Jen and Tom got re-married on the beach in St Lucia after one of our live events!

6

HOW TO FORGIVE ANYTHING

BY STACEY MARTINO

"The practice of forgiveness is our most important contribution to the healing of the world."
—MARIANNE WILLIAMSON

"Forgiveness sets you free to move past the pain and on into a life of loving and serving."
—DR. WAYNE DYER

U nfortunately, there's a dynamic that I see all too often.

People come to me in pain. Truly suffering every day. They want to transform their relationship, create a better life, be a good role model for their kids, and have an unshakable love and unleashed passion.

Yet they feel stuck in their suffering.

When I dig deeper with them, I often find that what is keeping them stuck is something that they cannot yet forgive. Something they are holding onto is keeping them from having everything they so desperately want.

You simply can't have an unshakable love and rock-solid relationship if you leave things unforgiven. Hurts, betrayals, regrets, mistakes, pains of the past. By definition, these are things that come between you. Unforgiveness creates distance and a relationship that is susceptible to being shaken.

In some cases, we struggle to forgive our partners, and the distance builds over time. In other cases, the one we need to forgive most is ourselves.

I'm here to tell you that everything can be forgiven. Yes, everything.

Before you start swirling, hang on, let me explain. I'm not belittling. Trust me, in my work I have helped people navigate horrible things—some things you probably can imagine, and some things you will *never* imagine. And yes, *all* things can be forgiven.

By the end of this chapter, you will understand why I say that. Better yet, by the end of this chapter, you will not only believe that, you will walk through the rest of your life knowing that.

Whether the person you need to forgive is your partner, someone else in your world, or yourself … it's time to wipe the slate clean and start anew.

How?

Many years ago, Paul and I developed our proven 5-Step Forgiveness Process.

Of all the work that we do in the world, this is one of Paul's favorites because he is deeply passionate about helping people reclaim their life by freeing themselves from the unnecessary burden of unforgiveness! (I hope you come to one of our events where he takes you step-by-step through this process *live* … it's an experience not to be missed!)

After releasing any unforgiveness, stepping into forgiveness, and wiping the slate clean, you get your freedom back! You are …

Free from the past,

Free to move forward in your relationship (or begin one),

Free to create your life by design,

Free to create a rock-solid relationship, and

Free to create an unleashed passion.

This process is so powerful that, when our team sat down to talk about the tools and strategies that we *must* include in this book to empower you to transform your relationships, this one topped everyone's list!

5-Step Forgiveness Process

1. Release resistance to forgiving yourself and others.
2. Understand what forgiveness really is.
3. Find the gifts and get unstuck.
4. Change your story.
5. Decide and wipe the slate clean.

Are you ready? Let's do this!

Step One: Release Resistance!

Let's start with your resistance to forgiving yourself.

Can you think of something in your past that you struggle to forgive yourself for? Perhaps you said something hurtful in the heat of the moment and you wish you hadn't? Or maybe you've been living in regret because of a bad decision? Have you caused your loved ones pain through lying, infidelity, addictions, or some other harmful behavior?

After walking thousands of clients through forgiveness, the most common cause of resistance to forgiving themselves is a feeling that somehow they are paying their debt.

If there's something that you haven't been able to let go of and forgive yourself for, does that feeling resonate for you?

Is there a part of you that fears that forgiving yourself is somehow letting yourself *off* the hook, and that the only honorable thing to do is to keep yourself *on* the hook?

If so, has it helped?

Has holding yourself in unforgiveness actually *fixed* anything for you or any of the other parties involved?

If you reflect and answer truthfully, I'm willing to bet that neither you nor anyone else has benefited from your refusal to forgive yourself.

Let's be honest: your unforgiveness toward yourself hasn't actually fixed anything. Continuing in regret and self-flagellation only harms you and keeps you stuck.

Releasing resistance to forgiving yourself is the first step to starting anew.

We know this is easier said than done. It's not easy to do this work for yourself. If you could have forgiven yourself before this, you would have by now. Fortunately, we have developed many tools to help you. One of the most powerful is called the Version of You.

As human beings, we continue to grow and change throughout the course of our lives. Each day we are different from the day before. Therefore, whatever we say or do on any given day is dictated by who we are being at that point in time. We do the best we can do in the moment, based on our current level of development. Truly, when we know better, we can do better.

Our Version of You tool acknowledges this dynamic. We look back at something we regret and say to ourselves:

The version of me that I was, at that moment in time, did the best that I could with the skill set that I had. Today I am an even better version of myself, and I will do better.

Miracle Morning Opportunity: If this is an area of focus for you, consider adding that statement to your Miracle Morning Affirmations.

At this point you might be thinking, *Well, this tool is great for people who haven't done anything that bad, but you have no idea how much pain and damage I caused by what I said or did (or didn't do).*

I hear you. And I want you to know I get it—I really do. I've been there.

In 2010, I was stuck in this very place. The person I needed to forgive the most was myself, yet I didn't feel like I could because my failure had caused so much pain and damage to my family.

You see, back in 2009, Paul and I owned our own technology consulting business. We had been doing relationship coaching as our mission on the side, but we did technology consulting as our profession at the time.

Due to the global economic crisis at that time, which impacted so many families, we too experienced a very unexpected financial challenge that year. My idea was to recreate ourselves and invest in a solution that I hoped would pull us out of the crisis.

I was wrong. So very wrong. Instead of solving the problem, the avenue that we pursued speedily plunged us more deeply into financial crisis.

By 2010, we were down to $1,300 cash left in the world with two babies at home. We had six figures' worth of debt, and we were on the verge of going bankrupt and losing our home.

Fortunately, Paul and I had been doing personal development work together for years at that point, and, rather than letting the stress and regret tear us apart, we came together as a team and emerged stronger on the other side.

Paul and I hustled. We both took full-time corporate jobs and did everything we could to defy all the odds and pull ourselves out of financial disaster.

By 2011, just one year later, we began to come out of our financial crisis. Our relationship was stronger than ever, but I was still blaming and punishing myself for the financial damage I had caused. I just didn't know how to forgive myself ... but then came a defining moment in my life.

As I grew into my new corporate job, I hit a point where I was able to do it so well that I could easily exceed my goals and yet still get my work done in less than a typical forty-hour week. At that point, I felt ready to take on a second job to help my family, but I couldn't figure out what job I should do.

I asked my coach, mentor, and one of my best friends, Jon Vroman, to help me figure out what job or business to pursue next. I vividly remember every detail of what transpired next because our conversation that day became one of *the* defining moments in my life.

As I sat in his office, he started talking to me about my greatest passion: our long-standing mission to help people transform their relationships (as if that was a viable option for income!).

I remember telling him "No, no, no, Jon. I can't do more relationship coaching! *I need to spend my time doing something that I can make money doing.* I still have a lot of money to pay back!" (Remember those words, please.)

I asked Jon what he thought about my taking another side job in accounting, which is my former profession, or launching the online car-buying system that I had invented. (Seriously, I kid you not!)

Jon laughed, quickly dismissed those possibilities, and proceeded to tell me that anything that I am that passionate about will always come back to me in a financially rewarding way. It's unavoidable.

I heard what he said. I even believed what he said. Hell, I would even have told him the same thing if our roles had been reversed!

But ...

I had already failed in business. How could I even *think* about starting another one when that's what had caused this disaster in the first place?

Not to mention, I still had a lot of money to "pay back." In my mind, I owed that money to my family. It was my fault that we'd lost it, and I wouldn't stop until I paid it all back.

Jon is an incredibly perceptive coach, and the king of asking quality questions. He totally called me out on my unforgiveness toward myself with two pointed, powerful questions:

"Stacey, who are you paying back?"

"*Why* do you have to pay them back?"

As I reflected on my answers to those questions, I realized for the first time consciously that I was holding myself solely responsible for our near-bankruptcy, and that I was punishing myself until I paid my debt.

That revelation was a huge turning point for me. After I returned home that night, I shared my new awareness with Paul. Through tears, I confessed that I was so sorry I'd lost all the money we had in the world.

Paul's response stunned me!

Stacey, what are you talking about? You didn't make me *do anything! I made the same choice you did at the time. You didn't do* this *to us. We did this, together. And it wasn't a failure at all, Stacey. It was one of the greatest lessons we've learned in life. We learned so many lessons during that time that we will* need *to do what we are about to do in this world. Lessons I am grateful for. And we never* failed. *We triumphed! Not many other people could go from $1300 in the world, two babies at home, and being on the verge of losing their home ... to debt free, home paid off, and two six-figure salaries in less than 12 months. That's not a failure Stacey ... That's a* victory!

My mind was reeling. I was so confused.

All this time, I'd shouldered the blame for the entire situation. The voice of my conscience had taunted me so relentlessly over my failure that it had seemed like an obvious fact that I was solely responsible! Yet Paul, the person I am closest to in the world, the only one who could have held it against me, did not see it the same way at all. By refusing to forgive myself and punishing myself for the decisions I made at that time, I'd been keeping myself in unnecessary pain.

I truly believed I'd been doing an honorable thing by keeping myself on the hook to repay my debt, and yet all that time I was *wrong*.

The very next day, I started my relationship coaching business!

If I hadn't released my resistance and forgiven myself, who knows what might have happened?! I probably would have launched that online car buying guide on Clickbank. Holy crap! Can you imagine?

I think of the families we have served and supported in transforming their relationships: Where would they be today if I had stayed in resistance to forgiving myself, thinking I was doing the honorable thing? If I'd also continued to do relationship coaching for free, I would have had to remain employed full-time doing work that I'm not called to do.

Even worse, I would have had time to help only a minuscule fraction of the people that we do now.

Yet through saying "YES!" and stepping into my calling and destiny, hearts have healed, lives and relationships have been transformed, and children are in happier homes!

You can never achieve something positive by doing something negative! It's Universal Law.

Unforgiveness is a negative energy; therefore, holding yourself in unforgiveness can never actually resolve the challenges or make things better.

(Read that again!)

You can't do something negative (beat yourself up) and have it result in something positive (making the problem better). It's just a fact!

No matter what you think you can't forgive yourself for, the truth is that staying in unforgiveness is causing damage to you and everyone else. Again, how many people wouldn't have gotten the help they need if I hadn't forgiven myself and stepped into my calling?

Consider this ... what if everything YOU desire lies on the other side of forgiving yourself, too?

Your Resistance to Forgiving Another

Next, let's deal with resistance to forgiving someone else ...

When it comes to forgiving others, I've found that the resistance is created by a few major objections.

"I don't want to let them off the hook" is the biggest objection.

When someone feels they've been wronged, whether catastrophically or only mildly, it can leave that person stuck in resistance.

They feel that if they forgive, they will be affirming that what happened was OKAY, and letting the other person off the hook.

That feeling comes from misunderstanding what forgiveness really is, and we will address this thoroughly in step two of this process.

"I don't want to be a doormat" is the second most common objection that keeps you stuck in resistance to forgiving others.

You believe that if you forgive everything, then you are being a doormat and letting everyone walk all over you.

Here's the thing, Lovie. Staying in *un*forgiveness is not preventing you from being a doormat, today, in this moment. (Take that in for a moment.)

In fact, just the opposite occurs. According to Universal Law, by holding the experience of unforgiveness within you, and continually remembering it and associating to it, you are attracting more of it to you in the Now.

Since we attract circumstances that resonate with where we are emotionally, if we remain angry about someone treating us like a doormat, we attract *more* situations where someone will treat us like a doormat.

If you currently tell yourself that by staying in unforgiveness you are protecting yourself from this happening again, you are deceiving yourself.

How can you know if you're doing this?

Well, do you have any situations in your life that trigger you almost instantaneously?

Do you have any situations that make you rail with anger and wonder, *why does this* always *happen to me* ... or *why do* they *always* ... or *why don't* they *ever* ... ?

If so, then I can guarantee you have some underlying forgiveness work that needs to be done.

How do we bust through this?

Listen sweetie, we teach others how to treat us. To prevent yourself from being treated like a doormat in the future, combine the healing gift of forgiveness, along with the *wisdom* you've gained from what you've experienced, and set healthy boundaries.

Wisdom is the gift that will empower you to live better in the future.

Here's the catch, though: gleaning wisdom from the experience is not automatic. You must be intentional about pondering these questions about the offense:

- What did you learn from that experience?
- What can you shift about yourself?
- How can you learn from this so you can navigate the moment differently the next time and create a different outcome?

The wisdom revealed in the answers to those quality questions will surely help you create a better outcome in the future.

Wisdom is the source of your personal power and your protection in the future. Holding on to unforgiveness doesn't empower or protect you at all.

Since holding on to unforgiveness only guarantees future pain, the time to forgive is now!

Whether the person you need to forgive is yourself or another, it's time to release and be free! Empower yourself. Wipe the slate clean.

Decide that you want to forgive!

To overcome the resistance to forgiving yourself or someone else, flip the switch in this very moment and decide that today is the day you give yourself and others the gift of forgiveness!

Once you've made a decision and released all resistance to forgiveness, you are ready for the next step in the forgiveness process.

Step Two: Understand What Forgiveness Really Is!

The single most common reason most people are stuck and unable to forgive and wipe the slate clean is that most people don't understand what forgiveness actually is.

They believe the popular misconception that forgiveness means saying, "It's okay. It's okay that happened."

Darling, that is *not* what forgiveness is, and unfortunately it keeps a lot of good people stuck and unable to move forward.

You do *not* ever have to say that whatever happened is okay.

Many years ago, when I watched Oprah share her definition of forgiveness, I was left dumbfounded—jaw hanging open—sitting with this game-changing truth.

Forgiveness is giving up the hope that the past could be any different than it actually was.
—OPRAH WINFREY

(Let that sink in.)

It's a whole lot different than saying, "Oh, it's fine! All good. What you did was okay!"

After Oprah shared the definition that day, she went on to tell the audience an amazing story that demonstrated this point beautifully.

(I'm not going to do this story justice as I relay it to you because, let's face it, she's Oprah and it was her experience, but this is the gist of it, as Oprah told it.)

One day as Oprah was walking down Michigan Avenue in Chicago, she noticed a woman getting out of her limousine across the street.

Oprah instantly recognized her as someone she knew and despised. As she described it, years prior, this woman had wronged her. She was still seething mad at the woman and holding a big grudge against her.

As soon as she recognized her that day, she felt her anger skyrocket inside.

Then, the craziest thing happened!

From across the street, Oprah watched as the woman strolled into Tiffany's, laughing and smiling as if she didn't have a care in the world, with the person accompanying her.

Oprah told us that stopped her dead in her tracks right there.

She realized that the woman had no clue that Oprah was mad at her! She was laughing her way into Tiffany's, oblivious to the anger. In that moment, Oprah knew the grudge she was holding on to was *only* affecting *her*, and not the other woman!

Sweetie, unforgiveness is *always* like that. It affects only you, on the *inside*.

Likewise, forgiveness happens *within you*! It's *for* you, and not the other person.

Forgiveness does not happen *between* two people.

The minute Oprah decided to give up the hope that the past could have been any different than it actually was, forgiveness happened within her, and she was free from the effects of the anger and bitterness she'd carried.

Note: She did not need to walk across the street to Tiffany's and say to that woman, "I forgive you."

She could've done that, but that would've have been "making amends," which is not required for forgiveness.

Mind-Bender: Amends happen between two people, and forgiveness happens within one person.

That's a big difference. They are not the same concepts at all!

Many of us are taught that they are the same thing, and because of that, it's very common to stay stuck in unforgiveness because we believe that to forgive, we need to pick up the phone and say, "It's okay. I forgive you."

Sometimes, the person isn't safe to make contact with. Other times, they've already passed away. For a variety of reasons, we can't or don't want to make contact, so we feel like we can't forgive.

Making amends is not always possible because it involves two people. But forgiving is always possible, because it involves only you. A moment of decision. An act of your own will.

All you have to do is decide in your own heart and mind that you give up the hope that the past could have been any different than it actually was.

Feel the freedom and lightness of that! That's the gift of forgiveness within you!

Are you there? Can you feel it?

If not, you might be struggling with another very common problem.

At this point in the process, many people feel a whole new level of resistance around the need for "justice" to be served.

Mind-Bender: Unforgiveness does not equal justice.

By remaining in unforgiveness, you're not actually enacting justice on anyone, are you? If you were, you'd feel better by remaining in unforgiveness.

But you don't. The anger, rage, and bitterness is actually a cancerous energy that negatively affects you—spirit, soul, and body.

It doesn't enact justice on anybody because it doesn't transact that way. Unforgiveness has no capacity to impact the other person in a way that creates justice.

Injustice is the sense that something needs to happen to make things right again. An eye for an eye, a tooth for a tooth. Karma. But words can't be taken back. Actions can't be undone. Action can't be taken after the moment has passed. There is no way to make it like it never happened. We can't go back and change anything that happened in the past!

So what about justice then?

It is not your job to deliver the justice. That's not the way the universe works. The law of cause and effect is the most powerful of the universal laws.

The Universe will deliver justice using the law of cause and effect. Said differently, Newton's Third Law tells us, "For every action there is an equal and opposite reaction."

Many times you may view a situation and say to yourself, *There was no justice! They got off scot-free!*

It might seem that way, but in truth, that is not possible in the world we live in. The Universe is always self-correcting, and no one can escape it.

My friend, so much pain and suffering happens behind closed doors that you will never see. What you put out into the Universe comes back to you … and sometimes tenfold.

If someone did something—whether good or evil—it's going to boomerang back to them, many times over, in ways you may never see.

It's not your job to see! As Byron Katie, author of *The Work*, says, "There are three kinds of business: your business, someone else's business, and God's business." Justice falls squarely into the God's business category.

Sometimes you see a tycoon who embezzles millions and gets away with it ... but what you don't see is that he brings that same lack of integrity to his marriage, and he's reaping the consequences in his home. His neglected wife has an affair and then files for a divorce that leaves him financially devastated, or his neglected children are abusing drugs to numb the pain from their lack of connection and love from their dad. They might be stealing from him to buy drugs or much worse. The stolen money becomes a curse in his life. He never actually got away with anything.

These things happen every day in ways you will never know. *People always live in the results they create with their decisions.* No one escapes this. (Read that again.)

Holding on to unforgiveness does not create justice in the world. We think we are punishing the other person, but we are not. They go about their lives. They may or may not feel remorse, but either way, it has *nothing* to do with your holding on to that unforgiveness.

Do you see that now? Unforgiveness doesn't leave your physical, emotional, or spiritual body, and it has no power to create justice.

If you're still struggling with the need for justice, it's time to release any false belief that exacting justice lies within your power. You are not the deliverer of justice on this planet. That's not how things work here.

If you are operating under the notion that justice is within your power, you have slipped into *over-responsibility*. Release that desire and allow the Universe to do its work.

As you saw in Oprah's example, the other woman was laughing her way into Tiffany's. Oprah, while holding on to the unforgiveness, was hardly creating justice there.

What's more, staying in unforgiveness has the same consequence as blaming someone else. When you do, you put all the power in their hands to fix it. By doing so, you render yourself powerless in the situation—because they may or may not ever do something about it.

It's the same with unforgiveness: You give your power away!

Why? Well, in order for the transgressor to provide the justice you are looking for, so they can do right by you, *they* have to do something.

You could spend the rest of your life waiting for the people who've wronged you to magically turn around and make this right.

I hate to be the bearer of bad news, but that is unlikely to happen. And in the meantime, you get to stew in the negative energy that is disrupting your peace of mind, causing you to lose sleep, and keeping your muscles contracted in painful knots!

It's *so* not worth it! Unforgiveness is a self-created prison. Time spent in that cell only hurts you and holds you back from creating the life and love you want.

The good news is that you also have the *key* to get out of it because forgiveness is a gift you give yourself. Make the decision to gift yourself today so you can move on to the next step in the forgiveness process.

Miracle Morning Opportunity: If you have a strong intention to free yourself from unforgiveness of the past, create a powerful Affirmation for this to use during your Miracle Morning. **Example:** "Forgiveness is a *gift* I give myself. I thank the universe for enacting justice for me in more ways than I can see. Today I am free!"

Step Three: Find the Gifts and Get Unstuck

In step three, you will shift how you *feel* about the person or situation you previously couldn't forgive.

I know what you're thinking. *What? Forgiving is one thing, but how am I supposed to change how I feel about that horrible thing they did to me? You have no idea what they did, Stacey!*

Sweetie, I get it. And no, I don't know exactly what happened to you, but I have helped clients shift their feelings about the most grievous, heart-wrenching situations you can imagine (and some you can't).

The great news here is that it's possible to feel a whole lot better about any past hurts, while increasing the *wisdom* you gained from the experience at the same time.

Remember when we said that wisdom is the thing we need to protect ourselves in the future? Well, lucky for us, when we process the events in a certain way, wisdom and positivity are the resulting gifts that empower us to get unstuck and cross over into forgiveness!

Let's do an exercise together.

I'd like you to think back for a moment. Find an experience in your life that was unpleasant or painful, even horrible. Recall the details of the experience.

Now, as the person that you are *today*, please look back on that experience and answer the following question:

While you certainly don't want to ever go through that again, *is there something that came out of that experience that you can be grateful for today?*

- Maybe you got the wake-up call you needed to take charge of your life and become the person you are today?

- Did a relationship that ended with much heartache lead you to the marriage you are in today, and now you thank God for that divine redirection?

- Have you been fired or laid off from a job, and it prompted a career change more aligned with who you are?

- Maybe you were devastated about an opportunity that fell through, but looking back you realize that if it had come together, it would have taken your life on a different path, and you would've have missed out on the best things in your life today?

- Did someone hurt you so badly that you no longer speak to them? Sometimes, seeing the trajectory of their life since that time can help you appreciate that it was actually healthier for you and your family not to have been dragged through everything they were about to go through on their downward spiral.

- Perhaps the experience itself was so awful that there was *nothing* redeeming about the events themselves, yet today you have the depth, capacity, and compassion to help others who've experienced similar tragedies because you went through yours?

- Perhaps through navigating the worst tragedies that life holds, you experienced some of the goodness and compassion showered upon you from your friends and family, and that experience shifted you for the better as a human?

Can you relate to any of those circumstances? If you can't, what did they spark for you?

Wisdom is gleaned from a situation whenever we ask ourselves, "Where is the gift in this?"

Even and especially in our most painful and darkest times, there is a divine gift in the works.

Pain is a part of human life. If you believe it's possible to sail through this life without pain, you're setting yourself up for a lot of frustration and unhappiness. Even though pain is not pleasant, it is a fact of life for someone who is living fully and regularly taking the risks required to grow. In fact, if you are not aware of an experience of pain in your life, I can reasonably predict that you are playing too small, living from a place of self-protection and trying not to get hurt. Again, the key to navigating painful experiences in a way that brings personal growth and wisdom is to find the gift in them.

In every experience, you can always find something to be grateful for. The quickest way to cultivate gratitude for a crappy experience is to learn something from it.

As my greatest mentor Tony Robbins says, "Life gives us two kinds of experiences: enjoyable ones and learning lessons." If you don't learn the lesson from the experience, then it remains a crappy, yet pointless experience. But if you learn from it, you get to keep the gift of that learning and then use it to create the life you want. Life sends us learning lessons so we will grow. If we don't get the message, life will keep sending us lots of opportunities to learn that particular lesson. We don't fail the tests; we just take them over and over and over again until we *learn* and grow!

Take time to learn the lesson so life can stop sending you the same "challenge-tunities" again and again!

Client Example: One of my students, Karen, had the life lesson principle revealed in a powerful way through motherhood. One day, she called into one of our live Q&A sessions, and she told me that she had set an intention to be more patient with her kids.

The challenge was that from the moment she declared her intention, her kids had begun being *way* more challenging than before. Her patience was being tried on a daily basis, and she was frustrated.

Karen's mom, who knew of her intention to be more patient, turned to her and said, "Well, you asked to learn patience, so God is sending you lots of practice, Karen!"

Her mom is a wise woman. That's *exactly* how the Universe works! It will send you lots of extra practice until you learn the lesson, but the good news is that once you learn the lesson from the situation that you went through, you get to take that wisdom into the rest of your life with you.

The treasures from going through the trial are yours to keep, so learn the lesson, glean the wisdom, change how you show up, make different choices, take new action, and you will create a different outcome.

Everyone lives in the results of their decisions, no exceptions.

When you gain the wisdom from the crap you've been through, that wisdom will shift how you navigate the entire rest of your life. As a result, you don't actually need to protect yourself from that experience ever happening again. Once you've learned the lesson, become grateful for the hidden gifts, and released the unforgiveness, you will be on a different trajectory in your life, and the old experience will no longer be part of your path.

Marianne Williamson says, "You can have a grudge, or you can have a miracle, but you can't have both."

Joyce Meyer says, "You can be pitiful, or you can be powerful, but you can't be both!"

I'm asking you to love yourself as much as I love you and give yourself the gift of forgiveness. Remember, all it requires is "giving up the hope that the past could have been any different than it actually was."

Feel the freedom of that. Let the energy flow through you. The power of forgiveness is within you, and it's *for* you.

Find the gifts, learn from your experiences, and empower yourself to move forward as an even better and more authentic version of yourself. Once you've done that, you're free to move on to the next step in the forgiveness process!

Miracle Morning Opportunity: If you are struggling to receive the gifts from your experiences, use your Miracle Morning Visualization time to *feel* the joy and freedom of receiving that wisdom. See yourself staying in wonder and open to the moment when you will suddenly *know* the gift that came to you through that journey.

Affirmation: "Thank you, Universe for giving me these gifts on my journey through life. I am so grateful and blessed to have learned the life lessons of that experience so I can move forward into a new experience as a wiser and more compassionate version of me. Thank you again, Universe for always delivering grace to me in my darkest moments. And so it is."

Step Four: Change Your Story

The only thing keeping you from creating the life you want is the story you tell yourself about why you can't have it.
—TONY ROBBINS

There are two components to every situation: the facts and the story.

The *facts* of what happened are the verifiable, undisputable details of what actually occurred. For example, you were scheduled to meet your spouse at the movies at 7:30 p.m., and they didn't arrive until 7:50. Those are the facts. Simple. Verifiable.

The *story* is what we tell ourselves about the meaning of what happened.

In the movie date scenario above, you might say that your spouse doesn't respect you. You could conclude that the call that kept them from being on time was clearly more important to them than you were. You might tell yourself that your spouse lacks integrity to do what they say. You might say that they just don't care. Any of those, or all of those, might be the story you tell yourself about the situation. Those are not facts; those are the meanings you have assigned to the facts of the situation. It's the story you are telling yourself about the situation.

We become so emotionally invested in the story we tell about the meaning of things that happen that it becomes difficult for us to separate the facts from our story.

You may be thinking to yourself, *No, it's not a story, Stacey,* this *is true! This actually did happen!* I get that. Often we've lived with our story for so long, it becomes a comfortable old friend. We don't even recognize it for what it is.

Sweetie, no one is saying that the events didn't happen. Your story may be completely true. But, even if it's true, that doesn't mean that holding on to the story you're telling yourself about the events is serving you!

A much less popular, but nonetheless powerful, teaching from Tony Robbins is this one: "The only question you need to ask yourself about the story you tell yourself is, *'Does this story empower me* to move forward, or is it holding me back from having the life that I want?'" Our story about what has happened either keeps us stuck in unforgiveness or empowers us to find the gifts, learn the lessons, and move forward in our life.

Think about a painful situation you've experienced, something you found hard to forgive. What were the facts? And what was the story you made up about what it meant? Did your story empower you to move forward, or is it holding you back, keeping you stuck in blame and unforgiveness?

I'll give you an example of the power of facts vs. story in my relationship with Paul.

The facts were that 16 years ago Paul came home to me to tell me that our relationship was over and he was leaving.

We often refer to the story of that night as our hanging-by-a-thread moment. But from Paul's perspective, there wasn't even a thread left, because he was *done* before he ever came home that night.

Those were the simple facts.

Now, we'll examine the possible stories I could've created from the facts of that hanging-by-a-thread experience.

Story #1:

"It was the worst night of my life. I've never been hurt so deeply in all my life! He did that to me. I can never forgive him for that."

Story #2:

"We almost lost it all in one night. By the grace of God, we were given another chance! We pulled our relationship back from the brink and went on to create the unshakable love and unleashed passion we enjoy today. I would not be here right now if I hadn't broken open and gone through the unbearable pain of that dark night of the soul. I never want to go through that level of pain again, but I thank God that during the darkest moment of my life, He put Paul there beside me. As a result of everything we've been through, we're able to help others who are hurting and powerfully mentor them to create their own magnificent relationships."

Which story is true? Both stories are true!

But which story empowers me to create the life I want, and which story would hold me back?

That's the key question, and the answer is clear as day.

Now, would I have every right to hold on to the first story? Damn right I would! And you have every right to hold on to your disempowering story, too.

But please listen to me, Lovie. *Sometimes being righteous doesn't actually get you to the life you want to live.*

The truth is, it takes a lot more courage and vulnerability to live from the second story. But it's so worth it! Look at the life I get to live in because I was willing to be vulnerable, harness my courage, and tell myself a story that empowered me to create my life by design!

Creating a new and empowering story is a huge part of the work that we help people do. When you do the work, you get to live in the wonderful results that you create.

Miracle Morning Opportunity: Write down your new story and add it to your Affirmations so that you can repeat it to yourself every day. This repetition will help you change your neuropathways to imprint the new, empowering story and release the hold that the old one had.

Step Five: Decide and Wipe the Slate Clean

Here's the thing, no one else can do the forgiveness work for you, and no one is forcing you to carry unforgiveness around. You must make a decision, sweetie.

Will you decide to continue under the weighty burden and ill effects of unforgiveness?

Or will you decide to let it go and start with a clean slate?

Lovie, today I encourage you to follow the steps in this list:

- ✓ **Accept** that forgiveness is the best thing for you.
- ✓ **Understand** what forgiveness really is.
- ✓ **Release** your false belief that you are the deliverer of justice.
- ✓ **Find** the gift and feel grateful.
- ✓ **Learn** the lesson and take the wisdom into your life.
- ✓ **Choose** the empowering story to move forward.
- ✓ **Give** yourself the gift of forgiveness.
- ✓ **BE FREE!**

You get to decide! The moment you decide to forgive, forgiveness happens within you!

These are my great wishes for you …

- Take the perspective shift that you have experienced and apply some of these tools and strategies in your life, starting today.
- Be empowered to move past whatever hurts or betrayals you might have experienced in the past.

- Give yourself the freedom to start anew, leaving the past behind you, where it belongs.

- Live fully in the present moment.

Declare your commitment to start anew. Forgive and wipe the slate clean. Then let's start creating your life and love by design!

BONUS: Download a poster of the 5-Step Forgiveness Process, so that you can put it somewhere you'll actually see and remember it, at **RelationshipDevelopment.org/tmmbonus**.

Real Life Relationship Case Study

MEREDITH

Before

It was the darkest, most painful time in my life. My husband wasn't in love with me. He hadn't said the words "I love you" in seven years. I told no one. It was my deep, dark secret. I felt heartbroken but also ashamed to be rejected so blatantly.

This was the man I loved more than anything else in the world, and he had reciprocated that passionate, intense love for the first 10 years of our relationship. And then one day, he sat me down and told me he wanted a divorce.

I desperately wanted to save our marriage. I still loved him as much as I did on our wedding day. I loved my family with three kids aged 12, 10, and 5. I loved HIS family. I loved OUR friends.

I jumped into fix-it mode. I consumed marriage fitness boot camps, therapy, books, and everything else that offered a piece of hope. Nothing worked. Divorce was not an option. Divorce felt like shattering my entire life into pieces that I would never be able to put back together. 15 months later, an email appeared in my inbox with the subject line, "Why do people leave?" It was from Stacey Martino, and she finally offered me hope.

After

I remember asking Stacey, multiple times, "When do I get my rainbow?" The pain I had been through was intense and dark and heavy, and there had been days I didn't believe I had the strength to carry it one more day. The first breakthrough and transformation Stacey guided me through was opening up to the concept that there were two possible paths for me, and either one was going to result in happiness and a magnificent love. It was going to be either a saved marriage with my husband of 17 years or a loving co-parenting relationship and happy family.

For a long time, I mistakenly thought my rainbow would be my husband coming around OR a beautiful new, magnificent love. Stacey lovingly and beautifully guided me to my rainbow, and it wasn't either of those. My rainbow was me. Self-love. Emotional fitness. Understanding. A discovery of my feminine and appreciation of the masculine. And, once I discovered how to love myself and take control of and responsibility for my emotional fitness, I was able to harmoniously separate from my husband, and then a new love relationship came into my life.

Stacey helped me open up to the possibility of something better. She coached me through building both a harmonious co-parenting relationship AND a new relationship in the dating phase.

Finding myself dating again after 20 years was uncharted territory, and I desperately needed her help navigating that phase successfully. Stacey helped me to allow my new love to create the pace during the early phase. She helped me see him through the eyes of total appreciation for the masculine, when I would have defaulted to criticism and hurt. She planted the seed in my head that instead of seeing this as my family "breaking apart," our family could actually be even more beautiful with new members.

In my new committed relationship, watching the relationship that has developed between my kids and his children has been surprisingly easy and has been meaningful to watch.

Equally as great of a reward for doing the work is the relationship I now have with my ex-husband and father of my kids. It's remarkably good, solid, easy, supportive, and loving. We have a great, solid, loving happy family. That hasn't changed. The only thing that has changed is we live in different homes (less than a mile apart). We still spend a lot of time together as a family, including some holidays.

I never believed I could feel so happy, grateful, and optimistic for my future. I don't know what I would have done if I hadn't found Stacey and Paul. Thank you both so very much.

Keys to Her Success

- **Personal responsibility:** Meredith faced challenges during this time in her life. And each time, she was willing to refocus herself back to what *she* could do to create more transformation in her life.

- **Think differently:** Through doing the work, Meredith was able to repeatedly see how it was her own blueprint of how she *thought* things had to be that was keeping her in pain. Her willingness to do the work with me to shift her blueprint to open to a new possibility of what *happy* could look like was a game-changer for her.

- **Go all in:** Meredith was the one to go *all in*! Regardless of how scared or painful her journey was, she *committed* herself to this work and never gave up. She came to calls every week, attended live events, consumed the program curriculum—she did it all! Even when she was struggling through a tough time in her relationship, she always showed up, and did the work! Meredith continued to stay *open* and throw her whole self at her relationships, and that got her *huge* results!

7

DO THE WORK:

HOW TO CREATE YOUR UNSHAKEABLE LOVE

BY STACEY MARTINO

"Love is the oxygen of the soul."
—TONY ROBBINS

"Your task is not to seek for love, but merely to seek and find all of the barriers within yourself that you have built against it."
—RUMI

Creating a magnificent relationship *starts* with a Relationship Education, and we're so proud of you for taking the first step by reading this book! In doing so, you're clearly demonstrating that you refuse to settle for mediocrity in your life. Why should you, when you're perfectly capable of creating your life by design and having the love you desire? That is, once you learn effective tools and strategies to do so! Woohoo!

Sweetie, if you apply even a fraction of the tools and strategies that we've already shared in this book, you'll be amazed at the transformation you create!

It's Time to Do the Work!

Paul and I are wired to be strategic by nature, and this is one of the key differentiators in our relationship work! Over the past two decades, we've used this unique gift to create relationship tools and strategies that work for real families living real lives.

We created our Relationship Development tools and strategies by taking our real-life relationship successes and turning them into repeatable, actionable, strategic tools that we can teach you, so you can create the same kind of results in your life!

If you're willing to do the work, you *can* create an unshakable love and unleashed passion.

5 Key Principles for Relationship Transformation

1. It's not going to happen *to* you. You have to create it.

2. Your partner is not going to do it for you. You are going to create it.

3. You must do the work *for* you. You can't be attached to what your partner does or doesn't do as a result. Do this for yourself.

4. You will not create an unshakable love and unleashed passion just by learning the tools and strategies There's a big difference between learning it and living it.

5. You must take action on what you learn. This chapter is designed to give you the tools and strategies to start creating your unshakable love. In the next chapter we will give you the tools to create your unleashed passion.

Our tools and strategies are not theoretical! They work in real life, for real families.

What's real life? For most families today, real life resembles all or some of the following:

- Family looks like one of these:

    - » Mom and Dad both work (inside or outside the house) and are stretched way too thin;

    - » There is only one head of household shouldering everything that would normally be done by two people;

    - » They are single, and they want to find their forever love, but relationships haven't worked-out well in the past; or

    - » Mom and Dad are not together anymore, and trying to co-parent together is way harder than the relationship was when they were together.

- The relationship is strained due to financial stress.

- Employers expect them to prioritize work over family.

- They feel like they're failing as partners and parents.

- Parenting is a 24/7 responsibility with no end in sight, and no one really prepared them for how hard it is. They feel so guilty over how hard it is that they don't always enjoy it. They feel inferior because it seems like everyone else is doing it well, and they suck at it.

- One of the kids is really struggling, and they're not sure how to fix it.

- They don't know how to stop fighting with their partner all of the time.

- They're exhausted from trying to do it all.

- There's no time for fun!

- If they're even having sex anymore, it's not often, and when they do, it sure isn't hot.

- Someone is addicted to something, and they're trying to manage that.

- There is family drama causing pain or stress from one or both sides of the family.

- And ... oh yeah, one of them has had an affair, and they're not sure if they can even come back from that.

In the end, we are busy and overwhelmed taking care of children, pets, and aging parents; working a ton of hours with lots of crap going on; and no one ever taught us *how* to have a magnificent love affair in real life today.

This is real life, my friend. Real families are navigating all this and more. Yet somehow, in the midst of all that, we are supposed to have a fairy tale romance that just happens. I'm sure you've surmised by now that it doesn't work that way.

People handed us an *expectation* that we should be able to have this fairy tale romance ... but they never told us *how* to do that in real life. There was no model, no relationship education, and no methodology provided so that we could create it.

Enough is ENOUGH! This legacy has created too much unnecessary suffering and led to the disposable relationship society that we live today, in which when things get tough, people give up on the relationship because no one ever taught them another way.

Sweetie, you need *real* tools that work in the midst of all our modern day challenges. If relationship tools don't teach you how to navigate the scenario I described above, then they are worthless.

After all, it doesn't take much skill to have a magical romance while on vacation without kids when all your bills are paid. It doesn't take much skill to create hot sex with an exciting new dating partner, either.

It *does* take skill to create the kind of *unshakable love* where nothing and nobody can come between you, however. And it *does* take skill to create an *unleashed passion*, where the sex gets hotter the longer you've been together—especially in the midst of real life! This is when you *need* an unshakable love and unleashed passion.

How to Create the Rock-Solid Alignment You Want!

Let's look again at the Rumi quote I shared at the beginning of this chapter.

> *"Your task is not to seek for* **love,** *but merely to seek and find all the* **barriers** *within yourself that you have built against it."*
>
> —RUMI

Love is an inside job. It's already *in* you. You don't need to *find* love. The real work, however, is removing all the protection, barriers, false belief systems, rules, and mindset-crap that is blocking you from experiencing the love you desire.

You have the best of intentions. I know you, sweetie. You want a great love. You are wired for it.

And you can have it.

I am about to guide you through seeing the formerly invisible forces that have been tearing down the rock-solid relationship you desire. We will teach you how to stop doing what you have unknowingly been doing to contribute to this. And we will guide you on what to start doing that will rebuild the foundation to the unshakable love you deserve!

Your unshakable love is actually created in the little moments of your day.

The first step is to learn what you are unknowingly doing (on a daily basis) to *damage* your relationship and how to *stop it*!

Relationship Killer #1: Keeping Score

If you were born in the 70s like me, or later, you were most likely raised to want a 50-50 relationship. Most of us were taught to want a partnership where you would do *this* for your partner and expect that they would do *that* for you. It was a giant step forward from the male chauvinistic generations of the past. At least 50-50 was based on a desire for equality.

Unfortunately, the 50-50 relationship focus harbors an invisible consequence, and it's killing most relationships today.

Let me ask you a question: How would you know if your relationship is 50-50 and not 60-40 or even 90-10?

Answer: You are measuring.

To keep things equal at 50-50, you are measuring what you get from your partner in comparison to what you give, right?

In other words, you have to keep score.

That's the only way to know if you are *getting* as much as you are *giving* in a relationship. Even worse, you are consciously or unconsciously doing this relationship math in your head all day, every day, and it's designed to backfire on you every time. Why? Well, that leads us to the next problem …

Relationship Killer #2: Using Faulty Relationship Math

When you keep score, you're actually measuring what you *feel* **you are getting back from your partner versus what you** *feel* **you are giving to your partner in your relationship.**

Here's the problem with that: Your partner is a separate human being from you, and therefore by definition thinks, feels, processes, and acts differently.

So, when you measure what they are giving you, they will always come up short because they aren't *giving it to you the way you would have done it for yourself.* Friend, your partner will never be able to meet your expectations because they're based on how *you* would have thought, felt, processed, and acted. In other words, you expect to receive—from them—what *you* would have given to *you*, if you were them! (Read that one again!)

Another way to say that is that you expect your partner to respond precisely the way you would in every situation. But they're *not* you, and they don't respond the way you do, and so they continually come up short in your measuring. You're setting them up to fail, and you don't even realize it.

Oh, but it sure is different when *you* are the one giving. Since you respond or give to them exactly the way you'd want to receive, from your perspective, you are *giving* perfectly! According to your personal evaluation system (and only in your own mind), you're a rock star. Do you see how this dynamic always leaves you feeling like you are giving more than you are getting? That's why you always feel like crap!

Guess what, rock star? Your partner is running the same damn equation on you, and *you* are coming up short every freaking time in *their* faulty, score-keeping relationship math!

The bottom line is that 50-50 relationships, score keeping, and measuring using faulty relationship math all lead to *both* partners feeling like crap! If you're currently doing these things, and you want to create relationship transformation, you must stop immediately and here's why ...

Score keeping will actually block the relationship transformation process!

Practical Tip: Use the 100 percent-100 percent formula to create an unshakable love and unleashed passion The only way to *win* in love is **100-100 instead of 50-50.** You provide for them 100 percent, and they provide for you 100 percent.

You go first! You create the shift. You transform the relationship. You inspire them to shift in response to you. And eventually, as a result of doing the work, you will live in a relationship where your partner goes 100 percent all in for you!

Question: If you sit back and wait for your partner to give before you are willing to give (50-50 approach) and your partner is doing the *same* thing, what happens?

Answer: Nothing. Nothing happens. Because neither of you is giving. You both end up hanging back and looking at an empty relationship in between you waiting for "someone" to go all in. Guess what, my darling? It's *you*! That someone is *you*. You need to go all in to create the relationship you want. Regardless of what they do or do not do!

Your love relationship is not somewhere you show up to *get* something from your partner. It's somewhere that you go to *give* something to your partner. If both partners show up to the relationship to *get* something, there's *nothing* there because neither has anything to *give (but unfortunately, we do have everything to lose)*!

Practical Tip: Give love to your intimate partner without measuring—in the same way you do for your kids or beloved pet. In case you're protesting that you don't know how to go in 100 percent, consider the parents of an infant. The parents give 100 percent. There's no way the baby can do its fair share in the relationship. Do the parents love the baby any less because they're giving at 100 percent and the baby isn't? NO! And they don't punish the infant by withholding love just because things aren't fair and they're not getting what they want in return! They have *no expectations* for the baby, and therefore they don't keep score and they're not disappointed. The baby's smile, contentment, or snuggles are more than enough reward.

I tell my students all the time, "Trade your expectation for appreciation" and watch the transformation that unfolds!

The Only Winning Team

It's time to go *all in*, baby!

Are you ready to create *your* unshakable love?

Having an unshakable love means that you are aligned with your partner as a team, you fully support each other, and nothing and nobody can come between you.

Remember, unshakable love doesn't just happen. No one will hand that kind of alignment to you. You don't just find that. And your partner is not the one keeping you from having that!

We provide the tools and strategies, but you probably know what I'm going to say by now: employing them to create a rock-solid alignment with your partner is a *choice*! Are you willing to be the one to step up and do this for yourself? Awesome, because it begins now.

Four Steps to a Rock-Solid Relationship

Step One: Get Crystal Clear on the Hierarchy!

Do you know that, a very long time ago, one of the key elements in the wedding ceremony was that all the townspeople in the village would gather around, and the officiant would declare that everyone should be notified that, from this moment forward, the bride and groom would prioritize their new primary family above their families of origin? The ceremony was the vehicle for letting everyone know how things would be from then on.

Unfortunately, not only has this been left out of many modern wedding ceremonies, but also the intention has been completely lost. No one even teaches us that we're supposed to shift our priority to our spouse and children, let alone *how* to re-prioritize our relationship with our family of origin and all our other relationships.

If you want to create your rock-solid alignment, you must get crystal clear on the Rock-Solid Hierarchy:

PRIORITIES

1. Partner & Kids

2. Parents & Siblings

3. Extended Family & Friends

In theory, it's quite simple. Absolutely *no one* gets prioritized above your spouse. NO ONE! What's more, if your partner feels like *anybody* is more important than they are, your relationship is in trouble, and in your gut you know it.

I say "in theory" because there's a big gap between learning the Relationship Hierarchy tool and living it. And there's no faking it— either your partner *feels* that they are your number one, or they don't.

In truth, you either create or break down your alignment with your partner in every choice you make during the little moments throughout your day.

NOTE: One of my clients, Kara, once raised her hand and said, "I don't really have any relationships with my family of origin anymore. But I do have friends that are so loyal and so important in my world that they are like family. What do I do with tier two and tier three?"

My Response: Not everyone has biological family relationships that belong on tier two. You do *not* prioritize a family member to tier two if that person is not a healthy part of your life. We fully embrace and support you in designing your life in a way that is authentic for you. If you are blessed to have these beautiful friends in your life who love and cherish you, then it appears that the Universe has given you the family you needed. Please decide for yourself who among those friends are really your "family by choice" and prioritize those friends to tier two for yourself.

Family of Origin Real Life Example:

My student Debra once had a challenge prioritizing her husband and young son over her mother around the holidays. (Perhaps you can relate?)

Traditionally, Debra and her husband, Jeff, took their son Zack to Debra's parents on Christmas Eve. On one particular holiday, Debra was seven months pregnant, and Zack, being two years old, was struggling on the nights they didn't have him in bed by 7:30 p.m.

Jeff suggested to Debra that they start a new family tradition of staying home on Christmas Eve and visiting Debra's family on Christmas morning instead. Debra thought it was a great idea, but dreaded her mother's response to the suggestion.

When Debra mentioned it to her mom, the reaction was as bad as she'd feared! She may as well have initiated World War III.

Let's explore two possible scenarios where Debra will either create alignment with her husband or tear it down by prioritizing her mother:

Script for scenario #1, where Debra aligns with her family of origin instead of husband:

Debra (not owning her desire and using weather as an excuse): "Mom, the weather is bad; we are not going to come."

Mom (cranking up the guilt to get what she wants): "But you always come … it's Christmas!"

Debra (pleasing, to keep the peace): "Maybe we can come later, if it clears up …"

Mom (uses more guilt and shaming because she's still not getting what she wants): "Well, your brother is coming. He didn't think it was a problem …"

Debra (caving and pleasing again): "Okay, let me talk to Jeff and see what he thinks."

Debra asks Jeff about going anyway.

Jeff (who's thoroughly pissed off because she caves in to her mother every time, and he's sick of it): "We already talked about this …"

Debra (afraid of displeasing her mother, and wanting her husband to just go along with it to help her keep the peace): "I know but …"

Jeff (storms away, pissed-off that he never comes first and feeling like he is never heard and always steamrolled by Deborah's family!)

Script for scenario #2, when Debra aligns with husband first:

Debra (owning what she and Jeff want): "Mom, Jeff and I decided that this year, as our family is growing, it's time for us to create a holiday tradition that is best for our kids. From now on, we will enjoy Christmas Eve with our children here in our home, just like you did with us as kids. We love that tradition, so we're going to start it in our family. Weather permitting, we will come to you on Christmas day instead of Christmas Eve."

Mom (trying to use guilt to get her way): "But you always come … it's Christmas!"

Debra (acknowledging her mother's feelings, yet standing firm): "I understand you're disappointed, Mom, but our family is changing, and this is what Jeff and I feel is best for us."

Mom (trying the guilt and shame tactic one more time!): "But your brother is coming! He has *three* kids already, and it's not a problem for him!"

Debra (responding with resolve): "Mom, Pete does what's best for him, and Jeff and I do what's best for our family. We will be there on Christmas morning to celebrate with you all."

Mom (accepts the new terms because Debra won't budge): "Fine, Debra."

Before going into this scenario, Debra was clear that her first priority was her husband and son, so she knew what decision she had to make regarding her mother. She knew what she had to tell her mother, and she knew what the outcome of the conversation would be.

Once you have supreme clarity that your partner is *first*, you can more easily make priority-based decisions in the midst of the real-life, complicated situations that you find yourself in.

Now, although the decision making process becomes clear for you, the process with your family is not always going to be easy because most people resist change. Just like in the scenario with Debra, where she needed to make the choice either to disappoint her mom or to break down her alignment with her husband, you will have to make similar choices and then have difficult conversations with resistant loved ones.

Practical Tip: Learn tools to navigate difficult conversations in a way that builds relationships instead of tearing them down. The results are *so* worth the effort it takes to learn.

We know it's not easy. In fact, we spend a significant amount of time with our students teaching them how to have Brick Conversations, the ones that build a solid, brick foundation for a relationship so they're not walking on broken glass by tip-toeing around hot-button issues all of the time!

If you are anything like the students we serve, there are most likely many Brick Conversations that need to happen in your relationships. These are the tough conversations that you typically avoid because they are uncomfortable or just don't go well. The avoidance of these conversations, however, leads to persistent pain, frustration, and disappointment because things don't change.

Paul and I created a simple methodology to help our students navigate any conversation to a successful outcome. That doesn't mean that you *win* the conversation. Navigating the conversation successfully means that after having gone through it, you and your partner are closer on the other side. You have gained a deeper sense of heartfelt understanding for each other, you both feel heard, and you have put a big brick on the foundation of your relationship that you can build upon.

Paul and I have created a training video and workbook to give you, including a step-by-step, fill-in-the-blanks framework that you can use to map out any Brick Conversation successfully.

You can use this powerful tool in your marriage, with your family members, at work, and with your kids! (Anywhere you talk to humans.)

BONUS: Visit **RelationshipDevelopment.org/tmmbonus** for a free Brick Conversations training video and workbook!

The bottom line is, if you want an unshakable love, your partner and kids must come first, before anyone else!

Step Two: Never, Ever Bad-Mouth Your Partner

We've noticed a disturbing trend—an epidemic of people nitpicking, bad-mouthing, criticizing, competing with, and tearing down their partner in front of others.

Even worse, it's become socially acceptable! In fact, both men and women routinely bond with their friends by complaining about their partners.

Have you ever heard a scenario like this among a group of ladies?

> **Woman #1:** "I have to get home before Alex's soccer game to make him dinner or he will end up with cheese puffs and a soda pop if Bill does it."
>
> **Woman #2:** "Oh please, the other day John tried to 'make me a sandwich' … uh, no thanks!"
>
> **Woman #3:** "I can do better than that … Bob put Mikayla in her leotard for dance, and he put the tights on the outside of the leotard and sent her in that way!"

It's like a competition for a badge of honor for the woman who is putting up with the worst husband. Many years ago there was a magazine column called the Heinous-Husband Award, featuring quips by readers about their husbands. Whichever husband had screwed up the worst won the award. Ladies, think about this … how much national outrage would there be over a column in a men's magazine dedicated to guys bitching about their wives and giving out a Worthless-Wife Award?

I know it's done to be funny, but, honestly, it's not funny to the partners in those relationships.

If you're a woman, that's your man you are cutting down in front of other women. For what? To bond? To garner the pity of others? To gain empathy? To get laughs at his expense?

If you do this, and you want his 1000 percent support of your every dream, or for him to lay down his life to serve you, you're kidding yourself, my friend! Please open your eyes and see that your actions are tearing down the very foundation that you wish you had.

It's not just women who do this. Here's what that scenario sounds like with men:

> **Man #1:** "I'm at work for 10 hours a day. Nicole gets home three hours before me, and when I get home, the house is trashed, and she's looking at me expecting me to do something about it! What the hell does she do with her time?"

> **Man #2:** "I would happily do something about that. When I get home, Shelia doesn't stop talking about her day for like 20 minutes. It makes me wanna kill myself to make it stop, but I don't want to interrupt her, or she will start all over again!"

> **Man #3:** "At least you guys get to see your wives. Deb doesn't even make an effort to get home from the office before 11:00 anymore. She's so exhausted all of the time that she's never in the mood!"

If you're doing this, and you want her to honor you with her complete support and alignment, you're out of your mind!

By definition, every time you speak badly about your partner in front of anyone, you are breaking down the alignment that you say you want to create!

Don't believe the lie that "what they don't know won't hurt them," figuring it's all in fun as long as your partner isn't there to hear it. Wrong! They can feel it! And how you do anything is how you do everything! If you make it a habit to make sport of your partner, you will eventually slip up and do it in front of them (or the person you complained to will do it for you).

Besides, when you bad-mouth your partner, you are bringing an outsider in between the two of you! By definition, that makes your relationship shakable.

I'm taking a stand for your relationship, right now! Use the following practical tips to make sure you stop speaking badly about your partner:

Practical Tip #1: Take a pledge to never, ever speak badly about your partner to other people!

Does this mean that you can never have a negative feeling or thought about your partner again? No! You will. You're human. Keep reading to learn what to do about it!

Practical Tip #2: If something is bothering you, speak directly to your partner, and not others.

This is your opportunity. If something is going on for you, that's the signal there's work to be done. It's an opportunity to build up your relationship by making things better. Don't avoid it. Handle it. Speak directly to your partner about it. If your relationship is *not* yet in a place where you can have these conversations with your partner, then go to practical tip #3.

Practical Tip #3: Bring your challenge to a coach or mentor who can give you expert guidance on how to shift the situation you are struggling with and create a better outcome.

If there's something frustrating you, instead of complaining about it and watching nothing change, I can show you how to shift it without needing your partner to change first. Empower yourself and make your life better!

Practical Tip #4: Take personal responsibility instead of complaining!

A complaint is actually bad-mouthing your partner, and it does nothing to move your relationship or your conversation forward. It exposes and reflects your partner in a bad light to whomever you are talking to. Even worse, it leaves you feeling disempowered because, since it's their fault, there's nothing you can do until they change.

We teach our students how to share a challenge involving their partner by using a Personal Responsibility Statement. This tool allows you to share your frustration in a way that focuses on where *you* are stuck. It's sharing the same kind of struggle, but instead of complaining about *them*, it's all about *you* and what *you* can do to shift it.

Sample Personal Responsibility Script:

> *"I'm really struggling. I have this trigger when John comes in the door. If he's struggling or in a funk from his day, it's triggering me below the 50 Percent Line and triggering the kids. I know that I need to shift this so that I can stay above 50 percent and help the kids navigate this, but I haven't figured it out yet. I'm so frustrated with myself. HELP, please!"*

Practical Tip #5: Share your challenge with the right audience!

Clearly, you may not be able to share a Personal Responsibility Statement with just anyone in your life. Not everyone in your world will get it.

If you are working with a coach or mentor who is an expert in this area, you can achieve outstanding results. Also, if there are other people in your circle who are also happily on the Relationship Development journey, they will totally get you.

That's why our students say that our 7th Power Tribe is a life-changer for them. 7th Power is a term that refers to the people in your life that are on the personal development path with you. These are the people that you grow with. They will challenge you when you are not stretching yourself enough and they will pull you up when you stumble. They may not be doing exactly the same kind of development work as you, but they are into growth and they "get you."

That does not describe most people in your life. Lacking enough people in your 7th Power can be both painful and destructive to your progress. That's why we have created a trusted community of peeps for you.

So, are you ready to take the pledge? Yes? Good, repeat after me:

I declare that I will no longer engage in the destructive behavior of speaking badly about my partner to anyone!

Miracle Morning Opportunity: Add this Affirmation to your Miracle Morning!

Woohoo! You've taken the first step toward a rock-solid relationship!

Next, you need to understand that you are going to be "On the Spectrum" with this change, so you won't be discouraged when you inevitably slip up. This behavior has become so ingrained for most people that initially they're not even aware they're doing it until halfway through a rant when they catch themselves. That's okay! It's perfectly normal. Remember, all change happens on a spectrum. The first step is to decide to change! When you fall, get back up and keep moving forward!

Step Three: Never Agree with Anyone Who Bad-Mouths Your Partner

If you want an unshakable love, though, you can't stop at not speaking badly about your partner. If someone else says anything negative about your partner, you cannot agree with them. Even if you agree with the content of what they say, you cannot align with them against your partner!

This can be easier said than done. In the next step, I will give you clear tools, scripts, and an example that will help you understand what to do in this scenario.

Step Four: In the Presence of Something Negative Said about Your Partner, You Cannot Sit Silent, Either!

If you want to create an unshakable love, then in the presence of something negative said about your partner, you cannot sit silent. You must go above and beyond with positive statements about your partner to send a clear message.

This one is tough, especially if you happen to agree with what they say, like my coaching client Jackson did in a scenario he experienced with his wife. He asked what he should have done differently after recounting this scene to me during our Q&A call:

Saturday night we had planned to meet friends at the movie theater at 7:30. Tara was coming from somewhere across town, so she was going to meet me there. I arrived at 7:30. The other couple was there at 7:30. But NO sign of Tara. By around 7:55, my buddy, Brian, said, "Hey, where's Tara already, man? She's always late!" Before I could stop myself, I found myself saying, "Tell me about it. I have to live with this every day! I'll text her again."

I knew as soon as I'd said it that I shouldn't have. But what could I do? I totally agree with him. She didn't show up until 8:10! You know that drives me crazy, and I'm working on shifting that trigger, but what do I do when someone else complains about the exact thing that makes me crazy about my wife?"

I'm sure you'd like to know just I said to Jackson. Buckle up, buttercup, because here it comes.

"When you shift the meaning that you are giving to your wife's patterns around time, not only will this no longer trigger you in your life, but you will feel very congruent when addressing this promptly with others." Then I suggested a script like this:

"Brian, you know what I love most about Tara? She is so present and so in the moment that she takes in all the zest of life amplified to like 1000 percent! She really lives! She's so full of wonder and appreciation for every life experience that she's not as hung up on schedules and deadlines and bullshit. Every day, she teaches me how to live in the moment instead of missing out on life as it goes by. I'd rather watch her do that than watch this movie we are about to see!"

If it takes more than one occurrence of redirection like that, it likely will not take more than two occurrences before Brian gets the clear message not to pick on Tara, because Jackson isn't having any of it!

By the way, when Jackson did the work to shift his blueprint to appreciate Tara for those gifts that she brings, instead of judging her and letting his need for control get triggered, his relationship with his wife and his experience of life improved exponentially.

P.S. Tara was so inspired by Jackson's appreciation and how he showed up for her that she started creating systems for herself that allowed her to stay more punctual because she wanted to do that *for* Jackson! He inspired a shift in her! That's how it works.

Do the work! Do the work for you to shift how you feel about the thing that is triggering you regarding your partner. Don't speak badly about them. Do the work and shift things for the better!

These challenge-tunities are your opportunity to do the work that you NEED to do! It's FOR you!

While we teach countless actionable tools around creating your rock-solid relationship in real life, it begins with these foundational four steps to an unshakable alignment.

Now that you know what to stop doing and what to start doing to create the relationship you want, from today forward you can start taking new action and showing up differently in a way that starts building the foundation of that rock-solid alignment you want!

It's a skill, and it can be learned. It takes work, but it's so worth it because once you have created an unshakable love, you'll have a solid foundation for creating unleashed passion!

Real Life Relationship Case Study

GRACIE

Before

My marriage has always been loving, but it was lacking something I didn't even know was missing ... Passion! We hadn't gone on a date in about six months. With two kids (ages 1 and 4) we just figured that was one of the things you sacrifice when your children are younger and money is short.

My husband was not interested in participating in anything related to this relationship work. This is just not his thing ... at all. When Stacey said that it only takes ONE partner, that was the solution I needed.

Doing the Work

Soon after starting the online program, we had gone on several dates and were consistently planning more! Stacey offered great strategies for how to go on a date with your partner, even with little kids and a very lean budget, and they work!

In our marriage, our motto has always been "open, honest, real," but this material has given me the tools to be MORE open, honest, and real by learning more about myself and my partner. The understanding of masculine and feminine energy and the differences between men and women has been HUGE for me.

After

I've experienced so many shifts, so many aha moments, I can't begin to list them. Even my husband, who was initially resistant, has begun to notice the differences in me and our marriage, which is B-I-G!

We now navigate through upsets better and faster, and we return to intimacy faster after periods of distance. I've been overwhelmed with gratitude for the changes we've experienced! There is nothing that I have learned from Stacey and Paul that has failed to work for me. There is no doubt that Stacey and Paul really, truly, deeply care about changing people's intimate relationships, and in turn children's lives. But more than that, there is no doubt that they care about changing MY life! That's why I have been to TWO live events with them and will keep doing this work!

Thank you, Stacey and Paul, for the changes you have made possible for me, and the ones that are yet to come!

Keys to Her Success

- **Have faith:** Gracie really wanted to create an unshakable love and unleashed passion in her marriage, but she was concerned that our content would not support her spiritual beliefs. She stayed open, got curious, and explored our content with an open heart and a watchful eye. She was *delighted* that everything that we teach was completely in alignment with the spiritual beliefs that she holds so dear. In fact, she believes that learning how to love at a higher level through doing this work has helped her be an even better spiritual being!

- **Be willing to be the one to do the work:** Gracie was willing to do the work without her husband participating! The fact that her husband was not interested, and told her he would never be interested, did not stop her. Gracie went *all in* for her family and was willing to do the work and be the hero!

- **Cultivate Your 7th Power:** Every time Gracie does a program or event with us, she is building her 7th Power tribe! As a result, she has a strong tribe of support people in her life who "get her" and what she's doing!

Real Life Relationship Case Study

STEPHIE

Before

Before working with Stacey, things were starting to feel more and more disconnected between me and my husband. I knew that, although my husband and I had something amazing in our relationship, the passion was fizzled and the connection was slipping. We already had two little children and another baby on the way, so I wanted to take action.

We felt so busy and depleted. I knew we needed a booster shot of PASSION, but I didn't know where to start.

After

After working with Stacey and doing the program, the conversations, level of understanding, appreciation, and passionate connection that I created with my husband were absolutely PRICELESS!

This shift in our connection to one another has even led to a change in our relationship with our children (we're a TEAM) and in our support for one another. What's more, beyond the first module, I'm the only one doing the program! My hubby has been too busy to keep up with it!

The one thing I wanted, deeper connection and intimacy, has been OFF the charts after doing this program with Stacey and Paul! My marriage is SO passionate, beautiful, and exactly what I was seeking!

Keys to Her Success

- **See it for what it is:** Instead of looking backward at the amazing marriage she had before, Stephie recognized the changes that were happening as a result of having several children and being busy. She recognized that this new phase of marriage required something different and she started *seeking* the answers.

- **Be willing to be the one to do the work:** Stephie was willing to do the work without her husband participating! While her hubby was in favor of doing the work, he didn't actually have the time to follow through. Stephie was *not* score-keeping. She didn't *stop* doing the work when he stopped making time for the program. She went *all in*.

- **Shift how you show up day-to-day:** Stephie was willing to *shift* how she was showing up in her marriage! She brought a new level of vulnerability, trust, and openness to her husband and reignited the passion.

8

DO THE WORK:
HOW TO UNLEASH THE PASSION

BY STACEY MARTINO

*"I want to do with you what spring does
with the cherry trees."*
—PABLO NERUDA, Nobel Laureate for Literature

*"Freedom is not the ability to do whatever you want.
Freedom is the strength of character to do what is
good, true, noble, and right."*
—MATTHEW KELLY, Author and motivational speaker

P op Quiz: What's the difference between salad and garbage?

Do you know the answer? If you recall from our teaching about the Love and Passion Seesaw, the answer is … time!

Over time, passion organically fades in a long-term, committed relationship.

Since love comes from sameness, and passion comes from differences, as you go deeper and deeper into love, you build more sameness. This is great for love. But it's not so great for passion.

As you build more and more in common in a long-term relationship, you lose the differences you had in the beginning, and the passion fizzles out.

It's an organic and automatic process, but the good news is that if it's happened in your relationship, you can bring the passion back and make your relationship hotter than it ever was.

Bring the passion back by cultivating the differences between you.

While we teach dozens of differences between the masculine and feminine (and you learned some of those in chapter 5, unless you skipped right to this chapter), there is one difference that will give you the biggest bang for your buck (pun intended)! That difference is polarity, which is the energetic charge created between masculine and feminine when they come together!

NOTE: Please remember that at times I will use the word men to mean someone with a masculine energy core and the word woman to mean someone with a feminine energy core. If that is not the case for you, please don't let my vocabulary keep you from getting what you need from this content. Make the vocabulary switch in your head and keep going!

What we are seeing today is a reversed energy dynamic. Many men have disconnected from their masculine presence and cultivated their more caring and gentle feminine qualities. At the same time, more and more women have turned away from their open feminine radiance and instead cultivated their masculine mask and masculine tools because they perceive that they get rewarded for them at work or in business. This flip-flop of energies has caused the polarity to dim and the passion to fizzle, creating a passionless relationship epidemic in its wake.

Paul and I are extremely passionate about helping others restore the polarity and bring the passion back to their relationships because this used to be one of our greatest struggles. We suffered from the flip-flopped energy dynamic, so I want to share what that looked like for us to see if you can relate.

As you may know, I was formerly known as the Ice Princess because I was very cold, driven, focused, hardened, and tough. I was proud of how I had protected myself from getting hurt and that I provided for myself extremely well without relying on anyone to provide anything for me that I needed! I was living in my masculine and had suppressed my feminine energy so I wouldn't be weak or vulnerable. I was very successful, too. I achieved a lot all by myself and never depended on anyone else for anything.

I was a great success on the outside, but I felt empty inside. I felt very lonely because I'd isolated my heart—guarding it behind walls of self-protection. The irony is that, despite the protection, I felt more afraid than ever.

Paul had disconnected from his strong masculine presence when he was a kid. His intensity as an adolescent was **not** *welcome at home or at school. He learned at a young age how to disconnect from his masculine energy to seem less threatening to the people around him. For Paul, it felt as though he woke up every day tasked with holding a tiger underfoot so it wouldn't come out. Eventually, he got better and better at making that side of him wrong. He disconnected from this masculine energy, which caused him to lose his passion and feel dead inside. He never quite felt like he was being his true self.*

As a result of our flip-flopped energies, passion and sex were a huge struggle for us! Once I began to learn about masculine and feminine energy, I knew that was the problem we were having, but I had no idea how to get unstuck. It was a very painful time in my life. For two years, I was stuck in that space of knowing what the problem was and not having the means to fix it. I knew I was screwing up every day, operating from my masculine and triggering the crap out of Paul. I didn't want to trigger him, yet I didn't know what to do differently so I could stop. It was a dark time for me.

Today, Paul and I live by the motto that everything happens for a reason and a purpose. We now understand that our struggle, exhaustive study, and trial-and-error effort to break free was by design. We were destined to figure this out the hard way, so we would teach others like you!

Today, I am passionate about teaching women (feminine core energy) how to open to their feminine, and Paul is passionate about teaching men (masculine core energy) how to re-root to their mature masculine! Most importantly, we demonstrate and model what this looks and feels like for our students so they have a reference for what to move toward themselves.

Ladies, if your authentic core energy is feminine and you are operating from the masculine, it's time to realign yourself with your open feminine energy flow!

Men, if your authentic core energy is masculine and you are disconnected from that energy or operating more from your feminine, it is time to re-root yourself to your mature masculine energy!

What is Feminine Energy?

Feminine energy is so wildly misunderstood today that it's helpful to define what it isn't first.

Feminine energy has nothing to do with your hair, clothes, or makeup! Feminine energy is not a look, it's all about your energy.

Furthermore, there isn't just one flavor of feminine energy. Your flavor of feminine energy is as unique to you as your fingerprint. It's part of your authenticity.

When we ask people to describe what feminine is, they sometimes will describe a woman with a long, flowing skirt and flowers in her hair (like a tampon commercial). Then they think, *that must be feminine, and I'm not that.* Wrong.

Others will describe a woman with a tight skirt and sexy top, hair and makeup done like she walked out of a magazine. They think, *that must be feminine, and I'm not that.* Wrong again.

The biggest misconception of all is that feminine energy is weakness! No, it's not!

Too many women are stuck in their masculine because they think that being in their feminine is weak, and they don't want that. Feminine energy is not weakness. In fact, if you have a feminine core, it can be your greatest strength, which you will see in a moment.

So what is feminine energy? Only two qualities define feminine energy:

1. An openness
2. A willingness to be vulnerable

That's all feminine energy is. Yet, if you are anything like me or the thousands of people I teach, that concept of femininity can be elusive.

The best way for me to teach you how to access your feminine is to first explain what it feels like when a woman operates from the masculine:

- If you are a feminine core, when you operate from your masculine, you will feel tense and your muscles will feel tight. You are guarded. You intentionally close your heart. You spend your energy controlling, directing, driving, pushing, and "efforting." You feel depleted and exhausted too much of the time.

- In an effort to protect, you unconsciously use masculine weapons like correcting others, withdrawing, punishing others by withholding, or holding back to protect yourself from being hurt.

Here are some real-life examples of what operating from the masculine looks like ...

1. Stephanie sees her husband loading the dishwasher the "wrong" way. He is wasting *so* much space that it makes her skin crawl. Instead of allowing him to do it his way, and being grateful for the help, she gets frustrated and steps in to do it herself!

2. Lucy and her team have been assigned a project that is due in four days. Each of them is supposed to take ownership of a piece of the project and then collaborate to bring the pieces together. Knowing that the results of this project are going to impact her advancement, she goes home that night, maps out each piece of the project and how it should be done, and creates the fundamental pieces of work for each area of the project. The next day, she hands everyone their assignments and her helpful starting point (which was more like 75 percent of the way there). She then volunteers to compile the end results when everyone is finished. Instead of being helpful, her real motive is to have the opportunity to redo any of the pieces she feels are wrong or inadequate so that it doesn't negatively impact her chance for advancement.

3. Mark calls his wife, Sherri, on his way home and offers to pick up the blank name tags, plastic badge holders, and lanyards she needs for an event the next day. Sherri tells him the card stock number, the measurements of the badge holders, and the measurement and color of the lanyards. She warns him about the other options at the store and to be careful "not to get any of those other ones by mistake." After painfully going over all the details, she realizes she's still not feeling confident about his ability to find the right supplies. She doesn't want to risk his screwing up, so she finally says, "You know what? Forget it. I'll just get it all myself!"

As you can see from the above examples, when a woman is operating from the masculine, her motive for doing so is fear. She doesn't believe she can count on anyone or anything, so she feels a need to either do everything herself or control the way others do things to get her way. She will push and drive others, micromanage circumstances, and close herself off to both pain and possibility out of self-protection.

Very often when I give examples like these, women who are stuck operating from the masculine will pose an objection: "So, to come from my feminine, I just have to allow him to load the dishwasher in the wrong way, be okay with people on my team doing a project incorrectly, and be fine with him coming home with the wrong name tag supplies?"

No! That's not what feminine energy is about, but I can understand why you'd think that. It's often described, incorrectly, as being a "go with the flow and let everyone walk all over you" kind of energy.

To illustrate the point, I'll go through each of the examples again, and show a feminine approach ...

1. Stephanie sees her husband loading the dishwasher *his* way. She knows that if it's loaded that way, the family's daily dishes won't all fit in. Here are two different feminine ways to handle it.

    a. In the first way to approach the situation, Stephanie is *so* happy her husband has finally started loading the dishwasher every day, taking the task off her hands after she had asked him for help the other day! She reasons, "Hmm ... they're not all going to fit, but he's a smart guy, he'll figure it out and find a way to get all of the dishes clean in one shot, come hell or high water!" Besides, she laughs to herself, "In any event, no children or small animals will be harmed, and the world won't end if a couple of dishes don't fit!"

    b. The second way would be for her to ask him, "Bill, would it be okay if I showed you a strategy for getting more dishes to fit into the dishwasher in one shot?" She knows that she has showed him this before, and she sees that he already did one of the things she'd shown him that time. She appreciates that he is trying and understands that this is not how he naturally "sees" the dishwasher. She reminds herself how grateful she is to have a husband who (a) makes an effort to load the dishwasher and (b) smiles when she offers to teach him.

2. Lucy and her team have been assigned a project that is due in four days. Each of them is supposed to take ownership of

a piece of the project and then collaborate to bring the pieces together. Knowing that the results of this project are going to impact her advancement, she goes home that night, and maps out the project. She thinks about each team member's unique strengths and natural wiring. She assigns each piece of the project to the team member who would really thrive with that piece. She knows Connie is a data person and will appreciate doing the research. Brad is more kinesthetic and likes to work with his hands, so she assigns the model build to him. Lisa is more connection-focused, so Lucy assigns the interview piece to her. Since writing is her own strength, she volunteers to compile the report. Staying curious for the journey, she's grateful to have people on her team who have strengths that are different from hers.

3. Mark calls Sherri on his way home and offers to pick up the blank name tags, plastic badge holders, and lanyards she needs for an event the next day. Sherri says, "Oh my gosh, thank you so much, babe, that would be a huge help! I'll text you the details. I love you so much!" Sherri pulls out the empty boxes from the first 100 name badges, snaps a quick picture of each with her phone, and texts them to her hubby because he is a very visual guy and needs to "see" what he's looking for. When Mark comes home, he has three boxes of name tags and badge holders in his hands. "What happened?" Sherri asks curiously. Mark responds, "I'm so frustrated with that store. They had the name tags that you texted me, but they didn't have the clear plastic holders that go with that one! Why? Why would they do that? It makes no sense! Anyway, I brought you a box of those just in case you or Darla had extra name badge holders around." (Sherri shakes her head no with a smile.) "No? Okay, I'll take those back. Anyway, here are the three sets they did have. These are the card sizes, and these are the holders. This one is the closest in size to the one you sent me, but this one is the same thickness in paper. I didn't know which one you wanted, babe, so I brought you full sets of each. Pick the one that works, and I'll take the others back."

Sherri hugs him and says, "OMG! You are the greatest husband in the world! Thank you, baby! I think this box is going to be great. Would you please help me reformat the name tag file on the computer so it works with these instead?" Smiling and satisfied that he served her he replies, "Of course!"

That's feminine energy! It's open and not controlling. Open to pleasure, possibility, and, yes, even the pain of being disappointed sometimes because she knows that life's not perfect, nor is any person. She's collaborative and curious while still focused on a great outcome. She really "sees" others, instead of making everything about her. She allows and helps others to thrive, knowing that it will be better for her, too. She speaks up about her needs and desires to other people, and then considers their needs and desires, instead of steamrolling them. Her open energy triggers others to step up and happily serve her, using their very best effort! Feminine energy is happy to shower others with praise and appreciation and willing to allow others to make her happy! Can you feel how vulnerable it is to operate this way? Feminine energy is not weakness by any stretch of the imagination! It takes strength and courage to live like this!

Now that you've seen what it looks like when a feminine energy core is operating in her masculine versus what it looks like when she's operating in her feminine, it's time to do a bit of self-reflection. If you're a woman with an authentic feminine core, and feminine energy is willing to be vulnerable and open, the question becomes …

How Open Are You?

I want you to take a moment to reflect on that and then rate your openness on a zero-to-ten scale. Ten means fully open, allowing each moment of life to flow without trying to control anything or anyone while allowing every experience in without walls of self-protection. A score of zero means you're pretty much closed, protecting and driving in every waking moment. Where has your center of gravity been, day to day?

Don't be afraid to be honest with yourself about where you are now. It's only a starting point, that's all. If your score is low, there's absolutely no judgment about that.

In the immortal words of Master Oogway from the movie Kung Fu Panda, "There is just news. There is no good or bad."

When you're travelling and you get lost, you need to find out where you are to figure out a route to get to where you want to be. It's the same with this work.

Miracle Morning Opportunity: If opening to your feminine is important to you, use your visualization time to connect with your feminine energy inside and then create an affirmation that will help you shift!

Sample Affirmation: "My feminine energy is part of my authenticity. It is the real me inside. My openness brings out the best in everyone around me. When I operate from my feminine, people go out of their way to serve and support me. Every day, I appreciate the opportunity to harness my courage and *open* myself to the joy and love that life has to offer."

Before we go any further, let's chat about vulnerability …

That word tends to be a huge trigger for women when they first begin the work to reconnect to their feminine.

Why would anyone in their right mind ever purposely be vulnerable? It sounds crazy, right?

At this point in your life, odds are that you have had some less-than-pleasant experiences that you wished you hadn't gone through. (Believe me, I get it, and I'm so sorry you had those experiences and incurred the pain you felt along the way!) Most of us, especially those of us who are feminine, experienced this pain and learned how to protect ourselves for the next time. We vow, "I'm never going to let that happen again!"

Because we aren't taught the skills we need to successfully navigate these painful experiences, we do the only thing we know how to do: shut down in self-protection. We don't want to hurt anymore! We put up walls, we keep people out, we open only so far, we push for things to go a certain way so that we can be happy, and we depend on ourselves so no one ever disappoints us again. The problem is that, to do all of this, we have to close to our feminine.

The unfortunate part about closing is we keep out the good along with the bad. We are not aware of that at the time, of course. But that's what happens.

The level at which you block the bad from coming in is the same level at which you block the good from coming in.

Likewise, the levels of joy, love, and ecstasy accessible to you will be capped by the level of pain you're willing to risk experiencing.

My Example:

In my early 20s, I was willing to be in a committed relationship, live together, date, and have sex. I was not willing to depend financially on anyone else. I was not willing to give myself to someone else. I was not willing to stop leading my single life. I was not willing to move out of my house or even leave my city. I was not willing to let my partner see the parts of me that I was ashamed of. I was not willing to allow him to serve me or take care of me in case I liked it and then he stopped doing that one day.

As a result, I felt happy about my relationship some of the time, and it pissed me off other times. I enjoyed his company some of the time, and also liked being on my own. I felt empowered by providing completely for myself, but I felt overburdened at times because I was the only one providing for me. I felt closer to my friends, whom I allowed to see more of me than I did my boyfriend. The sex was okay, but not great. I liked him, but I didn't feel swept away by love. I never hungered for him. I didn't feel the kinds of love and passion that musicians spoke of in songs. I didn't experience ecstasy. My experience of being in a committed relationship at that time was one of living my single life, with the addition of a companion.

I was comfortable only with being open enough to experience connection, companionship, and friendship, and so I was limited to experiencing the level of love that matched that level of openness. It was very vanilla!

Years later, when I was in a committed relationship with Paul, things were very different. When I first experienced my moment of breaking open during the night we affectionately refer to as our "hanging by a thread" moment, the feeling was unlike anything I had ever experienced in my life up to then.

I thought I'd been protecting myself, yet when he was going to leave me, I felt this tremendous surge of pain, desperation, despair, and hopelessness. It was agonizing. I felt so lost. It felt as if everything I thought I knew about life was unraveling underneath me.

"You failed. You failed. You failed," the voice in my mind kept taunting. Not because I'd failed at the relationship. After all, I was the Ice Princess, so that was not a surprise! No, the real terror I felt coming up was because I had failed to protect myself from the very pain I was experiencing.

I cried hysterically in disbelief that I was experiencing so much pain. I wondered WTF was going on. I had spent my whole life protecting myself from this agony that was searing through my heart and scaring the ever-loving crap out of me. How could I have a broken heart? I wasn't in love!

It's a brutal and humbling moment when you simultaneously discover (a) what you are feeling is the greatest love possible for humans and (b) you have lost it forever because you did everything wrong.

F'n A!

In my 29 years of life, I never knew it was possible to feel love like that for anyone! The surge of love I felt for Paul was so overpowering, so all-encompassing, it's hard to explain. It took me to another level of life.

It's said that love is the only experience on our planet that connects us to the 4th dimension. I believe it. That's what I experienced for the first time that night. It was transcendent.

I didn't want to feel that way. Trust me. If there was anything I could have done to make it stop, I would have. In fact, after Paul said the words "our relationship is over," I'd spent the next two or three hours of hysteria trying to use my old rational brain to make it stop. Today, I thank God that didn't work!

As Oprah says, "Now you know. And you can't unknow it."

After a while, I came to terms with the fact that I would never be able to "unfeel" this, or unknow the experience of this level of love!

Suffering over the thought of losing that love forever, when I had only just discovered this rare and most precious experience, felt so brutal to me. There are almost no words to describe the agony. I didn't think I could breathe without Paul, and trust me, that was terrifying for me! It was in that moment of breaking open that I came to understand a new truth I never could unknow:

If I can't protect myself from the pain, and it's possible to experience this level of love for another person, then I have to do whatever it takes to live and love at this level!

I'd spent my whole life protecting myself and trying not to get hurt, and I'd failed. If it's possible to feel this level of love and elation, I reasoned, then it's worth the risk of opening myself to the experience. I decided to jump in with both feet. I wanted to live my life full-out.

I'd rather play full-out and risk the shit hitting the fan once in a while than live a low-grade shit life every day trying not to get hurt.

Paul and I now live by that motto. Back then, I concluded that, whether my love with Paul would continue to be part of my life, I was done hiding. It was worth jumping in with both feet because I finally decided that I was worth it!

That was my awakening.

It takes a hell of a lot of courage to live this way. I allow life to come in. And I'm willing to go through the pains that come my way as a result. But I also get to experience the heights of life and love as a result.

When you do the work, you can develop yourself so that the pains come fewer and further in between. Eventually, you'll look back at the most painful experience of your life and say, "I'm so grateful to God for giving me that experience! If I hadn't gone through that, my life would not be what it is today."

I thank God for putting Paul Martino next to me when I traveled through my dark night of the soul!

The rewards are well worth the risk that it takes to be to open and be vulnerable!

Sadly, that's just not how most women operate today. We have an epidemic of women who are authentically feminine core energy, but operating from their masculine every day, like I had been.

How Did We Get Here?

In the words of Barney from *How I Met Your Mother*, this was an overcorrection.

Women's liberation was an amazing and necessary elevation for all humankind. Women deserve every bit of equality afforded to anyone else on this planet. Our society needed to evolve, and we evolved it.

Women made great progress toward equality and became independent, capable, and able to provide for themselves and their families, which is a good thing because another big change was upon us as a society.

Divorce became more accessible and prevalent for the first time. With this new opportunity to leave, men started abandoning or divorcing their wives in droves. As a generation, we watched our mothers suffer because they were wildly unprepared to fend for themselves at the time.

Heeding the lessons passed down to us from those women, girls understood they should never depend on a man. Instead, they should provide for themselves.

At the same time, in the wake of being left or betrayed by their husbands, mothers started teaching their boys to be nice guys and not to act like a jerk!

And ...

An overcorrection took place. In school, in the workplace, and at home, many women were taught to be more like men. Authentic feminine energy was perceived as weakness and got lumped in with the inferiority we were rebelling against.

We got all the glory of our independence, but in the process, we overcorrected and adopted a false belief that we should never rely on anyone else. There was no such thing as a relationship education to help us all appreciate and cherish the differences between the masculine and feminine core energies. Femininity got slammed as weakness and became the unfortunate scapegoat of that time period.

Look around today at all the woman who are stuck in their masculine, and you will see the nasty wake of this overcorrection.

Women being in their feminine had not caused the pain of the women who went before us, but rather, a lack of elevated thinking, fueled by fear, created the pain. Unfortunately, many women associated pain with femininity. As a result, they've been distancing themselves from feminine energy ever since, believing that it demonstrated neediness and was somehow inferior.

When our generation of women entered the corporate workplace, we were taught to man up. Right, ladies?

> "There's no crying at work."

> "Don't be so emotional about this. It's just business."

> "Don't *feel* anything about it, just focus, push through, get it done, and produce results!"

Those were the messages we received, loud and clear!

Over time, we adapted to the workplace. We got really good at using our masculine masks and masculine tools. We learned to drive, push, control, direct, punish, withdraw, close up, tighten, and use our strong wit to emasculate others. Unfortunately, we then became so stuck in our masculine that we brought it home and into all our relationships! When a love relationship broke our hearts, we shut off another layer of feeling and closed ourselves off to protect ourselves.

Any feminine energy we had withered away.

We learned how to be strong and successful, and yet, we were unhappy and unfulfilled.

Why?

It's quite simple: if your core authentic energy is feminine, and you are operating from your masculine every day, then you are not operating from your most powerful authentic self.

Fact: You can be your most powerful only when you operate from your most authentic self.

Fact: If you are a feminine core energy being, then you can't possibly be at your most powerful by operating from your masculine.

If you've been stuck in your masculine, then you're tired. Life is harder than you thought it would be. Your relationship is not what you dreamed it would be. You're irritable. And did I mention that you are tired? That's an understatement, right? You're exhausted!

You deserve the gift of energy that your feminine core holds for you. It's time to start coming home to yourself. As you know, this is where I was painfully stuck for so long, trying to figure out how to be something I felt I was not.

While I could spend three days teaching you how to open to your feminine and allow yourself to operate from your greatest power, you can begin using the following four powerful strategies today.

Stacey's Strategies for Opening to Your Authentic Feminine Energy

Strategy #1: Courage

Opening to your feminine requires the courage to put down your masculine mask and tools and just *be* feminine, open, and vulnerable. That takes courage.

After Paul just told me he was leaving, and described, in detail, all the reasons why I wasn't the right love partner for him, choosing to look into his eyes, through my tears, and ask him for another chance took *courage*!

Similarly, staying open in the little moments of your day takes courage. In our example above, it took courage for Lucy to allow her team members to do their part of the project without trying to control them. It took courage for Sherri to allow Mark to figure out the name badge supplies on his own instead of pushing for him to do it the way she wanted it done.

It's an act of courage to open yourself to allowing and being willing to be disappointed, hurt or rejected if things don't go well. It's not easy, but it's always worthwhile.

Strategy #2: Practice

You will cultivate your level of connection with your feminine energy through practice. I am a big advocate of using the Intervals of Time strategy for this.

Set aside ten minutes and decide you are going to stay open, without closing, for that interval of time.

This is not quiet time, meditation, or alone time. This is ten minutes of living real life and operating from your feminine instead of your masculine.

During your ten minutes, intentionally decide not to fall into protecting, directing, controlling, pushing, driving, or closing.

Instead, choose to remain open and allow yourself to be vulnerable for just ten minutes. Connect with this open energy within you so that your nervous system starts to recognize what it feels like. Do this over and over again to start training yourself.

When you can master ten minutes at a time for several days in a row, extend it to fifteen minutes. As you master that interval, extend it again.

Strategy #3: Set Yourself up for Success

When you choose to have the courage to open to your feminine for an interval of time, be mindful of when, where, and with whom you do this. Set yourself up for success by choosing the environment where you feel the safest. If you are going to intentionally focus on "not protecting" then it makes sense that you will be the most successful when you begin doing so where you feel the safest to be the "real you."

Paul was that person for me, so I practiced with him. It took me *years* of mastering my feminine in other areas of my life (with my kids, with friends and family, and in the community) before I was willing to bring *any* feminine energy to my corporate job.

One of my clients, Sue, had the opposite experience when she first started this work. She loves her work since it's creative and allows her to connect with many wonderful people. When she first came to me, given the state of the relationship with her husband, she couldn't be sure that he had her best interest at heart. Because she felt safer at work, Sue started her intervals there and continued until she had strengthened her ability to come from her feminine consistently.

Strategy #4: Role Model

Find a role model who is fully open and living from her feminine energy. Easier said than done, I know, but this is the most effective strategy you can use, especially if you are struggling to figure out what feminine energy feels like.

When you are in the presence of a woman in her feminine, your nervous system will pick up on her feminine energy, and it will create a resonance with your feminine energy deep inside of you, creating a shortcut for your nervous system.

Think of the model as your own personal, feminine tuning fork!

Bonus Strategy: Experience the Energetic Interchange of Mature Masculine and Feminine

If you can spend time with a feminine role model in the presence of her mature masculine man, you've hit the jackpot! That is the winning combination! Talk about leveraging the ultimate short cut—your nervous system will pick up on what is feminine and mature masculine, *while* experiencing what the mix feels like in one fell swoop.

Additionally, when *your* nervous system experiences her energy while being fully protected and served by her man, it will help you drop your defenses and believe that being in your feminine and experiencing the protection of the mature masculine is not only possible, it's real!

Our students tell us time and time again that, while they learn a ton from all the content we pack into our live event experiences, they get just as much value from watching us interact for days. As our client Shelley once said,

Even if you and Paul showed up here, hung out for three days and taught nothing, my life would transform just from what I'm able to experience by being in your presence and watching you interact and be with each other.

I hope one day you'll bless me with the gift of coming to a live event so that I can take you through the experiential breakthrough of opening to your feminine.

Reclaim the Power of Your Feminine Energy

The great news is that when you learn how to stop operating from an inauthentic masculine and start using your feminine energy as your driving force, you will feel a burst of energy surge through you!

What will it look like when you're in your feminine?

- Life will begin to *flow* in ways that it never has before!

- People will respond more favorably to you.

- All manner of resources and opportunities will come your way, more effortlessly.

- You will experience a renewed passion in your intimate relationship.

- Your man will step up to serve you in ways he never has before!

- You will no longer feel the weight of the burden you used to shoulder.

- You will have a newfound energy instead of the depletion of being burned-out.

Who wouldn't have a burst of energy when experiencing all of that? Woohoo! That, my friend, is the power of living from your feminine.

Yes, I do realize that all sounded like a commercial for a fairy tale, where a woman in a flowing dress is practically floating through the world with everyone at her beck and call, granting her heart's every desire so that she has everything she could possibly want. The entire world, including plants and animals, align for her as she walks by! Turtles throw themselves in her path so she doesn't have to walk on puddles, and elephants protect her beautiful locks from rain showers with their ears.

Ha! Okay, so life is not quite like that when you operate in your feminine. But in all seriousness, it might feel like that seemingly unrealistic portrait. And there's a good reason why once you understand how the masculine is wired!

The masculine is wired to step up and serve the feminine.

At one of our recent live events, Paul wanted to demonstrate how differently men and women communicate. He turned to our student Jared, and asked him a telling question.

> "Jared, if I picked up the phone in the middle of the day, called you while you were at work, and said, 'Hey Jared! How's your day going? I just thought I'd call to share my experiences of the day with you,' would you enjoy that call?"
>
> The idea of it was hysterically funny. Jared laughingly joked back, "Yeah, and then you can tell me about what you're wearing today!"
>
> When the room erupted with laughter, Paul drove the point home. "Obviously, if I did that, Jared would never take my call again."

Why was that so ludicrous? Because that's not how men treat other men! Paul would never say that to another guy.

Listen up, this is serious now …

Guys interact with other guys in a certain predictable way.

If a man needs help from another man, he will ask for it directly and any mature masculine man will step up and gladly serve his brother in need. However, without being asked, a masculine man will not just show up and start giving support or protection to another guy!

Ladies, if you are consistently showing up in your masculine and wondering why your man is not "serving, protecting, and providing," then I have an answer for you. It's because you are showing up as a guy in the relationship, and your masculine energy is triggering him to treat you like another guy.

Guys interact with other guys differently than they interact with the feminine. When you show up in your masculine, you are triggering him to treat you like "one of the guys." Only the feminine will organically trigger him to serve, protect, and provide for you.

I know you don't intentionally trigger him not to step up for you. We have a saying in our Relationship Development community, "You may not be the cause of the crap you don't like from your partner, but you sure as hell are the trigger." It's true! We are always teaching others how to treat us, and your masculine is triggering him to treat you like one of the guys.

The good news is, when you open to your feminine, and show up in an energy that allows for him to serve, protect, and provide for you, you will trigger that response from him … naturally!

Unfortunately, many women fear opening to their feminine because they've had a bad experience with the masculine before. This is unfortunate because if they were wounded in the past, it was by the immature masculine and not the mature masculine. There is a huge difference, and it's best explained by Paul in the following section.

What is Masculine Energy?
By Paul

Masculine energy, at its core, is rooted, focused, unwavering, decisive, confident, assertive, and outcome-focused. It knows what it wants, enjoys breaking through challenges, likes to engage in conflict head-on, is fully focused, and nothing will stop it.

In pursuit of a goal, the obstacles encountered along the way are just part of the fun for men. The fulfillment felt by masculine energy is realized in achieving the goal, but the level of satisfaction, in part, depends on the challenges encountered. If the path to the goal is easy, there is little or no fulfillment value. Conversely, when the path to the goal is particularly grueling, there is huge fulfillment value gained, which deeply satisfies the core of masculine energy. Achieving our outcomes gives masculine energy a sense of purpose in life. Without purpose, masculine energy will eventually feel hollow and dead inside.

Don't get me wrong, masculine energy isn't masochistic in nature. It's not that we love to suffer. Rather, when we are in a masculine flow state and committed to achieving our objective, we don't focus on the obstacles or the suffering we may be experiencing. We are so single-focused on the goal that we tend to not notice the suffering. Once the goal is achieved, we feel the full value of the victory, and only then do we focus on what we experienced and overcame along the path to victory. These accomplishments feed our own sense of self-worth.

Masculine energy is a powerful force that rises up from within us. It is outcome-oriented. There's a lot of energy driving that objective.

Unfortunately, there are very few positive, mature masculine role models today, so it can be difficult for men to understand how to access and use their greatest power—their masculine energy—to serve others in a way that is fueled by integrity and honor.

The Differences Between Mature Masculine and Immature Masculine

Many, if not most, women can recall an experience in their life when they encountered a man who possessed focused, driven, seemingly confident and decisive masculine energy (those are traits that both immature and mature masculine possess). You may have been sexually attracted and willingly pulled into it, only to be left deeply hurt, disappointed, and confused by how that man eventually treated you. Unfortunately, that is the result of an experience with the immature masculine. It leaves a woman believing all men are jerks, or worse.

There is a big difference between mature and immature masculine, however, and it has nothing to do with someone's physical age. Plenty of younger men are in their mature masculine energy, and plenty of older men are wildly stuck in their immature masculine energy.

How can that be? Hang in there, it's simple!

The fundamental difference between mature and immature masculine energy is that immature-masculine-energy men are driven from their ego, and mature-masculine-energy men are driven from their heart and soul.

Let me explain …

The immature masculine man will use the powerful masculine energies to meet his own needs; even when it is at the direct expense of others, including his partner. Immature masculine is inherently selfish in nature, egotistical, short-sighted, reactive, and untrustworthy.

I am not saying you can never trust the immature masculine. However, since immature masculine is selfish in nature, by definition, others could only reasonably trust such a man when their interests happen to be the same as his.

Immature masculine energy is constantly looking for the next accomplishment, or a reason to get a sense of temporary fulfillment, because it lacks the true inner strength and inner peace that mature masculine energy owns completely.

Immature masculine energy, on the surface, appears deceptively similar to all of the qualities that feminine energy finds so attractive in men. It can still be driven, decisive, and confident, know what it wants, and seem powerful on the outside. Women find it attractive because these same characteristics are the mark of someone who will be a strong protector, provider, and leader for the feminine. As a result, women often find themselves attracted to a masculine energy that they thought would protect and provide for them, only to find afterward that the opposite was the case. In reality, the immature masculine energy was far more interested in taking what it wanted from her, instead of protecting or providing for her. When feminine women find themselves in a relationship with the immature masculine, his selfishness and ego challenges will lead to a lot of negative experiences for her.

Immature masculine energy is the side of the spectrum that wrongly gives masculinity a bum rap. When women mistakenly categorize all men as being like this immature masculine energy, it leads to even more confusion, misunderstandings, and relationship problems down the road, on both sides of this equation.

Women tend to overcorrect and seek out a gentler man who seems less threatening. Unfortunately, when that happens, the woman will eventually discover that this gentle nice guy is not connected to his masculine energy. As a result, he does not protect or lead her, and she feels disappointed and burdened by having to continue doing all of those things for herself.

Examples:

1. Bob's sister calls to let him know that his niece Claire's graduation party is the second Sunday in May. Looking at the calendar, he realizes that falls on his wife Bonnie's birthday weekend.

   a. Immature masculine response: Bob pleases his sister and family of origin by telling them that he and the family will come to the graduation party. He knows that Bonnie will be unhappy, but he figures she'll get over it, and, anyway, "What could he do?"

   b. Mature masculine response: Bob politely declines the party invitation, letting his sister know that they can't attend because it's Bonnie's birthday weekend. He tells his sister how proud he is for Claire and tells her that they will make separate arrangements to take Claire out another time to celebrate. Later that evening he lets Bonnie know that Claire's party happens to be on her birthday weekend, and that he already declined and put a reminder in his phone to take Claire to brunch and the museum the first weekend in June. Bonnie smiles and adds the date for brunch to her calendar.

2. Barb was scheduled to fly home from Seattle on Thursday morning. Her flight got delayed and now she won't land until 7:30 in the evening. She's been away since Sunday working her tail off and she's exhausted. Bryan has a networking event on Thursday that starts at 7 p.m.

   a. Immature masculine response: Bryan texts Barb, "Did you arrange for a sitter? What are you going to do about the girls? You know I won't be home—I have a networking thing at 7. Let me know what you are doing before I leave."

b. Mature masculine response: Bryan has been on the phone with Barb all morning to help her with her flight delays, but this time he has good news:

Bryan: "Babe, I got you on a flight that connects through Chicago O'Hare and will get you home by 7:30. Head to Gate C. You have about an hour. Did you eat? There's a salad place at that gate. Get something for the plane, sweetie."

Barb: "I love you, Bry. Thanks. I'm so sorry about your networking meeting tonight, baby. I know I'm screwing up your plans. I really thought I would be home long before you needed to head out."

Bryan: "Barb, I don't give a shit about networking, don't worry about that. I've got a sitter for the girls, I'm coming to pick you up at the airport, baby."

Barb: "Babe, you don't have to do that. I can Uber."

Bryan: "No way, babe. This day has been too much for you. I'll be there. Besides, then I get to see you ninety minutes sooner. And only I can bring your favorite coffee!"

Barb: "Oh, you are so getting lucky tonight."

Bryan: "That's what I'm talking about!"

Mature Masculine

Mature masculine energy gets fulfillment from serving, providing, and protecting. Mature masculine is selfless in nature. It's an outward-focused energy, not inward. It is completely lit up and fueled by a sense of purpose, inner strength, honor, and integrity.

Mature masculine is always about doing what's right, no matter how difficult or what the personal cost may be. Honor, purpose, and freedom are some of the most powerful ingredients in the mature masculine mindset. Mature masculine energy will literally and willingly die for others, doing what he believes is right. Mature masculine energy can lead others effectively by inspiring them to willingly follow. A mature-masculine-energy-man owns himself completely and is supremely confident in his power to influence the world around him without needing to compromise his integrity and honor in the process.

Since he is confident in his own ability to meet his own needs, the mature masculine has no interest in taking anything from anyone. Because he's driven by virtues such as honor and integrity, he makes for a highly trustworthy partner in a relationship.

Admittedly, throughout history the immature masculine has provided the feminine plenty of ammunition for taking shots at modern men. When combined with the overcorrections of the equality movement for women, where men were taught to suppress their masculinity or to otherwise play small, it has created a powerful, polarity-killing cocktail that current generations have been drinking for far too long!

As a mature masculine man, it is deeply saddening for me to watch men go through life honorably doing what they believe is right, but at their own expense. They were conditioned to be gentler to seem less threatening. This leaves them feeling emasculated and dead inside. As a result of this dynamic, both men and women are losing in so many ways! Women are forced to become more masculine because their man seems too gentle to protect them. Men check out and disconnect because they don't see their purpose in the relationship.

Masculine energy is actually magnificent, deeply honorable, and badly needed in this world. Masculine energy is the same energy that drives a fireman to kick doors in and rush into a burning building to rescue people he does not know, willingly putting his life on the line to protect them from harm. Mature masculine energy is intense, powerful, and unstoppable, but it is not threatening. It is protective, because it is solidly founded in honor, integrity, and doing what is right, regardless of the personal cost to himself or how difficult the path.

The mature masculine of that fireman is exactly as described above: rooted, focused, unwavering, decisive, confident, assertive, and outcome-focused. He knows what he wants, enjoys breaking through challenges, likes to engage in conflict head-on, is fully focused, and nothing will stop him from saving a complete stranger's life. And he knows that if he did die trying, it was worth it. Isn't that the kind of energy and commitment you so badly want from your partner, ladies?

Stacey and I have created a bonus video for you so that you can experience the mature masculine in action!

So much unnecessary pain and frustration in our relationships come from situations where the man is disconnected from his masculine energy and/or the woman has assumed the masculine role in its absence, like the flip-flop predicament that Stacey explained earlier.

The good news is that either side can flip the switch in the relationship. For that to happen, men and women need to stop making their core energies wrong, not only for themselves, but also for their partners.

Interaction between Mature and Immature Masculine

A mature masculine man can identify an immature masculine man 10 miles away. We don't like them, and we don't trust them. Ladies, pay attention. If a mature masculine man in your life refers to another guy as a dick or a total ass, steer clear: he has spotted an immature masculine man. You should trust his instincts.

Mature masculine energy will conflict with immature masculine energy due to the lack of honor and integrity in the immature masculine. Immature masculine energy does not like to be around mature masculine energy because the character gap is too great, and it makes him feel inferior. Immature masculine men justify their behavior by seeing mature masculine men as overly full of themselves.

How the Mature Masculine Brings Out the Feminine

Men, for a woman to let go like she so badly wants to, she must feel safe enough to open to you and trust that you will lead her for her best interest.

(Read that sentence several times because this one simple fact is wildly important for the longevity and happiness of your love relationship.)

Stop looking to your woman to be more in her feminine. If you are not firmly rooted in your mature masculine and serving her for her best interest consistently, she just won't open to her feminine. Said differently, she won't stop being the guy until you prove that you are the man for that job!

She instinctively knows she cannot let go of the driving, pushing, and control in the relationship unless mature masculine energy is present and acting in her best interests to protect, lead, and provide for her. Who can she let go to if you are not driving the ship?

If you want a feminine woman who happily and willingly opens to you and surrenders to your lead, then you must cultivate your mature masculine energy and masculine presence. It's a skill, and it can be learned. The immature masculine can evolve into the mature masculine, and men who operate from their feminine can get back to their authentic core masculine energy.

The motivation to change comes either from inspiration or desperation. However, I find that, without actionable tools, many men struggle to access and live from their mature masculine. For that reason, I teach and model mature masculine presence to the students at our events, and it powerfully connects men to their authentic, mature masculine.

Whatever path you choose to get back to your authentic core, the goal is for you to experience the deeply satisfying wholeness that comes from operating from your mature masculine core! It's who you are! And it's time to come home, brothers!

The Impact of Mature Masculine Presence on the Feminine

Real mature masculine energy has tremendous power that is capable of opening the flower of femininity quickly in profound and incredibly rejuvenating ways.

Masculine presence seems like such an elusive thing to so many men. You can exude masculine energy when you are fully connected to your masculine core. The sheer confidence, power, and focus of real mature masculine energy will create a vibe that will be felt by all those around you.

Masculine energy is not monolithic! Like the feminine, it comes in different flavors and intensities, because it's part of your authenticity. Moreover, mature masculine is available to any man who wants to own it, just as its feminine counterpart is available to all women who want to fully embrace their own essence.

Masculine presence is masculine energy that is fully owned. When your woman can truly feel your masculine presence, it provides the missing key that unlocks her ability to let go of her forced masculine energy and resume her true femininity. When she consistently feels your mature masculine presence, even a completely overwhelmed and exhausted woman will begin to blossom before your eyes as she begins to experience her ability to surrender to your lead.

Masculine presence happens when you are deeply connected to your masculine, fully present, and focused on her in such a way that nothing else exists. Through this focus, you become deeply connected with her and in tune with what she is feeling.

When you successfully bring your masculine presence, you will experience the power that your presence has to free your woman within seconds. At some of our live events, I demonstrate masculine presence in a very visceral and visual experience with Stacey. Whenever that happens, Stacey says it's like her brain shuts off. This is how she describes it:

When Paul brings his presence to me, I can feel him approaching before he ever reaches me. It's as if I'm the only thing that exists in the room, and he has thoughts of nothing but me. His confidence and pres-

ence overpowers the chatter in my mind, and it's like my brain shuts off. I can feel him fully connected to me. I feel a tremendous sense of trust for him, and I know that I am fully protected in that moment. Twenty-five ninjas could drop from the ceiling, and nothing would happen to me. Paul is completely present and in total control of everything in that moment. I have a deep knowing that my fake masculine is no match for this power he brings. Any tightness, driving, or pushing that I may have slipped into (masculine operating) falls away like an outer shell. I melt into him. It feels amazing to let go of everything and allow him to take over for me. It's like a vacation for my brain.

Paul can bring varying levels of masculine presence to me at different times. He is fully present for me on a day-to-day basis. Rarely does he drop his level of being fully connected. He has an operational level of masculine presence where I know he's got this always. Paul is my leader. He clears the path for me, for my best interest, at all times. He selflessly creates our life to serve me, and he makes all my dreams come true.

At times when I get "crunchy," caught up in a moment of controlling, pushing, or fearfulness, Paul will turn up the volume on his masculine presence so I can let it all go. The energy level (volume) of his presence must be able to overpower the level of my crunchiness, if he is going to break through to me. And he delivers every time! God, I love that man!

Just so this point does not go unnoticed, in Stacey's description can you see how one person (me) is creating a change in the relationship just by showing up differently?

Men, cultivating your masculine presence in a way that can shift your woman in an instant is a skill, and it can be learned!

Reconnecting to Mature Masculine

First, know this: If you have a masculine core energy, you are masculine. You didn't lose your masculinity somewhere on your path through life, and nobody took it away from you. Rather, you have simply learned to suppress it, or you've lost touch with it for so long you can no longer readily connect with it.

Strategies for Cultivating Your Mature Masculine Presence and Energy

Strategy #1: Face a challenge and break through

Seek out activities that force you to overcome a challenge and break through to the next level. Some examples might be working out, martial arts, and sports. As you participate in these activities and overcome the challenges, you will start to resonate with feeling powerful, unstoppable, confident, and focused in a way that only masculine energy understands. When you feel that natural resonance, that's your masculine core energy. Cultivate that even more.

Miracle Morning Opportunity: Use your Exercise time during your Miracle Morning to choose an activity that connects you to your masculine core.

Strategy #2: Put her first

To exercise being in your mature masculine you must continuously put her needs ahead of your own. You must have a clear understanding of her needs, which does not come naturally. When you study Relationship Development work more deeply, you will cultivate the ability to understand her needs in a way that becomes second nature to you. In the meantime, here's what you can do:

1. **Commit to mastering your relationship education and the differences between masculine and feminine.** This is an absolute nonnegotiable. You can't serve a woman if you don't fully embrace how different women are and attain mastery of these differences. (Don't guess, you'll be wrong!) Your Reading time during TMM is a great time for this.

2. **Study her. Take notes.** Figure out what motivates her to feel different feelings or say the things she says. I keep an app on

my phone for this purpose (I like Evernote). I have an entire section for Stacey. When I learn something new about her, I record it in my app immediately.

3. **Cultivate your sensory acuity to pick up on what she is feeling underneath her words.** This is contrary to the natural male response of listening for the purpose of conversation or a problem to be fixed. This will not be easy at first. But it is a skill, and it can be learned. Continually tell yourself, "Instead of listening to the words she is using, I will listen for what she is feeling about the subject." *Respond to the feeling, and not the words.* (You will thank me for this one tool alone!)

Miracle Morning Opportunity: Add an Affirmation to your Miracle Morning for this. "Today I will listen for what she is *feeling* instead of getting caught up in the words. Every opportunity to practice this is honing my mastery of this skill, so I cannot fail!"

Strategy #3 Role Model

The number one strategy for cultivating your mature masculine energy is to spend time with men in their mature masculine so that your nervous system can pick up on their energy and become familiar with it at a resonance level.

If you currently struggle to bring your masculine presence forward, and reading about it feels elusive, I suggest you spend more time with a mature masculine man, especially when he is with his feminine woman.

I highly recommend that you join us one day at one of our live events so you can experience this for yourself. And beyond experiencing Stacey and me together, you will also get to be around the great men in our Relationship Development tribe who are on their journey and doing the work.

In the next section, Stacey will teach on the impact that realigning with your authentic core energy has on your relationship.

Mature Masculine and Feminine, Together, Create Sparks!
By Stacey

When you truly begin to live in your authentic energy, whether that is masculine or feminine, it dramatically restores your passion for each other and for life itself.

The mature masculine gets to lead, serve, protect, and provide as he is wired to do. The feminine allows him to step up and serve. Her appreciation and gratitude are the only gifts he needs in return, and she fulfills his deepest desire when she is open and happy!

Once that happens, you will feel the intense spark of passion that has been missing, and the sex will be off the charts! But that's not all. You'll begin to experience the secret benefits of doing this work: a surge of energy and true happiness, living as your best and most authentic self, in a rock-solid relationship with your partner!

Bonus Download: Visit **RelationshipDevelopment.org/tmmbonus** for free videos of Paul and me teaching masculine and feminine energy live! If you thought reading about it was powerful, wait until you see Paul and me demonstrate it on video!

A Sex Problem is Rarely a SEX Problem

Many people come to me struggling with a lack of passion, playfulness, and flirting in their relationship. They want more sex and better sex. I often hear requests like this one: "Yeah, everything you teach is great, and I'll do all that, but can we start with the sex and the passion?"

No, you cannot.

The gateway to ravishing intimacy for women is vulnerability. Only through her willingness to open to her vulnerability and surrender to her man can a woman achieve levels of unleashed passion!

The gateway to being a rock star in the bedroom for men is to be able to lead your woman! You can't lead your woman inside the bedroom if you are not leading her outside the bedroom. Master your masculine presence, and she will open to you.

That's why I often say, "A sex problem is rarely a sex problem."

Ladies, open to your feminine energy. Men, cultivate your mature masculine energy.

It's a skill set, and it can be learned.

It does not happen overnight. This is a journey, but it doesn't have to be a long journey. It will take work. It will stretch you, and there will be some bumps and bruises along the way. But if you implement, you will see and feel the progress you want!

There are a few tools that I want to give you to help you get better results with this. These tools are exactly what you need to keep you moving forward. If you are committed to taking this journey to your unshakable love and unleashed passion, the keys to preventing setbacks are in the next chapter for you!

Real Life Relationship Case Study

JON

Before

My wife and I knew about Stacey and her coaching, but we had a 'good relationship' so I actually said, "Do we really need this coaching?" I'm SO glad that I have an underlying belief that I can get better at anything! Just because we are satisfied with our relationship, it doesn't mean we shouldn't try to take it to another level and make it extraordinary!

Doing the Work

During the first coaching call with Stacey, my wife was in tears and I was in tears. Not 'bad' tears ... tears of joy, connection and love! We said, "Thank goodness we're doing this!" I never would have been able to predict the breakthrough that we had!

I'll never forget attending one of Stacey and Paul's live events because I had a tremendous breakthrough during one of the sessions on masculine and feminine energy. On the next break, I took Tatyana aside and said five words to her that would change our marriage forever. I told her, "I will never leave you." She collapsed on me crying and told me, "If you never told me you loved me again but you only told me those words forever, I'd be the happiest woman on the planet Jonny, that's all I need."

It was the experience of being at the immersion event that gave me the powerful insight and answers that I needed ... and I just knew that was what Tatyana had needed from me all this time, and I never saw it before.

After

We have had such a tremendous breakthrough, I was kicking myself for not doing it earlier! My marriage to my wife has never been stronger, more aligned, or more passionate. Experiencing this transformation has been a game changer for me as a man, as a husband, and as a father.

If your relationship is in a tough spot (many people are), you need tto start using this advice, now. And if your relationship is in a great spot, you need this now. You don't want to put your relationship on 'auto pilot'; you always want to be making it better.

Stacey, thank you for all that you have done for myself, Tatyana, and our family! Good luck everybody ... Stacey Martino is gonna Rock Your World ... GET READY!

Keys to His Success:

- **Not willing to settle for 'good enough':** Jon is committed to making every area of his life outstanding and is willing to do the work it takes to create it. Jon is *not* a dabbler; he continues to cultivate himself to reach mastery.

- **Embracing the mature masculine:** Through doing this work, Jon catapulted his mature masculine forward to serve his wife in ways that he had never known were possible before. Even as a great leader in other areas of his life, Jon was able to learn so much more about how the mature masculine can serve as a leader for his wife and children in ways that took him to a whole new level.

- **Remains curious:** Regardless of how much personal development work Jon has done or who he has coached with, Jon is always willing to keep learning, growing, and taking action so that he can become the best version of himself.

— 9 —

YOUR ROADMAP TO RELATIONSHIP MASTERY

BY STACEY MARTINO

"I fear not the man who has practiced 10,000 kicks once, but I fear the man who has practiced one kick 10,000 times."

—BRUCE LEE

"It's not about how hard you hit. It's about how hard you can get hit and keep moving forward. How much you can take and keep moving forward. That's how winning is done."

—ROCKY BALBOA

Better relationships equal a better life.

If you want a better life, you'll want to create better relationships with your partner, your kids, your clients, your prospects, your co-workers, your boss, your family of origin, your friends, your community, and your Creator, too. Phew! That's quite the list!

If you had to work on improving all those relationships individually, it would be a daunting task indeed! There's only so much time you have in a day, or in a lifetime. Perhaps there's an easier way than trying to tackle them separately.

Maybe you can work on *one* thing that will transform every relationship? Let's see … what could that one thing be? I know! Who is the common denominator in all those relationships?

If you said, *"I am,"* you're right! The common denominator is *you*. If you want to leverage the *one* change that will improve *every* relationship in your life, you must master *yourself.*

Everything on planet Earth works through relationship, and therefore your success in marriage, parenting, friendship, work, or business will be capped by your relationship skills. Let's face it, the other people in your life are always doing something wrong, aggravating you, or making poor decisions that leave you wondering what the hell they were thinking.

Since all life works through relationship, you're always thinking or obsessing about relationship (romantic or otherwise) at least a little bit:

> "How do I deal with the employee I'm having a challenge with?"

> "My teen is getting into stuff that's disrupting the entire household—what should I do?"

> "I wonder what my boss meant by that comment? Does he think I handled that client poorly?"

> "My partner has been pretty distant lately, are we okay? Are they having an affair?"

The truth is, a lot of your energy already goes toward your relationships every day!

A percentage of that energy is productive and is getting you the results that you want, but a percentage of that energy is destructive, and it's causing you a lot of pain.

Your level of personal development and emotional fitness are what dictate those percentages. (Read that again.)

If you want to master relationships and increase the percentage of energy that is productively creating the results you desire, you must master these two components:

1. You

2. How you relate to others in the world around you.

Our motto around here is "Relationship Development, it's about *you* and how *you relate*."

Simple enough, but not necessarily easy. We're going much deeper on each of these, so buckle up, buttercup.

Mastering You

It only makes sense that we need to master ourselves before attempting to master how we relate to other humans. We're going to teach you the process to do so in a few steps.

Three Steps to Self-Mastery

Step 1: Master Your State

As we discussed in chapter 5, mastering your state means that you come from a high state most of the time, and only a few things can trigger you into a low state. Even when you get triggered below the 50 Percent Line, you have mastered the ability to get out of that low state in a matter of moments and *not* stay stuck there.

In the early years of dating Paul, I hadn't mastered my state yet. When I would find him behind the computer working at all hours, it would trigger me. I would have thoughts like, *When is he going to pick me? Why does he like work more than me? How many certifications are enough before he can get to me?* That would trigger me below the 50 Percent Line and usually resulted in the millionth argument over him working too much.

I didn't understand the masculine back then, so I didn't recognize that he was deeply focused on cultivating his professional skills so he could provide for me. I didn't appreciate that he was sacrificing for me to give me the life he felt I deserved. Nor did I appreciate his dedication to growth.

Once I got on the spectrum of state mastery with intentionality over situations like this, I started to see things differently and master *more* of *myself* in those moments. Eventually, staying in state became effortless.

Step 2: Understand and Up-level Your Blueprint

We touched on blueprints earlier, too, but in essence, your blueprint is comprised of your belief systems, meanings, rules, triggers, and emotional set points. It could be described as the playbook you're using every day or the software that's running your show. That is your blueprint. We all have one, but most of us go through life completely unaware of our own personal operating system. That's unfortunate, because our blueprint was created by the influencers in our lives when we were children.

We *must* understand our blueprints if we want to transform our lives, but the work doesn't stop at understanding, because it took a lot of conscious effort to manage my state in response to triggers, and the *efforting* is exhausting!

To make my ability to master my state *effortless*, I had to do the work at a deeper level so I could dismantle and eliminate the triggers altogether. No trigger, no response to manage.

Once I began the rewiring process, it didn't take quite as much effort to maintain my state above the 50 Percent Line. I continued to progress along the spectrum of mastery until my new software blueprint was completely installed, and *that* is the point when it became effortless enjoyment.

Step 3: Trust yourself to make good decisions, in any situation

The final step is all about deliberately designing your decision-making software, which is the unconscious process by which you are making decisions 24/7.

You are making decisions right now, even as you read this page:

"Is she for real?"

"Should I do the work?"

"How much more should I read right now?"

"Should I highlight that sentence?"

"Should I make myself some coffee or just take a nap?"

What's more, every decision you make shapes the results you see in your life! You *must understand and intentionally up-level* your decision-making software if you want different results.

If your decision-making software is allowed to run unconsciously, *it* will use *you* to create results based on the default blueprint you ended up with. However, if you create your software with intentionality, then *you* can use *it* to create the life you desire!

Lovie, it's *so worth* doing the work to purposefully design your decision-making software so you can live in the results you want!

Once you've attained this level of self-mastery, you'll no longer be easily knocked around by your outside world, and you'll remain consciously resourceful in virtually any circumstance.

Now that we've named and defined the three steps of self-mastery, we're ready to talk about how you relate to others. Becoming masterful at how you relate to others in the world is essential if you desire to inspire, lead others, and create a positive impact on their lives.

Mastering How You Relate to Others in the World Around You

If you want to relate successfully to other people, you must learn the following:

- Understand what motivates them.
- Build instant rapport.
- See things from their perspective in the moment.
- Use your tools and strategies to influence and inspire them.

These are critical skills, and they *can* be learned!

Through the principle of synergy, you will always be able to create more in relationship with others than you ever will on your own.

As Hellen Keller said, "Alone we can do so little. Together we can do so much."

I love that quote, but I want to highlight an important caveat: Just being *together* in relationship with other people won't to amount to *squat* unless you have mastery of yourself and mastery of the way you relate to the people you are *together with*. You must have the ability to influence and inspire them.

Since mastering how *you relate* to others in the world around you is critical to your experience of life, let's take a moment to do a self-assessment.

Question: What percentage of your life do you think is impacted by you and how you relate to other people? Ballpark figure?

Answer: 100 percent!

As you already know (even if you haven't yet admitted it to yourself), your love relationship impacts your life more than any other! It's your greatest opportunity for growth, and by design that means that it also can bring up your biggest and deepest fears. Truly, it's a gift for you (although you may not have been willing to unwrap that gift until now).

The state of your love relationship is impacting every area of your life:

Work

While I worked in a corporate environment, I saw many instances where one team member or manager was going through a rough divorce, or custody battle, which took down the morale and the productivity of the entire department.

Our personal relationships affect our work every day. How? Let's face it, when your love relationship sucks, everything feels hard. The opposite is also true: when your love relationship is rocking, you feel like you're on cloud nine and you can take on the world! You bring energy, happiness, and joy everywhere you go.

Business

If you are an entrepreneur, you have all the challenges of a regular workplace, but the stakes are even higher! Your love relationship directly impacts your income because your ability to acquire and retain clients is affected by the state of your relationship. If you're stressed about your love relationship when you engage with a prospect or client, they pick up on your negative energy. They have no idea that your negative vibe has nothing to do with them; they just know that they don't get a warm-fuzzy vibe from you, and it impacts their decision on whether or not to work with you.

The state of your love relationship is either making you more client-attractive, or less client-attractive. And there's something even more impactful than that ...

The biggest impact that your love relationship has on your business is an invisible force that you might not see. The ceiling on your love relationship is the ceiling on your business right now because the degree to which you feel supported in your love relationship determines how far you're willing take your business without risking harming or losing your relationship.

In other words, *the state of your love relationship is an invisible thermostat on your business right now.*

Finances

The state of your love relationship absolutely impacts your finances and financial decisions. Usually when two people fall in love, they have different money mindsets. One's a saver, one's a spender; or one's a saver, one's an avoider. Almost every time! Disagreement about money causes *major* kerfuffles!

Parenting

If you're a parent, are you and your partner on the same page with your parenting philosophy and practices? When our students begin working with us, the answer to that question is almost always *no*. That's not a parenting issue, that's a relationship alignment challenge. If you are not aligned in your parenting, you are not operating as an indivisible team in life. It's affecting more areas of your life than just your parenting, even if that is where you feel it the hardest.

Furthermore, when it comes to your children, are you modeling the quality of relationship you'd like your children to create for themselves as adults? (They're learning what relationship is by watching you!)

Health and Vitality

When things are crappy between you and your partner, it's stressful, and the research clearly shows that chronic negative stress has a detrimental impact on your entire body. The state of your love relationship impacts your energy levels. Your love relationship either fuels you up or sucks the life right out of you!

The state of your love relationship dramatically impacts your ability to achieve your goals in every area of your life! That, in turn, impacts your confidence level, happiness, and eventually your self-worth!

Today, I know what it feels like to walk through my day feeling so loved it's unbelievable. I feel impervious to the kinds of things that stress out most people. I walk through my day knowing that I am the most important person in the world to the most important man in the world to me! I get to feel charged up with desire and craving for him, and it's *amazing!*

It wasn't always like this, though …

Years ago, my lack of self-mastery and relational mastery cost me a $150,000-per-year corporate job!

Here's what happened: I'd had a job I really liked working in corporate tax accounting. After six years, a new manager came in (I'll call her Cathy). Between you and me, I thought Cathy was a witch with a capital B! I saw her as evil, and she hated me! Everything turned to crap for me once she came on the scene. I was pregnant with our son Jake at the time, and that made it even more unbearable. I got very sick from stress, put on 80 pounds in four months, and had to go on bed rest, which she did not like at all.

Even though I loved my clients, Cathy was ruining every client engagement because she interfered in everything I did.

One of my best friends at the time, Anne, also worked in my department. She was fighting leukemia, and she died, at only 34 years old, six weeks before Jake was born. I was depressed and unhappy.

Cathy was so unbearable that I quit my job after Jake was born. Since I hadn't fixed our working relationship *before* Jake was born, I knew there was *no way* I could deal with her *after*, what with caring for a new baby and getting absolutely no sleep.

It was a disaster.

I had not mastered *me*, and because of that, I had zero influence with Cathy. I made it all her fault, and therefore she had all the power.

If anything was going to change, she was going to have to change it because I hadn't done anything wrong! (Sound familiar?)

Was she going to change? Hell no, but if I had known about these tools back then, I could have turned that situation around in a matter of days. Instead, my inability to master myself and master how I relate with other people ended up costing me that $150,000 corporate job at a time when we *really* needed the money. We had just had a baby, and we'd moved into a bigger house that year to accommodate our expanding family! I walked away from a salary that was *very* large for us at the time.

I became depressed and miserable, and I stayed stuck that way for months, continuing to gain weight even after I gave birth to Jake.

I wish that was the only time that my inability to master how I relate to other people in the world had cost me financially, emotionally, or spiritually, but it wasn't.

Do I regret going through that? No, I don't because it made me who I am today. I'm 100 percent committed to mastering myself, my state, my ability to influence, and my ability to relate.

I love who I am, knowing that tomorrow I will grow into an even better, more authentic version of myself than I am today because I am relentless about my own growth!

So no, I don't regret it ... *but it did cost me.*

How about you? What has a lack of self or relational mastery cost you?

Are there situations that you couldn't turn around?

Have you been passed over for opportunities?

If so, what were the spiritual, emotional, and financial costs involved?

You simply must master yourself and how you relate to others if you want to stop suffering. Shitty relationships equal a shitty life. Better relationships equal a better life. Magnificent relationships equal a magnificent life! It really is that simple.

When you do start creating masterful relationships, particularly creating your unshakable love relationship, you will discover that your life changes in unexpected ways.

Paint the OWL!

For one of my birthdays, Paul took the kids and me out to paint ceramics. When Paul asked me what I wanted to do for my birthday, I told him that I wanted to go painting with my family and actually paint something myself for the first time ever.

I was so excited. Paul set the whole thing up. Coffee in hand and wearing a dress (my kinda painting), I was off to paint! Before we could start painting, we each had to walk through a room lined with shelves of plain pottery and pick something to paint.

I had such a tough time picking just one thing because it all looked great to me. I wondered if I should choose a coffee cup, because I love coffee cups. I have a collection, and I want them all to be unique. I reasoned, *I'll paint my own coffee mug; it will definitely be one of a kind.*

Just then, I noticed an owl sitting on the shelf, and I said, "Oh, my God, I *love* that owl!"

Actually, I loved the *sample* owl because it was already painted with colorful, intricate detail designed to make the owl pop and stand out. To make a new one look like that sample, I would have had to carefully paint the plain, white, egg-shaped blob of an owl by hand, and I lacked the confidence in my ability to make that happen.

"Wow," I said, "I don't think I can swing that. I think I'll do the mug."

Paul believed I could do it, though, and he wouldn't let me settle. He immediately came up behind me and said, "Paint that owl."

"Babe, this looks like a pretty big undertaking," I said, shaking my head in doubt.

Paul still insisted. "Paint that owl." He was giving me that look that he gives me. My husband is quite immovable when he chooses to be. He was as still as a mountain standing behind me.

"I like the mug. I'm going to paint the mug."

Paul stood firm with his masculine presence and assertive tone: "Stacey Martino, you paint that owl."

When Paul Martino takes a stand for me, I listen! He had my full attention!

"All right, all right, Big Man!" I said playfully. "I'm painting the owl. Go ahead, pay for it. I'm painting it."

I painted that freaking owl, and it came out *amazing*! Have you seen it? It's gorgeous!

That owl sits in my office, where I see it every day for good reason. Yes, I love it, but it also reminds me of how much Paul believes in me and how he won't let me settle. He has faith in me, even when I don't believe in myself, and that's enough to carry me through.

If Paul hadn't taken a stand for me, I'd be drinking out of the mug every day. The mug was great, but it's not the owl. And, I *did* it.

Having this kind of love relationship gives you the confidence you need when you can't find yours.

Your partner infuses you with their faith in you when you've lost yours. They shower you with love and appreciation, even when you feel as if you've failed and you can't see your way out. You float on unconditional love when your husband looks at you and says, "I don't really care if the four of us end up in a cardboard box, Stacey, as long as I have you."

Even better, once you've mastered these tools and created this kind of unshakable love and unleashed passion, you can successfully apply these same tools to *all* the relationships in your life. You will improve your relationships with your kids, clients, prospects, team, boss, co-workers, family of origin, and friends.

Most importantly, this will transform your relationship with yourself!

You will love how you show up every day.

You will feel proud and confident.

You will feel happy on a consistent basis.

You will fall in love with the person you are now and person you will be tomorrow.

You will be a great example for others.

> *Everyone's life is either a warning or an example.*
> —TONY ROBBINS

You have the power to choose what your life will be.

The great news is that you never fail on the Relationship Development journey; you just get to keep taking the test over again until you pass it.

My friend, magnificent relationships are created; they are certainly not found, and it only takes one person to transform a relationship … any relationship.

The question isn't "*Can you* transform your relationship?" It's "*Will you?*"

Do the work for you, because you take *you* into every situation. It's *for* you.

At this point, I need to make you aware of a few obstacles you might encounter while doing the work. They'll hinder your progress and keep you stuck if you don't recognize them and use the tools you need to break through barriers and defy setbacks.

Obstacle #1: Your Resistance Set Point

There is a huge threat to your ability to do the work. This same threat is impacting everyone every minute of every day. No one escapes this, regardless of who you are. It impacts me, Paul, Hal, Tony Robbins, Oprah Winfrey, the greatest leaders of the world, and the greatest achievers of all time.

This threat to your ability to do the work is … resistance.

Let me explain. When you are learning something new that you have not yet mastered, there is a learning curve. Whether you are learning how to walk, how to ride a bike, or relate to others, there is a learning curve. There are going to be bumps and bruises along the way on that journey to mastery.

Are you with me so far? Great!

As you stretch, you will encounter moments of fear, doubt, worry, upset, and kerfuffle. Your nervous system will want you to stop when you perceive those things. This is a key factor in determining whether you succeed or fail on your path to mastery, so please pay attention.

Your resistance set point is the point at which you allow your nervous system to stop your progress on the path to your next level.

Some people have conditioned themselves to have a very high resistance set point. They know that stretching their comfort zone, walking into the fear, and blowing through doubts are all required for growth. They accept it as part of the journey to get the massive results they want, so they bust right through it. We see these people as courageous, determined, resourceful, committed, relentless, and unstoppable.

Other people have a very low resistance set point. When their nervous system perceives fear, doubt, uncertainty, and upset, they stop and retreat.

Perhaps you've been unaware of your resistance set point until now? If so, then even though you know your net worth, IQ, FICO score, or any other statistic about yourself, if you don't know your resistance set point, you are blind to the force that has the biggest impact on whether you succeed or fail!

To help you understand what I mean, let's go back to my story about that witch Cathy I was working for when Jake was born.

I had a very low resistance set point back then. Cathy came in, and I started to spiral. I was always trying to cover my ass or create agreements that would protect me. I would do things like copy her boss on communications so he would see how crazy she was. I was always in fight-or-flight mode. First I fought. When I realized I couldn't fight my way out, I flew. If you recall, I quit.

Back then my life was all about control, so I focused on controlling every situation to get the outcome I wanted. My driving force was protection, so my goal was to avoid pain.

I had a low resistance set point, so I experienced a low quality of life.

Eventually, I did the work; I attained self-mastery (and I'm still attaining new levels of mastery every day). I mastered my ability to relate to and influence others. I now fully accept the fact that fear, pain, and discomfort are all part of the journey because I choose to live as someone who blows through comfort zones really fast to get to my next level.

I never quit anything. Not now, because I've learned the secrets to raising my resistance set point.

Unfortunately, most of the people I see are unconscious about this force just like I was. They make decisions out of fear and a desire to protect themselves from emotional upset, pain, and uncertainty.

Low resistance set points are also fueling this disposable relationship society we are in right now. People today get into a relationship, and when life inevitably throws them some crap they were not prepared to handle, they get upset and unhappy and can't find their way out of it. Then, because they have a low resistance set point, they make a decision and say, "I can't deal with this! I'm out of here. It's too much pain."

Without the tools and strategies to master yourself and raise your resistance set point, you will give up or check out before victory—both in love and in life!

These are some of my favorite quotes from people who understand the need to press past, and raise, their resistance set point …

It ain't about how hard you get hit, it's about how hard you get hit and keep moving forward; how much you can take and keep moving forward—that's how winning is done!
—SYLVESTER STALLONE (AKA ROCKY)

Pain is temporary. It may last for a minute, or an hour, or a day, or a year, but eventually, it will subside and something else will take its place. If I quit, however, it lasts forever.
—LANCE ARMSTRONG

Most of you say you want to be successful. But you don't want it bad. You just kinda want it. You don't want it badder than you wanna party. You don't want it as much as you want to be cool. Most of you don't want success as much as you want to sleep!
—ERIC THOMAS

Don't cry to give up, cry to keep going. Don't cry to quit. You are already in pain, you are already hurt! Get a reward from it!
—ERIC THOMAS

Miracle Morning Opportunity: Any of those quotes would make an excellent addition for your Miracle Morning!

Now that you know about your resistance set point, you can't unknow it. You have two choices. You can stay unconscious, letting your nervous system kick in and stop you every time before you reach your next level. Or you can get conscious and see that the stretch, though uncomfortable, is part of the journey. Master the tools to raise your resistance set points and break through to your next level.

What's your decision?

As Rocky says, "Now if you know what you're worth, then go out and get what you're worth. But ya gotta be willing to take the hits, and not pointing fingers, saying you ain't where you wanna be because of him, or her, or anybody!"

That quote brings us to the second biggest obstacle …

Obstacle #2: The Habit of Blaming Others

In my story about the job I quit when Jake was born, who did I blame? Cathy! Therefore, who had the power to change the situation? Only Cathy.

I had rendered myself powerless to change anything the minute I started blaming her because if anything was going to change, she'd have to be the one to do it. That left me powerless and out of a job when she didn't change. That's why Rocky says, "Cowards do that and that ain't you! You're better than that!"

Are you giving your power away? Ask yourself …

- Who have you been blaming for a situation that you're in right now?
- Who have you been blaming for what's wrong in your life right now?
- Where in your life have you been waiting for a situation, or another person, to turn around and go your way?
- What has this cost you?
- How would things be different if you had mastery of yourself and how you relate to others?

To do the work, you need to check your blame at the door and take 100 percent personal responsibility for your life from here forward.

Many people resist taking personal responsibility in life because it feels too hard or overwhelming.

The work doesn't have to be hard. With the right tools, step-by-step solutions, proven methodologies, shortcuts, community, support, accountability, and love … it can be easy. But it will stretch you. Paul and I often tell our students, "We will give you what you want, *and* we'll give you what you need!"

What do we mean by that?

We give our students what they want:

- Answers
- Breakthroughs
- Support
- Community
- Accountability
- Expert guidance for their journey because we've travelled the path already, then guided tens of thousands of other people down the same road.

In addition to what they want, we also give our students what we know they need to grow:

- Stretching beyond their current comfort zone
- Support as they walk right through the fear and discomfort of their resistance set points
- Unconditional love and acceptance
- Insistence that they remain in nonjudgment of others
- Help to release the painful things they've been running from so they can be free
- Insistence that they take 100 percent personal responsibility for everything in their lives
- Help to embrace and move through painful growing experiences so they can break through to what they say they want

Obstacle 3#: The Dabbler vs. The Master

There's a big difference between "knowing" something and mastering it. Dabblers learn or hear something new and think, *Cool, what's next?* while someone on the path to mastery learns something new and begins implementing it into her life. She listens/reads again and again, as she integrates the new pattern until it becomes second nature for her.

Mastery requires a willingness to take things in repetitively, practice, and continually improve.

> *Talent you have naturally. Skill is only developed by hours and hours of beating on your craft.*
>
> —WILL SMITH

Dabblers learn something new, and once they've learned it they look for more *new* information.

Unfortunately, life will throw them a curveball designed to test what they *thought* they had learned, and then they find themselves ill-equipped to navigate it. Why? Because they never *mastered* it. They'd only ever heard it before.

They can't understand what went wrong and will usually complain, "But I already *know* this. Why am I still struggling?"

It's because they fell into the I-already-know-that trap.

After hanging out with growth-oriented people for more than two decades, I've noted a phenomenon among people who read or study a lot. They claim to know something because they've heard it, yet they are still struggling to live it.

Have you ever had that experience? Perhaps even while reading this book? Maybe you learned something, intending to apply it in your relationship. And yet you totally forgot in the moment and afterwards realized, "Dang it, I know better now, why did I still react that way?"

Sound familiar? If it does, that's okay! It should.

This is part of a very normal, predictable pattern in the growth process. It's just that, until now, it has been invisible to you.

If you want *transformation* in your life, you must get on the path to *mastery*! There's no other route. Look at anyone who has achieved a massive level of success in some area, and you will find they took the path to mastery.

Hal spoke earlier about repetition being a requirement to attain mastery. Dabblers *never* achieve mastery because they resist repetition! I remember one time Hal was at an event and he shared a photo of a quote up on the screen ...

> *Upon hearing something he has heard before, the novice says,*
> *"I already know that," but the Master says,*
> *"Thank you for reminding me."*
> —UNKNOWN

If you want to become a master, instead of a dabbler, whenever you learn something new, you must stay on the spectrum to mastery until it is wired into your blueprint so you effortlessly operate from the change you want embody. There are actually five levels to mastery.

Five Levels of Mastery

There are five levels to mastering any change that you want to make in your life.

Let's say you decide to master your state, and your goal is to maintain it above the 50 Percent Line. This is what the Five Levels of State Mastery would look like.

Level One: Unaware

"I'm unaware even that there is such a thing as state mastery. I'm just going through my day minding my own business."

Level Two: Awareness

"Oh, I get it. I heard this thing. There is something called state mastery. Yeah, I've heard of that."

Level Three: Cognitive Mastery

At this level, you've not only heard it, you've studied how it operates, and you understand the principles. You have done a deep-dive study on it and consumed massive amounts of information, so you have no remaining questions about it. You've got it.

Level Four: Emotional Congruency

At this level, not only do you understand it, but you feel emotionally congruent with the shift you are making. That means you feel that keeping your state above the 50 Percent Line is absolutely the best thing for you. You have no energetic snags or internal conflicts holding you back from operating that way. You can clearly *feel* when you are above the 50 Percent Line, and you are equally clear on what it feels like for you to fall below the line. Additionally, you possess the emotional acuity to feel this in others around you. You can tell when they are either above or below the line.

You can have state mastery at times. You have moments of being able to stay above 50 percent. But you also have times when you are not able to live it. There are triggers and frustrations that kick you below the 50 Percent Line, and many times you still must make an effort to stay above it. It takes conscious work on your part to do this. At this level, your life certainly reflects these improved results. You have made tremendous progress, and you should celebrate this massive achievement!

Level Five: Physical Integration into Your Blueprint

At this level, operating from the change that you want is *effortless*. You have rewired your blueprint for this change, and now that is simply who you are. You no longer have to remember to do things the new way. You have effortless enjoyment of this change!

When you have attained state mastery at level five, you stay above the 50 Percent Line most of the time effortlessly. You no longer feel the triggers you used to feel (and then had to choose and act to stay above the 50 Percent Line). Those triggers aren't there anymore. You have rewired yourself to move through life with a level of state mastery where you can effortlessly maintain your state, regardless of the environment or situation. Dropping below the 50 Percent Line happens rarely, and when it does, you can come back up above the line in a matter of moments—you don't stay stuck there.

During the first four levels to mastery, you make continual progress that comes from efforting and trying. Because you're learning something new, sometimes you will succeed, and other times you won't. That's okay! That progress should be celebrated. It's part of the spectrum to mastery.

Dabblers usually hover somewhere between levels two and three.

Don't be a dabbler; keep going until you reach level five mastery, where you experience effortless enjoyment of the life that you've created by design.

When Theresa, one of my clients, learned the Five Levels of Mastery for the first time, she came up to me and said, "I have been a professional dabbler my whole life. I had been taught to keep learning, and I had *no* idea that was why I was struggling so much. I'm *done* with dabbling, and I'm committed to mastery!"

I recently saw Theresa, and I reflected on her progress and her "dabbler-revelation" moment. Today, she is unrecognizable compared to the woman she was then. She has blossomed in her marriage and in her career as a physician. I've never seen her so happy. That level of joy, love, and passion comes from living the change you want instead of just knowing it!

If you want an unshakable love and unleashed passion, you cannot be a dabbler! You must commit to doing whatever it takes to achieve level five mastery!

If you really want everything that we have been introducing you to in this book, you must decide and make a commitment!

As the great T. D. Jakes says, "You will never really know what you could be, until you throw your *whole* self in!"

Don't just put this book on the shelf and make it shelf-help. Make a commitment to yourself. If you feel pulled to actually create an unshakable love and unleashed passion, then *do it*! Make the commitment!

What's your *why*?

To be successful on this journey, you must be clear about what you must have and why you must have it. If you don't possess this clarity, this book is just some cool info, but it will not be enough to help you break through to the life you dream about.

It's time to declare your intention. Answer the following questions in a journal or use your *Do The Work-Book*:

- *What **must** you have?*

- *Why **must** you have it?*

Once you are clear on your big *why*, you can't just put this book down and do nothing! It's time to act and *begin* the work!

- *What has your lack of skills in this area already cost you in life?*

- *What is your lack of mastery costing you today with each day that goes by?*

- *What are you going to do when life throws you something you don't yet know how to handle?*

- *If you refuse to take a deep dive into attaining mastery in you and how you relate to others, what will this cost you in the future?*

So …

What is your plan for tomorrow?

We've jammed a ton of content into this book for you so that you would have it. Don't get overwhelmed. Most likely it's more than you can implement and integrate on your own in one fell swoop! Don't be hard on yourself as you go through your day and recognize moments where you are not yet living what you have already learned.

The difference between learning it and living it is huge, and it takes repetition, time, implementation, practice, expert guidance, and support!

And there's even more for you to learn beyond this level! I have been on my Relationship Development path now for about two decades, and have *lots* more to teach you!

Miracle Morning Opportunity: Use your Miracle Morning time to declare your commitment and your Big Why to yourself every day! Create an affirmation from your why exercise above so that each day you imprint your why onto your nervous system to propel you forward.

Here's an Affirmation for you about commitment: "I am 100 percent committed to mastering *me* and how I *relate* to others in the world around me! I refuse to continue life as a dabbler! Every day I will experience exactly what it feels like to throw my *whole* self into my relationship development! This is the standard I have set for myself, and my life reflects those decisions and actions!"

What's your plan to navigate the journey toward creating an unshakable love and unleashed passion?

Here Are the Next Steps I Recommend:

1. DECIDE to stay plugged in to this journey.

2. GRAB your Bonus content from the Bonus Downloads page: TMMbook.com (for Miracle Morning Bonus content) and RelationshipDevelopment.org/tmmbonus (for Relationship Development Bonus content)..

3. JOIN our FB Community so you can surround yourself with a tribe that is on the same journey as you! Visit MyTMMCommunity.com and MyRelationshipDevelopmentCommunity.com.

4. COMMIT to begin reading this book again as soon as you finish it. Remember that repetition is the key mastery, since the first time we read any book, we're merely being exposed to new information. However, when we re-read a book we deepen our understanding and accelerate our ability to implement what we've learned.

5. ATTEND a live event with us or start one of our online programs: RelationshipDevelopment.org/events.

6. JOIN our RelationshipU program, when you're ready: RelationshipDevelopment.org/programs.

— 10 —

THE MIRACLE MORNING
30-DAY TRANSFORMATION CHALLENGE

BY HAL ELROD

*"An extraordinary life is all about daily, continuous
improvements, in the areas that matter most."*
—ROBIN SHARMA.

Let's play devil's advocate for a moment. Can practicing the Miracle Morning each day really transform your life, or business, in just 30 days? Can Stacey and Paul's Relationship Development work be the catalyst to giving you an unshakable LOVE and unleashed PASSION that will truly last a lifetime? Can anything really make *that* significant of an impact for you and your relationship, that quickly?

Of course! Consider that both the Miracle Morning and Paul and Stacey's Relationship Development work have already done this for hundreds of thousands of individuals, and couples. Therefore, when you put both into practice, it can and will absolutely work for you.

Also keep in mind that incorporating or changing any habit requires an acclimation period, so don't expect this to be effortless from day one. However, by making a commitment to yourself to stick with this, beginning each day with a Miracle Morning and leveraging the S.A.V.E.R.S. will quickly become the foundational habit that makes all others possible. Remember: *Win the morning, and you set yourself up to win the day.*

The seemingly unbearable first few days changing a habit are only temporary. While there's a lot of debate about how long it takes to implement a new habit, there is a powerful 3-phase strategy that has proven successful for the hundreds of thousands of individuals who have learned how to conquer the snooze button, who now wake up every day for their Miracle Morning.

From Unbearable to Unstoppable

The 3-Phase Strategy to Implement Any Habit in 30 Days

As you take the Miracle Morning 30-Day Life Transformation Challenge, here's arguably the simplest and most effective strategy for implementing and sustaining any new habit, in just 30 days. This will give you the mindset and approach you can take on as you build your new routine.

Phase One: Unbearable (Days 1–10)

Phase One is when any new activity requires the most amount of conscious effort, and getting up early is no different. You're fighting existing habits, the very habits that have been entrenched in *who you are* for years.

In this phase, it's mind over matter—and if you don't mind, it'll definitely matter! The habit hitting snooze, and not making the most of your day are the same habits that hold you back from becoming the superstar _____ you have always known you can be. So dig in and hold strong.

In Phase One, while you battle existing patterns and limiting beliefs, you'll find out what you're made of and what you're capable of. You need to keep pushing, stay committed to your vision, and hang in there. Trust me when I say you can do this!

I know it can be daunting on day five to realize you still have twenty-five days to go before your transformation is complete and you've become a bona fide morning person. Keep in mind that on day five, you're actually more than halfway through the first phase and well on your way. Remember: your initial feelings are not going to last forever. In fact, you owe it to yourself to persevere because, in no time at all, you'll be getting the exact results you want as you become the person you've always wanted to be!

Phase Two: Uncomfortable (Days 11–20)

In Phase Two, your body and mind begin to acclimate to waking up earlier. You'll notice that getting up starts to get a tiny bit easier, but it's not yet a habit—it's not quite who you are and likely won't feel natural yet.

The biggest temptation at this level is to reward yourself by taking a break, especially on the weekends. A question posted quite often in The Miracle Morning Community is, "How many days a week do you get up early for your Miracle Morning?" Our answer—and the one that's most common from longtime Miracle Morning practitioners—is *every single day*.

Once you've made it through Phase One, you're past the hardest period. So keep going! Why on earth would you want to go through that first phase again by taking one or two days off? Trust me, you wouldn't, so don't!

Phase Three: Unstoppable (Days 21–30)

Early rising is now not only a habit, it has literally become part of *who you are*, part of your identity. Your body and mind will have become accustomed to your new way of being. These next ten days are important for cementing the habit in yourself and your life.

As you engage in the Miracle Morning practice, you will also develop an appreciation for the three distinct phases of habit change. A side benefit is you will realize you can identify, develop, and adopt any habit that serves you—including the habits of exceptional <u>relationships</u> that we have included in this book.

Now that you've learned the simplest and most effective strategy for successfully implementing and sustaining any new habit in 30 days, you know the mindset and approach that you need to complete *The Miracle Morning 30-Day Transformation Challenge*. All that's required is for you to commit to get started and follow through.

Consider the Rewards

When you commit to *The Miracle Morning 30-Day Transformation Challenge*, you will be building a foundation for success in every area of your life, for the rest of your life. By waking up each morning and practicing *The Miracle Morning*, you will begin each day with extraordinary levels of **discipline** (the crucial ability to get yourself to follow through with your commitments), **clarity** (the power you'll generate from focusing on what's most important), and **personal development** (perhaps the single most significant determining factor in your success). Thus, in the next 30 days you'll find yourself quickly *becoming the person* you need to be to create the extraordinary levels of personal, professional, and financial success you truly desire.

You'll also be transforming *The Miracle Morning* from a concept that you may be excited (and possibly a little nervous) to "try" into a lifelong habit, one that will continue to develop you into the person you need to be to create the life you've always wanted. You'll begin to fulfill your potential and see results in your life far beyond what you've ever experienced before.

In addition to developing successful habits, you'll also be developing the **mindset** you need to improve your life—both internally and externally. By practicing the *Life S.A.V.E.R.S.* each day, you'll be experiencing the physical, intellectual, emotional, and spiritual benefits of *Silence, **Affirmations**, Visualization, Exercise, **Reading***, and *Scribing*. You'll immediately feel less stressed, more centered, focused, happier and more excited about your life. You'll be generating more energy, clarity and motivation to move towards your highest goals and dreams (especially those you've been putting off far too long).

Remember, your life situation will improve after—but only *after*—you develop yourself into the person you need to be to improve it. That's exactly what these next 30 days of your life can be—a new beginning, and a new you.

You Can Do This!

If you're feeling nervous, hesitant, or concerned about whether or not you will be able to follow through with this for 30 days, relax—it's completely normal to feel that way. This is especially true if waking up in the morning is something you've found challenging in the past. It's not only expected that you would be a bit hesitant or nervous, but it's actually a very good sign! It's a sign that you're *ready* to commit, otherwise you wouldn't be nervous.

Here we go…

3.1 Steps to Begin The Miracle Morning (30-Day) Life Transformation Challenge

Step 1: Get The Miracle Morning 30-Day Transformation Challenge Fast Start Kit

Visit www.TMMBook.com to download your free *Miracle Morning 30-Day Life Transformation Challenge* Fast Start Kit—complete with the exercises, affirmations, daily checklists, tracking sheets, and everything else you need to make starting and completing *The Miracle Morning 30-Day Life Transformation Challenge* as easy as possible. Please take a minute to do this now.

Step 2: Plan Your First Miracle Morning for Tomorrow

If you haven't already began, commit to (and schedule) your first *Miracle Morning* as soon as possible—ideally *tomorrow*. Yes, actually write it into your schedule, and decide where it will take place. Remember, it's recommended that you leave your bedroom and remove yourself from the temptations of your bed altogether. My *Miracle Morning* takes place every day on my living room couch while everyone else in my house is still sound asleep. I've heard from people who do their *Miracle Morning* sitting outside in nature, such as on their porch or deck, or at a nearby park. Do yours where you feel most comfortable, but also where you won't be interrupted.

Step 3: Read Page-1 of the Fast Start Kit and Do the Exercises

Read the introduction in your *Miracle Morning 30-Day Life Transformation Challenge* Fast Start Kit, then please follow the instructions, and complete the exercises. Like anything in life that's worthwhile, successfully completing *The Miracle Morning 30-Day Life Transformation Challenge* requires a bit of preparation. It's important that you do the initial exercises in your Fast Start Kit (which shouldn't take you more than 30-60 minutes) and keep in mind that your *Miracle Morning* will always start with the *preparation* you do the day or night before to get yourself ready mentally, emotionally, and logistically for *The Miracle Morning*. This preparation includes following the steps in *Chapter 5: The 5-Step Snooze-Proof Wake Up Strategy.*

(Optional) Step 3.2: Get an Accountability Partner

The overwhelming evidence for the corelation between success and accountability is undeniable. While most people resist being held accountable, it is hugely beneficial to have someone who will hold us to higher standards than we'll hold ourselves to. All of us can benefit from the support of an accountability partner, so it's highly recommended—but definitely not required—that you reach out to someone in your circle of influence (famliy, friend, colleague, significant other, etc.) and invite them to join you in *The Miracle Morning 30-Day Life Transformation Challenge.*

Not only does having someone to hold us accountable increase the odds that we will follow through, but joining forces with someone else is simply more fun! Consider that when you're excited about something and committed to doing it on your own, there is a certain level of power in that excitement and in your individual commitment. However, when you have someone else in your life—a friend, family member, or co-worker—and they're as excited about it and committed to it as you are, it's much more powerful.

Call, text, or email one or more people today, and invite them to join you for *The Miracle Morning 30-Day Life Transformation Challenge.* The quickest way to get them up to speed is to send them the link to www.MiracleMorning.com so they can get free and immediate access to *The Miracle Morning Fast Start Kit:*

    »   **The FREE Miracle Morning Video training**

    »   **The FREE Miracle Morning Audio training**

    »   **Two FREE Chapters of *The Miracle Morning* book**

It will cost them nothing, and you'll be teaming up with someone who is also committed to taking their life to the next level, so the two of you can support, encourage, and hold each other accountable.

In less than an hour, they'll be fully capable of being your *Miracle Morning* accountability partner—and probably a little inspired.

Are You Ready to Take Your Life to the Next Level?

What is the next level in your personal or professional life? Which areas need to be transformed in order for you to reach that level? Give yourself the gift of investing the next 30 days to make significant improvements in your life, and your most important relationship, one day at a time. No matter what your past has been, you *can* change your future, by changing the present.

In the next chapter, we have an awesome bonus for you! Paul and Stacey are going to reveal the *Relationship Manifestation Equation* to help you to achieve what you desire, faster, so that you can accelerate the massive results you create for yourself, in love and in life!

THE RELATIONSHIP MANIFESTATION MIRACLE EQUATION:
FOLLOW YOUR YELLOW BRICK ROAD

BY STACEY & PAUL MARTINO

"Faith is taking the first step, even when you don't see the whole staircase."

—DR. MARTIN LUTHER KING, JR.

"God does not call the QUALIFIED, he qualifies the CALLED ... through the YES!"

—T. D. JAKES, Pastor and author

We all want something. Something "more" in some area or facet of our life. We want a better relationship, better health, more money, more impact, a better job, to lose weight—something that seems out of easy reach from where we are right now. So, we create goals in our mind of things that we wish to be, do, or have.

Upon setting a new goal, we start off feeling the gap, or sense of lack, between what we currently have and the result we want to obtain. It's human nature. For some people, that is as far as they get. They stop at the wanting phase because the gap feels too great and insurmountable. Conceding defeat before they take the slightest action toward their goal, they simply stop ... and then focus on what they do not have, which is in some ways worse than not identifying the goal in the first place.

Luckily, you are not one of those people who will stop at the wanting phase. I know you don't stop because you've already demonstrated more commitment than that by reading this book. Take a moment to celebrate this about yourself! You are one of the "few who do" versus the "many who talk."

For people like you who refuse to accept mediocrity as the standard for your life, there is a road ahead that must be navigated if you are to be successful in achieving your desired result. Let's call it a yellow brick road for now. Understand that your wish will materialize when you reach the end of it. Just like in the movie *The Wizard of Oz*, we should expect quite a few challenges to overcome along the journey. Let's face it, if the road ahead were straight, completely visible, and obstruction-free, this wouldn't be a goal. In the words of another one of my great mentors, Keith J. Cunningham, "The answer to all of your problems is just outside of your current comfort zone. If it wasn't, it wouldn't be a problem!"

Right now, all you have is the knowledge about where you are currently standing and an awareness of what you want, but that is about it. Since the yellow brick road ahead immediately starts winding around the hill in front of you, the next thing that typically happens is that your mind starts racing with questions about how to prepare for this move forward and how to ensure you're successful in getting to the end of the road where your desired outcome lies.

Right away, you'll have some challenges to deal with, not the least of which is the fact that you do not have a map of the yellow brick road. What if there are forks in the road, or even off-ramps to other yellow brick road superhighways going in other directions? To make matters worse, you already know you're not entirely clear about what the Oz at the end of your path looks like. After all, you're not going to be staying in your hometown in Kansas on this one, and you've never been to where you are going. To further complicate matters, you start to wonder what you should pack and bring with you to be ready to handle the inevitable surprises along the way.

Oh, what to do, Toto ... What to do?

At this point, imagine that you start rummaging through your backpack looking for something that could help with these challenges. This is obviously uncharted territory, so there is no hope of finding a good map of it; however, you realize that if you just had a compass, it would still be helpful in choosing the right path ahead since you know the general direction you want to go. You also realize that some tools and supplies will be needed to help you prepare for the unknown challenges you will inevitably encounter on this trip.

Dang it! No compass, no matches, and no Swiss Army knife! All you find in your bag is one old protein bar and a bottle of water, which isn't enough for you to be comfortable. Looks like you're going to have to stay a bit hungry on this trip.

Frustrated and concerned that you seem to be very unprepared for the path ahead, you look up to the sky and make a wish for help.

You wait a bit for some kind of sign or response. And you wait ... and wait ... and wait some more ... Ugh, nothing is happening!

When you look back at the sky again, this time you notice how breathtakingly beautiful the clouds and sky are. It is getting close to sundown, and the sky is a mix of the most beautiful blues, golds, and purples you ever remember seeing. The white glowing clouds have textures and strokes that could have only been crafted by a deft master painter. The setting summer sun is still warm on your face and body, and the gentle breezes seem to soothe your soul somehow.

While still caught up in awe of the beauty of the moment, you inexplicably flash back to a moment two weeks earlier when you were hanging out with your friends Stacey and Paul. In your head, you can see and hear Paul saying, "It is only when you are fully committed to the goal, and start taking physical action toward it, that the universe will start guiding you and providing you with exactly what you'll need …" Paul's voice trails off as you snap out of that vision.

In that moment, you suddenly realize that you never fully committed to this goal, that you have not been playing full-out in this area of your life, and that your current results reflect those facts. As the sun starts going down, you suddenly feel a tremendous yearning rising up from inside you for the future. You can almost feel how the clock is ticking. You refuse to just let the days of your life drift by any longer without going for what you want. Your yearning grows into a fire inside you, and your goal suddenly becomes a *must* for you.

Just then, a magical presence appears in front of you, and it says, "Fret not, I'm here to provide you with all you will need for you to be successful in your journey to Oz. You will not only be able to navigate this (and any other) unknown path ahead, but your powers will grow in a way that will uniquely prepare you to receive your desired outcome at the end of the journey."

After the shock of what you are seeing begins to fade, you recover your senses enough and think to ask, "How? Will you accompany me on this journey, or is this something that you can give to me now?"

At this point, the magical presence laughs loudly in a knowing kind of way and nods. She says, "The answer is both … and neither!"

At this point, you start thinking to yourself, *why do all of these magical characters always have to answer questions with riddles?*

Just then, she touches your head, and in your mind's eye, you see a crystal clear message that says,

The Relationship Manifestation Equation: SAVERS + RTS + EGS = Relationship Miracles (RM)

While blinking slowly, you stare into your consciousness at the message while trying to make sense of what it means.

At this point, the magical presence says, "What you see in front of you now is all that you were missing. You already have everything else you needed to get you to your goal successfully."

That statement jars you back to your own thoughts again. You ask, "Really? That equation, a protein bar, a bottle of water, and *me?*" Inside, you start thinking, *I'm so screwed! If I make my wish again, I wonder if I can get a good map, a GPS, some tools, and more supplies?*

The magical presence does not respond to these thoughts and lovingly continues speaking to you, saying, "I've looked into your heart, and I feel that what you strongly desire is to have a magnificent love relationship with your intimate partner. You have no idea how wise this desire is. Love is the most powerful force that any human can possess! Love is not only the greatest possible fuel for your human experiences, it's also the connection between your world and mine. We could not be happier to support you on the journey you have chosen! Now, I will explain the meaning of this Miracle Equation to you."

Instantly, the image in your mind changes, and now all that you see is

The S.A.V.E.R.S.

The magical presence then resumes her teaching …

For me to actively assist you with our magic along this journey, you will need to regularly put intentional focus into seeing yourself already living in your magnificent love life, very grateful and happy for what you have. You must cultivate your ability to visualize this, even though you cannot yet see it in your current physical life. This is <u>faith</u>. In the beginning, release all doubts and tap into the feelings you want to feel when you have the unshakable love and unleashed passion you want.

Each time you do your Miracle Morning, we will send you the strength and resources you need to navigate the circumstances and opportunities of your day so you can overcome the obstacles that would otherwise have been beyond your ability to influence.

This Miracle Morning is also how I will stay present with you during the journey, although you will not be able to physically see me like you can

right now. You must hold on to your faith that I am guiding you on your yellow brick road to Oz.

You will use the Miracle Morning as follows to help you get to your goal as fast as humanly possible.

1. *Silence—It is within the silence that I will transfer insights and guidance to you. Listen for me; I will be the quiet knowing (not the loud chatter).*

2. *Affirmations—You must keep strong during your trip! Your Miracle Morning affirmations will allow you to start each day with a renewed vigor and resilience, regardless of how difficult your day ended the night before. If times get difficult as you leave your comfort zone, your Miracle Morning affirmations will also reinforce your momentum and your faith. With each affirmation, you are becoming the version of yourself who will be ready to receive what awaits you in Oz.*

3. *Visualization—To achieve your goal, you must first become very clear about what your version of a magnificent relationship looks and feels like. As a great human, Zig Ziglar, once said, "You can't hit a target that you can't see." Your Miracle Morning visualization will give you that clarity and continuously guide all of us toward your goal. When you visualize, feel in your heart what you truly desire, and I will receive those requests and start creating them for you in Oz.*

4. *Exercise—Build your strength and endurance so that you have the physical energy to complete the trip. It will also nourish your mind, helping you quickly remove emotional stressors that can drag your state down. Remember, when your state goes down, so does your ability to be resourceful and to hear our guidance.*

5. *Reading—Learning through reading is a great way to remove limiting belief patterns and to expand your resourcefulness when dealing with challenges. Allow your sense of what makes you happy to guide you in choosing the right books and programs for you. I will work through those books and materials to teach you the rest of what you need to know to get to Oz.*

6. *Scribe—Through your journaling, capture each day's successes, both big and small. When you find yourself stuck, go back and review* *your celebrations so you remember how far you have already come. The reflection on how much you have achieved will create the certainty you need to rely on when things seem unclear. This is how you will strengthen your faith with each passing day!*

You ponder all the wisdom, and then just as you finish digesting all the information, the image in your head changes again. Now it says,

RTS = Relationship Transformation System®

The magical presence resumes teaching ...

The RTS in that formula stands for Relationship Transformation System. You will use Relationship Development content and resources to effectively handle the challenges you will inevitably find along your path. This will be your Swiss Army knife to prevent you from otherwise being knocked off your path or losing your faith along the way. You cannot simply learn your way there. You must empower yourself by growing your relationship development skills so you become the person who is capable of creating, having, and keeping the magnificent love relationship you have envisioned. Your growth on this path will be the first gift that you will receive for taking the journey. You get to keep that gift forever. Keep the tools and strategies top of mind, use them, and, most importantly, live them.

Your carefully designed Relationship Transformation System looks like this:

1. Seeing—Get clarity on what your magnificent relationship looks like. Use your Miracle Morning and Relationship Development tools to get crystal clear on what it will feel like when you are living in the magnificent relationship that is aligned for you. Release all thoughts of your current relationship and allow yourself to feel the way you want to feel. That will allow me to be clear on what you want me to create for you in Oz while you are journeying here.

2. Shifting—Your world will not change until your perspective changes. Stacey and Paul can be your masterful guides on this. On the path, you will free yourself from the disempowering beliefs that hold you back from having the relationship you desire! Whenever you feel frustrat-

ed, upset, unhappy, scared, or sad, look to your Relationship Development tools to help you shift how you are seeing the situation. Each perspective shift you experience will catapult you forward on your path to Oz.

3. Strategies—These are the tools you carry in your toolkit, which will prepare you to masterfully handle the challenges along the way. Any challenge you might encounter has already been solved for you by Stacey and Paul. Don't struggle on your own, or you will find yourself far off the yellow brick road. Use the tools in your Relationship Development toolkit.

4. Synergy—This is where you will create a rock-solid relationship, where nothing and nobody can come between you. Every day on the yellow brick road, you will be presented with an opportunity to build up or break down your relationship. When you use the Relationship Development tools to build up your relationship, we will power you up, and you will propel forward at 10 times your former speed. If you choose to break down your relationship in that moment, you will be set back a bit. Don't fret when that happens. I'll send you another opportunity to try again, and you will move forward even faster the second time.

5. Start Anew—Here, you will learn how to properly wipe the slate clean when it comes to your relationship. Think of your yellow brick road as having blocks or squares, like in the human game Candy Land, to take you on your path to Oz. Until you wipe the slate clean, you will continually feel pulled back to start. Follow Stacey and Paul's 5-Step Forgiveness Process. It's the answer you have been seeking. Just give yourself permission to release and trust that I've got you.

6. Sparks—This is the place where you will realign with your authentic core feminine or mature masculine energy and reignite your passion and desire. As you reach this place on your yellow brick road, I have placed an opportunity in every square on your path that is designed to allow you to experience your authentic core energy. Allow yourself to enjoy that moment and practice coming from your authentic self. Every time you show up in your authentic feminine or mature masculine, we will power you up, and you will progress at 10 times your former speed. Watch videos of Stacey and Paul (or go see them live) to get clearer and faster results with your core energy alignment. We delight in seeing you be *true to yourself. When you are, you will be amazed at how much easier your travels on the yellow brick road will become.*

7. S-Flirt—When you reach here, you will bring back the playfulness, fun, and flirting into your relationship. We are very excited for you to reach this point on your yellow brick road! Your smile and laughter are some of our favorite things about you, and we want to see more of them. To help you, I will give you opportunities in the form of interactions with other people. Each time you can choose to respond with playfulness, fun, and flirting or stay in the darkness you were in. The magic happens when you choose play! Each time, not only will you feel wonderful, but the energy you magnify will reshape your yellow brick road and remove the obstacles you would have found on your path had you not chosen to come from playfulness. The power that you possess to shape your journey is miraculous, and I'm delighted to watch you. When you see something particularly silly, just know that is me, giving you a reminder to make things easier for yourself today. (And yes, I invented farting for exactly that reason.)

8. Sensuality—When you reach this point, you will delight in the ecstasy of ravishing, satisfying sex with your partner. Remember, sex is an effect created by your relationship and not a cause. Every step of progress on your yellow brick road is creating results. You will experience some of the reward of your work through the effect it has manifested: more satisfying sex with your partner. Your Relationship Development tools will teach you how to open yourself to a level of sexual mastery and heightened sexual sensation that you didn't know humans could experience. You can have it! Lucky for you, it takes a lot of practice! Remember, unleashed passion is the outcome of transformation in your relationship. While you will experience better sex with each progressive step, unleashed sex is at the end of your journey, not the beginning.

The presence stops speaking and waits for you. Realizing that you do not have to do it alone and that you are empowered with so many incredible tools, you feel calm and confident, and for the first time you feel well prepared for the journey ahead. At this point, you find yourself wondering why you would need the rest of the formula.

The presence smiles broadly, thrilled to see your confidence, clarity, and resolve. Again, the presence resumes teaching …

The last piece of this formula is the EGS, which stands for Emotional Guidance Scale.

EGS = Emotional Guidance Scale*[1]

You wanted a compass. This is the most sophisticated compass ever created, and it has already been placed inside of your heart! This compass will tell you which path to take, even when you can't see the path. You will use the image below as your guide to knowing which direction you need to go.

1. Faith, Trust, Joy, Love, Appreciation, Gratitude	8. Boredom
	9. Pessimism
2. Passion	10. Frustration, Irritation, Impatience
3. Enthusiasm, Eagerness, Happiness	
	11. Overwhelm
4. Positive Expectation, Belief	12. Disappointment
	13. Doubt
5. Optimism	14. Worry
6. Hopefulness	15. Blame
7. Contentment	16. Discouragement
	17. Anger, Resentment
	18. Revenge
	19. Hatred, Rage
	20. Jealousy
	21. Insecurity, Guilt, Unworthiness
	22. Fear, Grief, Depression, Despair, Powerlessness

---

[1]   This EGS is from *Ask and It Is Given* by Esther and Jerry Hicks

Every time you find yourself unable to determine the next direction to take, or you wonder what is the right thing for you to do, you will simply connect with how you feel in your heart about each choice presented to you.

In the simplest terms, when you experience a feeling on the left side of the EGS, go! When you experience a feeling on the right side of the EGS, stop!

When your thought, action, or option gives you a feeling on the left side of the Emotional Guidance Scale, all is well. Each time you feel one of the emotions on the left side of the EGS, your hunch or intuition in that moment is being guided by me. Whatever you feel guided to do next will keep you on your yellow brick road. Move ahead with confidence!

When the thought, action, or option gives you a feeling on the right side of the Emotional Guidance Scale, you will stop! That thought or action would be taking you off your yellow brick road and into danger.

If you find yourself on the right side of the EGS, use the TMM and RDO tools to shift how you feel until you are on the left side again. Once on the left, you can take action and move forward again, knowing that you are back on your yellow brick road to Oz.

This is really important, my friend! As you journey your yellow brick road, you will come upon crossroads and off-ramps. They may seem inviting, and you may wonder, Should I go in this direction or that one?

Anytime you wonder which direction to take, consult the EGS I have put inside your heart. Start by focusing on path A. When you do so, do you feel the emotions on the left side of the EGS, or does it leave you feeling an emotion from the right side of the scale? Then consider path B. How does path B make you feel?

Dearest, when you look at the two paths, one of them will feel right to you, even though it may not make logical sense, and the path has never been traveled before. You may be concerned because of the unknown, but if you put that aside and assume all is well, then it is the path you are pulled to.

And if you look in your heart, the other path is only appealing because of the fear you feel. You are afraid of what you might miss out on, making a mistake, feeling disappointment, what others will think, or something else.

You'll find it is always the case that only one path feels right; you're only considering the other path out of fear or pain.

That's why I gave you the EGS in your heart.

When you feel one of the emotions on the right side of your EGS, that's me communicating that you are either off your yellow brick road or about to be.

When you feel yourself firmly in the emotions on the left side of the EGS, that's me communicating that you are safely on your yellow brick road and heading to Oz under my protection!

As you learn to trust in the wisdom of this guidance from us over time, you will be able to successfully navigate even the most invisible of paths and achieve the outcomes you desire. Your brain may become confused or deceived, but your heart always knows the right path to take.

You now have the greatest wisdom and tools in the world available to you to use throughout your journey to your Oz.

At that moment, the magical presence fades, and you come back to the present moment. You feel totally confident now that you know exactly what to do *for the first time ever*! Smiling, you take your first step down the yellow brick road ahead ...

SPECIAL INVITATIONS

(IN CASE YOU MISSED THEM THE FIRST TIME)

A Special Invitation from Hal

No one could have predicted that *The Miracle Morning Community* would become one of the most positive, engaged, and supportive online communities in the world, but it truly has. Made up of over 80,000 like-minded individuals, from more than 70 countries, I'm constantly astounded by the caliber and character of our members.

Just go to MyTMMCommunity.com and request to join **The Miracle Morning Community** on Facebook. It's free, and you'll immediately join 80,000+ like-minded individuals, from around the world, who are already practicing the Miracle Morning. While you'll find many who are just beginning their Miracle Morning journey, you'll discover even more who have been at it for years and who will happily share advice and guidance to accelerate your success.

I'll be helping to moderate the community and checking in daily, so I look forward to seeing you there! If you'd like to reach out to me personally on social media, follow @HalElrod on Twitter, @Hal_Elrod on Instagram, and on Facebook at Facebook.com/YoPalHal. Talk soon!

With Love & Gratitude,

- Hal

A Special Invitation from Stacey and Paul

Countless people around the world today are implementing the Relationship Development® tools and strategies we teach. They believe in creating an unshakable love and unleashed passion. They want to be a role model to their children! They believe in living and life by design and not living in a life by default.

And they have gathered with us in the most amazing community of like-minded, dedicated, positive, *fun* and extraordinary individuals! Our Relationship Development Community is designed to give you support, encouragement, insights, compassion, accountability, and love. It is a safe, judgment-free zone where real people come to be who they are and do the work to create the relationship transformation that they desire. In our community, you will find inspiration, dedication, fun, and enlightenment that will uplift you each day.

We invite you to join the Relationship Development Community. This is the secret advantage to *big* results! Surround yourself with like-minded people that are happily on this journey with you. Just go to MyRelationshipDevelomentCommunity.com and request to join. You will immediately be able to connect with people who are already doing this work.

If you would like to reach out to me and Paul personally, please email us at Support@RelationshipDevelopment.org, or connect with us on social media. Let's connect soon!

Sending love,

Stacey and Paul

CONCLUSION:
YOUR NEXT STEPS

The end of this book is not an ending, it's a *new beginning*! Please don't put this book on the shelf and let it become "shelf-help." The content in this book is just the tip of the iceberg. You cannot learn your way to a better relationship. You must implement what you have learned, shift how you show up, and keep going!

Continue to integrate until it becomes level five mastery and is part of your blueprint so you get effortless enjoyment!

We are here to help! Paul and I have designed programs and live events where you can get the expert guidance, support, compassion, accountability, and love you need for your journey!

We have designed our online programs, live events, and year-long programs to give you the next step that is a right fit for you!

Would you like to begin immediately with an online program? You can get instant access and start watching the videos, listening to the audios, and downloading the workbooks right now! This is an excellent way to immerse yourself and take your Relationship Development to the next level! Get details at RelationshipDevelopment.org/programs.

Are you a live event person? Join us at our next live event. We would love to see you there! Get details at RelationshipDevelopment.org/events.

Are you ready for mastery? *RelationshipU* is a year-long program designed for those who are committed to reaching Level Five Mastery with their Relationship Development tools. *RelationshipU* gives you in-person mastermind meetings with us, live weekly coaching calls, our private Facebook group for 24/7 support, online curriculum, and access to our live events! Get details at RelationshipDevelopment.org/programs and click on *RelationshipU*!

ACKNOWLEDGEMENTS

We stand on the shoulders of giants. To thank everyone who has shaped us into the version of ourselves that could create this book would take another entire book. We are so deeply grateful to every single person, mentor, student, team member, friend, and loved one who has shaped us on our journey. There are a few people that we would like to highlight, but this is by no means an exhaustive list.

To Hal Elrod for giving us the amazing opportunity to collaborate on a project to serve so many people.

To Jon & Tatyana Vroman for always believing in us, championing us, guiding us, and being close friends. (And for introducing us to Hal!)

To Honorée Corder for teaching us, guiding us, and helping us bring this book to life! You rock Honorée!

To our editor, Leslie Watts, thank you for taking our manuscript and helping us shape it into a best-seller! Your ability to make every paragraph more readable, digestible, and accessible for the reader is astounding.

To Carol Kus and Theresa Puckett, there really are not enough words to thank you for your contribution to shaping this book into what it is today. You read every line, you edited every page. Your edits and contributions took our book to a whole other level! You stayed up late and got up early! You cheered and smiled. You poured your hearts into these pages. You are the best collaboration team that Paul and I could ever ask for. We love you both endlessly.

To our team at RelationshipDevelopment.org, Amy Kazor, Carmie Buhalis, Jade Janusauske, Jennifer Gerhard, Theresa Puckett, and Carol Kus. Thank you so much for everything you did to create this book and rock this project! Your love, support, and dedication mean so much to us! We love you to pieces.

To our students in RelationshipU, we love and adore you. Thank you for inspiring us, helping us to continually shape this content to serve more people, and supporting us on our journey. You are our tribe and we love you.

To the authors, teachers and mentors who have inspired us, taught us, and guided us on our journey. We are forever grateful ... T. D. Jakes, Cloe Madanes, Keith J Cunningham, Blue Melnick and Bari Baumgardner, Matthew Kelley, and Michael Singer, thank you.

There have been books that shaped our journey. Thank you, Alison Armstrong, for writing *Keys to the Kingdom*. Thank you to our friends Bob Burg and John David Mann for writing *The Go Giver*. Thank you Dr. John Gottman for writing *7 Principles for Making Marriage Work*. Thank you, Marianne Williamson, for writing *A Return to Love*.

To Fabienne and Derek Fredrickson, there are not enough words to thank you. Without the two of you, we never would have grown into the organization that can serve so many through this book. Thank you for promising me it would always be the four of us together facing the world! Gratitude is not enough to express how we feel for you both. We love you endlessly.

Tony Robbins. There has been no greater force that has shaped us into the versions of who we are today than you, sir. For over two decades, you have taught us how to become the best and most authentic versions of ourselves. You have shifted our destiny in ways that no one else could have. We are so grateful to live at the same time that you are alive. There are not enough words to thank you for your contribution to who we are today. Not only did you do that for us, but then you taught us how to do that for others. We honor you by paying it forward, one life at a time. Thank you, Tony.

To you, the reader. Thank you for giving us the opportunity to serve you. Thank you for opening to the possibility of a different perspective and new approach. Thank you for stepping forward and doing the work!

ABOUT THE AUTHORS

HAL ELROD is on a mission to *Elevate the Consciousness of Humanity, One Morning at a Time.* As one of the highest rated keynote speakers in the America, creator of one of the fastest growing and most engaged online communities in existence and author of one of the highest rated books in the world, *The Miracle Morning*—which has been translated into 27 languages, has over 2,000 five-star Amazon reviews and is practiced daily by over 500,000 people in 70+ countries—he is doing exactly that.

The seed for Hal's life's work was planted at age twenty, when Hal was found dead at the scene of a horrific car accident. Hit head-on by a drunk driver at seventy miles per hour, he broke eleven bones, died for six minutes, and suffered permanent brain damage. After six days in a coma, he woke to face his unimaginable reality—which included being told by doctors that he would never walk again. Defying the logic of doctors and proving that all of us can overcome even seemingly insurmountable adversity to achieve anything we set our minds to, Hal went on to not only walk but to run a 52-mile ultra-marathon and become a hall of fame business achiever—all before the age of 30.

Then, in November of 2016, Hal nearly died again. With his kidneys, lungs, and heart of the verge of failing, he was diagnosed with a very rare, very aggressive form of leukemia and given a 30% chance of living. After enduring the most difficult year of his life, Hal is now cancer-free and furthering his mission as the Executive Producer of *The Miracle Morning Movie*.

Most importantly, Hal is beyond grateful to be sharing his life with the woman of his dreams, Ursula Elrod, and their two children in Austin, Texas.

For more information on Hal's keynote speaking, live events, books, the movie and more, visit www.HalElrod.com..

STACEY & PAUL MARTINO believe that it only takes ONE partner to transform a relationship...ANY relationship! They are passionate about empowering people with the relationship education that no one ever teaches us!

The Martino's are the founders of RelationshipDevelopment.org and creators of RelationshipU®. Relationship Development® is personal development for your relationship.

Today, through their strategic coaching, online programs and packed live events, Stacey and Paul have helped tens of thousands of people around the world to transform their love relationship! And as a happy bonus, you get to apply the same strategies to improve all your relationships.

Trained and certified by Tony Robbins, Stacey is a certified marriage educator and divorce preventionist. An international best-selling author, Stacey is a sought-after relationship expert, passionate and engaging speaker and media guest and is the Relationship Expert for Aspire Magazine.

After being together for over two decades, the Martino's live the unshakable love and unleashed passion they now teach others to have. They are also proud parents to their two children, Jake 13 and Grace 9.

HONORÉE CORDER is the author of dozens of books, including *You Must Write a Book, The Prosperous Writers* book series, *Like a Boss* book series, *Vision to Reality, Business Dating, The Successful Single Mom* book series, *If Divorce is a Game, These are the Rules,* and *The Divorced Phoenix.* She is also Hal Elrod's business partner in *The Miracle Morning* book series. Honorée coaches business professionals, writers, and aspiring non-fiction authors who want to publish their books to bestseller status, create a platform, and develop multiple streams of income. She also does all sorts of other magical things, and her badassery is legendary. You can find out more at HonoreeCorder.com.

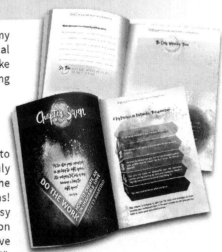

HAL ELROD & JON BERGHOFF

PRESENT...

ONE WEEKEND CAN CHANGE YOUR LIFE.
JOIN US FOR THIS ONCE-IN-A-LIFETIME EXPERIENCE.

www.BestYearEverLive.com

Most personal development events cause "information overload" and often leave attendees feeling more overwhelmed than when they arrived. You end up with pages and pages of notes, then you go home and have to figure out how and when to implement everything you've learned.

Co-hosted by experiential trainer, Jon Berghoff, the **Best Year Ever Blueprint LIVE** event won't just teach you how to change your life, you'll actually starting taking steps to *change your life while you're still at the event*.

"I truly had a life changing weekend during BYEB2015. I feel as if my mind has hit a 'reset' button. Reading The Miracle Morning and coming to the live event has been a gift, and the best investment in myself I've ever made. I am excited to take this momentum and create my level 10 life next year!"

Ericka Staples

Learn more about the Best Year Ever event online at
WWW.BESTYEAREVERLIVE.COM

LET'S DO THIS!

ARE YOU READY TO
CATAPULT YOUR RELATIONSHIPS TO THE NEXT LEVEL?
Come to a live immersion event or join an online program!

Work with Stacey and Paul

GREAT RELATIONSHIPS ARE CREATED, NOT FOUND.
The transformation you really want is closer than you think...

Relationship 101
DEVELOPMENT®
▶THE QUICK START™

For Details and Program Registration visit
RELATIONSHIPDEVELOPMENT.ORG/PROGRAMS

Come to a Live Event

CATAPULT YOUR RELATIONSHIP
TO THE NEXT LEVEL IN THIS
3-DAY IMMERSION
EVENT EXPERIENCE!

Relationship
BREAKTHROUGH
RETREAT™

3-DAY
LIVE
INTENSIVE

For Details and Event Registration visit
RELATIONSHIPDEVELOPMENT.ORG/EVENTS

THE MIRACLE MORNING SERIES

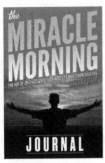

The Journal

for Salespeople

for Real Estate
Agents

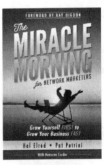

for Network
Marketers

for Writers

for Entrepreneurs

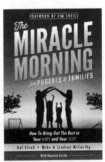

for Parents &
Families

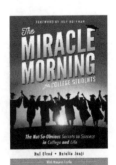

for College
Students

COMPANION GUIDES & WORKBOOKS

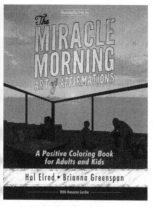

Art of Affirmations

for Network Marketers
90-Day Action Plan

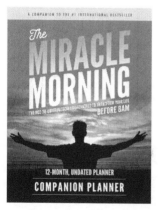

Companion Planner

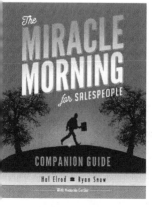

for Salespeople
Companion Guide

for College Students
Companion Planner

Made in the USA
San Bernardino, CA
03 April 2019